THE HARLEM RENAISSANCE: REVALUATIONS

CRITICAL STUDIES ON
BLACK LIFE AND CULTURE
(Professor Henry-Louis Gates, Advisory Editor)
VOL. 17

GARLAND REFERENCE LIBRARY
OF THE HUMANITIES
VOL. 837

CRITICAL STUDIES ON BLACK LIFE AND CULTURE
Professor Henry-Louis Gates, Advisory Editor

THE HARLEM RENAISSANCE: REVALUATIONS

Amritjit Singh
William S. Shiver
Stanley Brodwin

GARLAND PUBLISHING, INC. • NEW YORK & LONDON
1989

Published under the auspices of Hofstra University

The conference and these proceedings have been made possible by a
grant from the National Endowment for the Humanities

Library of Congress Cataloging-in-Publication Data

The Harlem renaissance: revaluations / [edited by] Amritjit Singh,
William S. Shiver, Stanley Brodwin.
    p.   cm. — (Critical studies on Black life and culture ; vol.
17) (Garland reference library of the humanities; vol. 837)
    Papers presented at a conference held May 2–4, 1985, and sponsored
by the Hofstra University Cultural Center.
    Includes bibliographies, index.
    ISBN 0–8240–5739–2 (alk. paper)
    1. American literature—Afro-American authors—History and
criticism—Congresses. 2. American literature—New York (N.Y.)—
History and criticism—Congresses. 3. American literature—20th
century—History and criticism—Congresses. 4. Harlem Renaissance—
Congresses. 5. Afro-American arts—New York (N.Y.)—Congresses.
I. Singh, Amritjit. II. Shiver, William S. III. Brodwin, Stanley.
IV. Hofstra University Cultural Center. V. Series. VI. Series: Critical
studies on Black life and culture; v. 17.
PS153.N5H264 1989   88–3930
810'.9'896073—dc19   CIP

Printed on acid-free, 250-year-life paper
Manufactured in the United States of America

In memoriam
Joseph G. Astman
1916–1985

CONTENTS

INTRODUCTION

This volume contains a selection of papers presented at a three-day conference, May 2–4, 1985, sponsored by the Hofstra University Cultural Center with a grant-in-aid from the National Endowment for the Humanities. The title of the conference, "Heritage: A Reappraisal of the Harlem Renaissance," alludes significantly to the well-known Countee Cullen poem. Indeed, our purpose was to present a comprehensive, interdisciplinary study of the legacy bequeathed to our contemporary society by this remarkable period and its outstanding figures and to examine in fresh ways the social dynamics of the movement itself, as it was shaped by earlier historical events and the particular cultural concerns of the 1920s. We believed there was much to be gained by analyzing in new ways the inner workings of a movement that was doubtless, in many ways, a precursor to the "black consciousness" strivings of the 1960s. If this later period owed something to those who expounded the earlier concept of the "New Negro," indeed the Harlem Renaissance itself, in a similar manner, evolved from historical forces that generated parallel movements in Latin America, the Caribbean, and West Africa. So, for the conference as for this volume, we welcomed papers on general themes related to historical background, black music, and women writers, as well as studies devoted entirely to an individual writer or artist.

In selecting articles for publication, we have been guided more by a contributor's focus or comprehensiveness than by a preconceived scheme of classification for the volume. Although a "method" might become apparent to a discerning eye, we have hesitated to impose categories. The papers included, therefore, reflect something of the multifaceted nature of the Harlem Renaissance itself as well as the various critical approaches of contemporary scholarship, though occurring most frequently are the historical, formalist, and "new critical" perspectives. Each author, of course, speaks for his or her own critical point of view.

In organizing this conference, our objective was to highlight, or bring into sharper focus, those areas of critical investigation that have received inadequate attention in the hitherto published scholarship. At the same time, we welcomed fresh approaches to the more frequently studied figures of the period, as well as the fascinating new work on influences—the effect on individuals of the interaction among painters, sculptors, musicians, poets, and novelists, as among journalists, politicians, and sociologists. It appears now that artists working in different mediums and academics from all disciplines contributed to the emergence of a "new" Afro-American psychology, philosophy, and political stance; and many of them were, in turn, influenced by this nationwide phenomenon, as revealed in various art forms and polemical writings reflecting the power of a *change* in black consciousness already announced by the beginning of the postwar period.

Still other related phenomena of the 1920s and early 1930s, we felt, deserved notice. Indeed, an especially important aspect of our interdisciplinary perspective concerned the concepts of Negritude in some Afro-French literatures. At the same time, following the lead of Sterling Brown, we hoped to provide some exhaustive historical examinations of the contributions made to the black artistic resurgence by persons in cities other than New York, in cities such as Philadelphia, Nashville, Kansas City, Chicago, Cleveland, Los Angeles, and Washington, D.C. Finally, we wished to learn more about neglected minor figures and about such enigmatic and controversial writers as Wallace

Thurman, that "voice of protest" against the common enterprise.

These were the directions, then, that we had wished to pursue. Perhaps inevitably, not all of our expectations were fulfilled. The gap between what we had hoped to receive from the scholars in the field and what actually came to us might well be instructive—of where contemporary scholarship is headed and also of the areas where more work is called for. While we were pleased to note the burgeoning interest in women writers such as Zora Neale Hurston and Nella Larsen, we were puzzled by the fact that so little was submitted on important figures such as Countee Cullen, Arna Bontemps, and Wallace Thurman. And yet, we do have James W. Tuttleton's work—his unearthing of Countee Cullen's undergraduate thesis on Edna St. Vincent Millay is, we believe, an important contribution to the understanding of the poet's aesthetic development. The title of this volume, *Harlem Renaissance: Revaluations*, approximates more closely what the conference actually achieved than the more ambitious objectives suggested by our original title for the conference. Our volume will, we hope, serve as a step toward a full reappraisal of the period.

The conference was well attended, and it brought together a wide range of scholars, white and black, American and international. About sixty papers from among some eighty that we received were presented. The panels were wide-ranging in their coverage: cultural and socio-political meaning; women writers; African and Caribbean connections; poetry and fiction; music, theater, and painting; patrons and supporters. Most sessions were led by moderators who have distinguished themselves in Afro-American scholarship, and there was plenty of discussion to provoke thought and stimulate new perspectives. Some conference papers by several well-known scholars that we would have liked to appear in this volume could not be included, mainly because of copyright problems; they will no doubt be found in print elsewhere.

We wish especially to acknowledge the contributions of those guests who shared their memories of life and art in the 1920s and 1930s at a special evening session, which was indeed the highlight of the conference. The guests were Bruce Nugent, Mrs. Hale Woodruff, Mrs. Selma Burke, and Mrs. Countee Cullen (sadly, Mrs. Cullen and Bruce Nugent passed away in 1986 and 1987 respectively). They were joined in a roundtable by a conference participant, Mrs. Ethel Ray Nance, who served as Charles S. Johnson's secretary during his *Opportunity* years. In sharing with us their memories and experiences of people and events in the Harlem of the 1920s and the 1930s, these individuals brought to the conference a most delightful evocation of that exciting era. The play *Zora*, by Laurence Holder, starring Yvonne Sutherland, and a dance-celebration, "Three Moods of the Renaissance," led and directed by Jacqui Malone-O'Meally of Wesleyan University, both, in their own special ways, brought the period alive to the conference participants. The conference also hosted two exhibits organized by the Hofstra staff, entitled "Heritage" and "1935: The Year and the Arts," the latter viewed at a special reception, where the University Jazz Quintet entertained the participants with familiar numbers from the period.

The conference ended with an evaluation session led ably and perceptively by Professors Charles H. Nichols, Richard Barksdale, and Arnold Rampersad. Through their own comments and the responses elicited from the audience, the conference as a whole attained a focus—its strengths and weaknesses were clearly delineated. Some of the suggestions made in this exchange of impressions and ideas were most important. First, there was a strong sense, indeed consensus, that there ought to be some formal structure or structures that would instill a sense of community among Harlem Renaissance scholars, perhaps a society to meet annually at the MLA, or, what many participants felt was sorely needed, a quarterly or bi-annual journal devoted to the growing interdisciplinary scholarship of the period; at the very least, a newsletter could be inaugurated. Second, many participants suggested there be a "follow-up" conference to this one in another five to ten years, at Hofstra University or possibly at another institution with a strong Black Studies program, or at an institution that houses important materials on the period. Third, a number of people voiced the need for new or updated biographies (a need that is being gradually realized in studies such as Robert Hemenway's on Zora Neale Hurston, Arnold Rampersad's on Langston Hughes, Nellie McKay's on Jean Toomer, Wayne Cooper's on Claude McKay, and projected biographies of Nella Larsen, Jessie Fauset, and others), more work on folklore and theater, and new projects in oral history to obtain more intensely personal revelations of those formative and creative years. Finally, there was a clear call to the scholarly community to determine, in ever-widening contexts, the true nature of Harlem Renaissance's legacy for black Americans, Americans in general, and the world at large. Indeed, such probings may well lead to a radically new or revitalized canon. Given the vigorous and fresh critical perspectives developed by many scholars working on the problems and issues of the Harlem Renaissance—some of which, we hope, are reflected in the essays included here—we can perhaps look forward to a time when the full and complex meaning of that time, and its consequences, are fully revealed.

As we look back at the several months of careful preparation for the conference during 1984–85 and at many more months since then in editing this volume for publication, we recall with gratitude the cooperation we have received from numerous friends and colleagues. We have dedicated this volume to the memory of the man to whom we owe our greatest debt—Joseph G. Astman, whose generosity and farsightedness left a stamp on everything he did during his long association with Hofstra University in various capacities. We extend our sincerest thanks for excellent support to Natalie Datlof, Alexej Ugrinsky, Athelene Collins, Jessica Richter, and others at the Hofstra University Cultural Center. Thanks are also due Joan McGreevy and Lisa Vines for serving most ably as editorial assistants for the project, and Mary Kate McGoldrick and Yan Shen for their help in proofreading.

AMRITJIT SINGH
WILLIAM S. SHIVER
STANLEY BRODWIN

The Harlem Renaissance: Revaluations

Primitivism as a Therapeutic Pursuit: Notes Toward a Reassessment of Harlem Renaissance Literature

ROBERT A. COLES and DIANE ISAACS

During the Harlem Renaissance one of the dominant cultural forces was the cult of primitivism, a therapeutic alternative to the insidious disease of Western culture, which was suffering from an overabundance of "civilization." In human terms, this disease was especially acute among alienated individuals who, after witnessing the First World War, were made abruptly aware of the self-destructive capacity of machinery and weaponry. Thus these individuals reflected their alienation by cultivating primitivism as a spiritual and cultural alternative to modern technological society and worked the cult into artistic themes, images, and symbols. Eventually its influence became so apparent that it grew into a literary and social doctrine with further implications in the Western world of the twentieth century.

Yet we become sensitive to the crystallization and conceptual development of primitivism during the 1920s because it functioned as a kind of inoculation against these destructive tendencies and the evils of civilization. It gave some reassurance to a number of artists, historians, and social theorists that they were striving to implement more vital and constructive human values to offset the spiritual failures of a culture suffering from what they loosely defined as a "psychic imbalance." That is to say, even though primitivism failed to understand that primitive alternatives did not exist and were essentially cultural pipe dreams, the mere fact that this cult searched for "better" (certainly different) human values made the pursuit an entirely healthy endeavor. Finally, it is important to distinguish this cult from exoticism or sensationalism, for the two are often mistaken for the same thing. Exoticism is quite different in that it exploits primitivism and makes it a kind of freak show for exoticism's own selfish indulgence.

Generally speaking, primitivism is a concept rooted historically in the development of Western culture that reflects a difficult and complex evolution. It functions as a critique of what it views as essential weaknesses and injustices in Western civilization. It disavows, for example, materialism, scientific thinking, faith and progress, and colonialism over other more human modes of thought and feeling. Although it had persisted as an idea in Euro-American culture since the eighteenth century, the doctrine did not become a dominant force in American art and literature until after World War I.

For some American whites who, prior to the war, believed in Western civilization as the world's salvation, the apparent barbarism witnessed in trench warfare certainly weakened the civilizing momentum. In short, primarily among some artists and thinkers and later among a broader base of people, the West had lost its golden glow. Here then, civilization came to reflect an essential spiritlessness and inhumanity with at best a tenuous future. Indeed, it was a commonplace among white American writers of the 1920s that the West might not survive unless it created an alternative set of values rooted in past societies that remain primitive, natural, and uncorrupted by destruction, alienation, and war. Thus these American whites began searching for an alternative, which, as it turned out, became the American Negro. Who else right within their homeland and not abroad in the remote jungles of Africa or the mountains of South America could have been a more convenient symbol of moral goodness?

The primitive cult functioned as a significant revolt by these white people to remake values for a more decent humankind. As one of these primitivists, Carl Van Vechten had been deeply involved in promoting some black writers. This involvement of Van Vechten is today generally accepted as genuine by many scholars. Even Harold Cruse, who felt that white participation in the Renaissance was primarily exploitative in that "the Negro's spiritual and aesthetic materials were taken over by many white artists,"[1] sees Van Vechten as an important element in the Renaissance, because "he was the first to establish some kind of link between the Harlem and Greenwich Village artistic movements. He subsequently became the leading white patron of Negro art and artists during the heyday of the Harlem movement of the 1920s."[2] Langston Hughes spoke similarly of Van Vechten's role during the Renaissance in saying:

> He never talks grandiloquently about democracy or Americanism. Nor makes a fetish of those qualities. But he lives with them with sincerity—and humor.[3]

Van Vechten's role during the Renaissance was crucial. Yet when his novel *Nigger Heaven* appeared in 1926, black newspaper and magazine critics reacted with anger and hostility; in particular, they were furious over the choice of his title with the apparent sensationalist appeal the novel made about blacks as exotic representations of the imagination. But here we must make a distinction, for it becomes apparent that the novel dramatizes a non-exploitative experience behind its ironic title. While it is true that some whites saw nothing in the Renaissance but gin and sex and a chance to go uptown and view the spectacle of uninhibited, strutting "darkies," Van Vechten certainly was not one of them.

For some American blacks, primitivism was strongly tied to the Africanization of the American Negro and the search for a more remote, naturally good, and uncorrupted Africa—free from the white racism manifested in Western civilization. This too was an escape but it had different sources than the primitivistic concepts that were popular among white people. Primitivism in this regard was basically political in its inception and had been greatly enhanced by Marcus Garvey's Back-to-Africa movement. The Harlem Renaissance, following this political thrust, cultivated Africanization in art, thus making the black artist turn inward or race-ward to see what was artistically significant. This meant denying one's own Western orientation in order to locate alternatives in an African past. This conflict is noticeably apparent in Claude McKay's well-known *Home to Harlem*, where Ray, representing a decadent Western culture, is influenced and ultimately spiritually renewed by Jake, who represents positive primitive values.

When *Home to Harlem* was first released in 1928, it caused some commotion, as had Van Vechten's *Nigger Heaven*. Again, the familiar slogans of attack were launched by the black middle class, the old guard who felt that the Renaissance should demonstrate black equality and achievement by attempting to uplift the race to some vague notion of respectability. McKay despised this kind of racial refinement and emasculation espoused by critics such as W.E.B. DuBois. Furthermore, McKay, who was decidedly and openly a primitivist, goes beyond the depiction of black lower-class life by juxtaposing the two main characters in order to force the reader to choose between what the two represent in the end. If one chooses Jake over Ray, which McKay intends, then one admits that the black folk tradition and the man of feeling are healthier than the educated black man who had denied his folk tradition and primitive vitality. Thus, for McKay, the primitive cult embodies the therapeutic potential of reuniting the mind with the body in order to create whole men and women. By rejecting middle-class denial, McKay's novels suggest that, indeed, one can and should go home again.

Except for Zora Neale Hurston, black women writers of the Harlem Renaissance did not embrace this cult of primitivism. One reason for this was that the cult of Negro Womanhood replaced the inherited stereotypes from slavery, like the mammy and the exotic loose woman, with the equally confining stereotypes of social convention. Elise McDougald's essay in *The New Negro* illustrates both the impact of class and the defensive attitude that particularly pressured black middle-class women writers to depict respectability as the moral imperative of race consciousness. She writes,

> We find the Negro woman, figuratively, struck in the face daily by contempt from the world about her. Within her soul, she knows little of peace and happiness. But through it all, she is standing erect, developing within herself the moral strength to rise above and conquer false attitudes.[4]

By emphasizing the physical beauty and spiritual virtue of their black women characters, these writers were paradoxically denying the uniqueness of black culture embodied not only in the cult of primitivism but also in the ideological underpinning of the New Negro movement.

Nella Larsen dramatizes this dilemma for black women writers in her novel *Quicksand*, published in 1928. Her somewhat autobiographical protagonist, Helga Crane, an upper-class mulatto, searches for her social and psychological identity in settings ranging from a Southern black college to Chicago, New York, and Copenhagen. Even with the advantage of such mobility, however, Helga Crane finds that being black and female means that her individuality is consistently ignored. As Barbara Christian asserts,

> Although Larsen employs elements of both the novel of convention and the primitive motif in *Quicksand*, she uses them as a means of demonstrating their limitations. The urban, sensitive, light-skinned heroine of the twenties is not free either in conventional, urban upperclass society or in "primitive," rural America. Given her options, she is doomed in Larsen's novels to become a self-centered, oppressed neurotic or a downtrodden, half-alive peasant.[5]

Thus, while McKay's novel provided a distinct and viable choice, Larsen's showed that rigid social categories stifle options for black women.

However, one black woman writer followed a different route and used primitivism as a means for resuscitation and redefinition. Zora Neale Hurston, whose work was recently rediscovered through the efforts of Alice Walker, was an anthropologist who had studied with Franz Boas at Columbia. Born in the all-black town of Eatonville, Florida, around 1901, Hurston studied with Alain Locke at Howard University, where her first published work appeared in its magazine *Stylus*. Between 1934 and 1948, she wrote four novels, two books on folklore, and an autobiography. This prolific writer, who "plunged her characters into the unselfconscious world of Black rural folk,"[6] combined her vision as an artist with her analytical perspective as an anthropologist to espouse psychic wholeness through black culture.

In particular, Hurston's novel, *Their Eyes Were Watching God* (1937), exemplifies the positive use of the primitive. The main character, Janie Crawford Killicks Starks Woods, returns to her black community to narrate the events of her life that have liberated her from the male authority and materialism inherent in white culture. Her struggle for self-definition and freedom from illusions reflects the best of primitivism. Janie's quest for the horizon and the blossoming pear tree metaphorically represent her self-fulfillment and renewal. And the circular plot structure, which allows the reader to overhear the story she tells to her friend Pheoby, establishes both the reality of the oral tradition and her reconciliation with her past.

Moreover, Janie's experiences illustrate the confining choices available to black women. Raised by her grandmother, Janie at sixteen is married to old Logan Killicks to achieve material security and thus avoid being "de mule uh de world." She soon flees from this loveless marriage to marry Joe Starks. He wanted her to accept a conventional role in the home, but he beat her when dinner was not prepared properly and did not let her talk with the

men who gathered on his porch. Thus he not only alienated
her from the community but also forced her to deny herself.
No wonder that his death twenty years later exposes the
allure of social status and wealth as an empty, lonely illusion.

Love enters Janie's life when she is forty and meets
Vergible (called Tea Cake) Woods, fifteen years her junior,
who treats her as an equal. He not only teaches her to shoot
and encourages her storytelling ability, but also takes her
into the Everglades, the Muck, where they can work
together. While earlier she had been prized for her
Caucasian features (straight hair and fair complexion), now
Janie is prized for herself. And most important, as Hurston
wrote, "her soul crawled out from its hiding place."[7] Through
her relationship with Tea Cake, she is spiritually renewed.

However, her Eden is destroyed when a rabid dog bites
Tea Cake and Janie has to kill Tea Cake to defend herself.
Ironically, the all-white jury finds her innocent while the
black community treats her as though she is guilty.
Nonetheless, she returns to her community to tell her story
and share her vision of liberating love. She succeeds because
indeed Pheoby feels ten feet tall after hearing the story and
Janie herself "pulled in her horizon like a great fish-net.
Pulled it in from around the waist of the world and draped it
over her shoulder. So much of life in its meshes! She called
in her soul to come and see."[8] Not only did Janie find her
identity but she found it "through her relationship with the
Black community rather than White society."[9]

Historian Paula Giddings praises Hurston's novel and
notes the critical reception it received: "Hurston's work was
controversial because she neither romanticized Black folk life
nor condemned it, thus falling between two schools of
cultural thought."[10] Like Janie, who was caught between the
American values of self-fulfillment and communal
responsibility, Zora Neale Hurston and her work were
judged by the New Negro critics for stepping outside assigned
categories. As one contemporary critic comments,

> Unlike Fauset, whose ladylike images were praised by Harlem
> Renaissance intellectuals, both Hurston and her characters were
> seen as irreverent. Her sensuality, her ability to secure money

from whites, her loud laughter, her nonconformist behavior, her
sometimes difficult and arrogant ways, were an affront to the
genteel spirit of the Renaissance.[11]

Thus Zora Neale Hurston's situation highlights the
contradictions of the Harlem Renaissance. In response to
criticism from Richard Wright, Alain Locke, and Langston
Hughes, she wrote "in defense of a people who had been
stereotyped as pseudoprimitive minstrels,"[12] according to her
biographer, Robert Hemenway.

Not only was Hurston criticized for using folklore, she
was also attacked because of her relationship to Mrs. C.
Osgood Mason of Park Avenue, a philanthropist who paid
her to collect folklore. Hurston signed a contract with her in
1928 whereby Mrs. Mason owned her work. Until 1931, Mrs.
Mason paid her to collect rather than to publish folk
materials on rural Southern black folk to document the
"primitive" in black people. An influential patron, she had
supported Hughes until he broke with her in the early 1930s;
but Hurston, hounded by financial worries, maintained an
almost obsequious relationship with this person whom she
addressed as "Godmother." Hurston once referred to her as
the "guard-mother who sits in the twelfth heaven and shapes
the destinies of primitives."[13] Whatever the complex
motivations behind this relationship, Hurston was dependent
on a patron who sought to promote the very stereotypes and
assumptions of cultural uniqueness for which Hurston was
criticized within Harlem's literary community. Perhaps
along with Janie, Zora Neale Hurston too was declaring her
independence in *Their Eyes Were Watching God.*

Hurston was a primitivist who both used her past and
paved the way for the future. As Barbara Christian notes,

> One of the first writers to use folk images and speech as well
> as the insular folk culture, Hurston anticipated future black women
> writers who would attempt to define themselves as persons within
> a specific culture rather than primarily through their relationships
> with whites. Fauset's characters, particularly in *The Chinaberry
> Tree*, also insulated themselves with a particular class, but
> Hurston's *Their Eyes Were Watching God* invokes not one class
> but the total community—its language, images, mores, and

prejudices—as its context. In so doing it articulates the Afro-
American experience not only as a condition but as a culture.[14]

Perhaps, then, we owe both Mason and Van Vechten a debt
of gratitude for espousing a philosophy that saw in black
culture positive alternative values and for encouraging black
writers to express those values through their work.

Contrary to the negative connotations that often surround
the concept of primitivism, it functioned as an affirmative
force in many ways during the Harlem Renaissance years.
This literary and social doctrine created a cult that spread
rapidly as an answer to some of modern civilization's
alienated population. Although it flowered and died, this
romantic pursuit was significant as a mechanism for the
search for human values. Finally, primitivism was a
therapeutic pursuit that enriched American art and its impact
continues to be felt among writers today.

NOTES

1. Harold Cruse, *The Crisis of the Negro Intellectual* (New York: William Morrow, 1967), p. 35.

2. Ibid., p. 26.

3. Langston Hughes, *The Big Sea* (New York: Knopf, 1940), p. 255.

4. Alain Locke, *The New Negro* (1925; rpt. New York: Arno Press, 1968), p. 382.

5. Barbara Christian, *Black Women Novelists: The Development of a Tradition 1892–1976* (Westport, Conn.: Greenwood, 1980), p. 53.

6. Paula Giddings, *When and Where I Enter: The Impact of Black Women on Race and Sex in America* (New York: William Morrow, 1984), p. 192.

7. Zora Neale Hurston, *Their Eyes Were Watching God* (1937; rpt. Urbana: University of Illinois Press, 1978), p. 192.

8. Ibid., p. 286.

9. Giddings, p. 193.

10. Ibid.

11. Christian, p. 61.

12. Robert E. Hemenway, *Zora Neale Hurston: A Literary Biography* (Urbana: University of Illinois Press, 1977), p. 243.

13. Ibid., p. 139.

14. Christian, p. 60.

White Writers and the Harlem Renaissance

JOHN COOLEY

After World War I, a new kind of black portraiture began to appear in writings by white Americans. Blacks were less frequently depicted in connection with Southern plantation society and less often portrayed in servile roles. In general, white writers showed a growing interest in urban black life, especially in Harlem during the 1920s. For an important group of white writers, Harlem and black culture came to symbolize a new and much-sought-after freedom from restraint, a new source of vitality and even sensuality. No matter how progressive and sophisticated black culture may have been during the Harlem Renaissance, for writers such as Eugene O'Neill, e.e. cummings, Waldo Frank, and Carl Van Vechten, it was primarily a happy hunting ground for portraits in the primitive.

In fact, this tendency in the imagination of these and other white writers to thrust into black character various guises of the primitive is the primary characteristic of white portraiture of black life during the Harlem Renaissance and beyond. As we will see, the primitivizing of black life, often into backwoods, jungle, or urban jungle settings, poses a number of difficulties for the critic, because the term, as it is used in different contexts, refers to several very different ideas. For instance, "primitive" is used with descriptive neutrality by the observer of landscape to designate that zone of nature that stretches away from city, beyond farm and pasture, to the wilderness or jungle. But "primitive" can also be a value judgment. It can serve handily for one wishing either to elevate or to denigrate the "primitive," depending entirely upon the concept of nature, or in this case, of race, on the part of the observer. The terms "savage" and "noble savage" reflect this contrariety of attitude. The black portraits by the four white writers mentioned above clearly reflect such a tendency either to denigrate or to elevate the black as primitive. Of particular interest is the extent to which these and other white writers avoided the clichés that dehumanized most earlier black portraits and captured the changing conditions and vitality of black life during the Harlem Renaissance.[1]

In 1917 Eugene O'Neill began experimenting with the possibility of using black themes and actors in his plays. The first of such productions was *The Moon Over the Caribbees*, a play set in the West Indies. It was produced by the Provincetown Players in 1918 with an all-white cast, who appeared in blackface where necessary. His next play, *The Dreamy Kid*, went a step further in racial borrowing, and it was produced at the Provincetown Playhouse in 1919—this time with an all-black cast. With each of these productions O'Neill pushed further into black life and further toward the open use of black actors in white theaters. These two productions paved the way to his history-making play, *The Emperor Jones*, which opened at the Provincetown Theatre, in Greenwich Village, on November 3, 1920.[2] The play was greeted with highly favorable reviews and practically overnight catapulted O'Neill and the Playhouse into national attention. Charles Gilpin, the black actor who played Emperor Brutus Jones, also received rave notices. The day after the opening, there was a long line of people waiting for tickets, and a thousand subscriptions were sold during the first week. The play ran for 490 performances before going on the road. It was followed by an opera that starred the black singer Paul Robeson in the title role.

The Emperor Jones broke new ground in American theater not only because it employed black and white actors on the same stage, but because it was the first major play to star and give its title role to a black. The play was perfectly attuned to its time—it responded to widespread white fascination with all aspects of black life. O'Neill also emerged briefly among white liberals as a champion of civil rights and human decency after the New York Drama League invited the black lead, Charles Gilpin, to come to their annual dinner and then reneged on the invitation when some members threatened to boycott the dinner. O'Neill exerted enough pressure so that the league reversed its decision and Gilpin actually attended the dinner.

Privately, O'Neill showed a very different face on another occasion. Gilpin substituted the words "black baby" for the term "nigger" that O'Neill had used in the script. When O'Neill discovered this, he told Gilpin, "If I ever catch you rewriting my lines again, you black bastard, I'm going to beat you up."[3] These two incidents are characteristic of O'Neill's racial ambivalence. He could both defend Gilpin against segregation, yet, unable to see the racial slur in his own lines, call Gilpin a "black bastard" for quietly rectifying the offense. On close reading of the play and its impact, it becomes apparent that O'Neill created a role which helped to establish the careers of both Charles Gilpin and Paul Robeson, yet he also approached his black portraits with insensitivity and maladroitness, perpetuating pejorative images of black life.

As the play opens, Brutus Jones, after fleeing from the United States, has established himself within two years as the emperor of a small island in the West Indies. In rising to his position of wealth and power, Jones has exhibited those qualities of free-enterprise leadership that he has assimilated from successful whites during his ten years as a Pullman car porter: shrewdness, aggressiveness, self-reliance, strength of will. Even though O'Neill establishes Jones as an individual with a particular past and distinct personality, the tone of his portrait is pejorative. The Emperor Jones is more clown than hero, ultimately a laughable pretender to be pitied and dismissed. O'Neill's bias reveals itself as the play progresses, presenting the defeat not of white colonialism and free enterprise, as some critics would have it, but of an "uppity" black man who presumed to model himself after successful white exploiters. The revenge of the play is complete as Jones reverts to a savage, is defeated, and then killed by his own people.

The Emperor Jones was wonderful theater, as its continuing popularity attests, and it provided a limelight for black actors, but it did so at considerable expense. Contrary to the efforts of the Harlem Renaissance, O'Neill uses some of the oldest and most annoying white stereotypes of black character. He tells us, in the opening description, that Jones's costume is "not *altogether* ridiculous" (emphasis added). His name Brutus implies even more. O'Neill establishes a mock-serious tone from the start, and puts Jones's position as emperor in comic jeopardy. The gaudy facade of the palace, pillars, and throne and the absence of subjects only add to this atmosphere. In the jungle he becomes a Sambo figure; his eyes pop out and he is too scared to run. The defeat of Brutus is clearly the defeat of a black pretender and not of the white colonial entrepreneurs he imitated.

Ironically, Langston Hughes, in his autobiography *The Big Sea*, describes the disastrous and abbreviated run of *The Emperor Jones* in Harlem. According to Hughes, the play that so captivated white audiences and obviously captured for them a telling image of black life was a counterfeit for their Harlem counterparts. As he describes the event, the black audience at the Lincoln Theatre on 135th Street "didn't know what to make of *The Emperor Jones*. . . . And when the Emperor started running naked through the forest, hearing the Little Frightened Fears, naturally they howled with laughter."[4] They shouted at Jones to "'. . . come on out o' that jungle—back to Harlem where you belong.'" Despite O'Neill's lack of imagination and originality in creating a black character commensurate with his originality in staging, he deserves credit for introducing white New York theater to black themes and black actors. In 1921 more black actors came downtown, this time to Broadway's 63rd St. Theatre with a record-breaking musical, *Shuffle Along*, and among the cast was the inimitable Eubie Blake.

The *enfant terrible* of the Lost Generation and sometime Village resident, e.e. cummings, was also fascinated with black character and life, but with quite different results than O'Neill's. It was against the conventional if not pietistic world of his father and of Boston itself that cummings revolted as he joined the American Expeditionary Force in France and signed on with the Norton-Harjes Ambulance Corps. Soon after cummings and his New York friend William Slater Brown joined their ambulance company, they were arrested and sent to a detention center for security risks. It seems that the censors had not liked the radical drift of Slater Brown's letters to Emma Goldman, back in Greenwich Village.

But cummings's imprisonment was a gift in disguise, providing the material for his autobiographical work, *The Enormous Room* (1922). As days of imprisonment turned to weeks, cummings discovered that he was on a pilgrimage from the diabolical desert of governments at war to the "delectable mountains" of human treasures. Among the many human treasures he discovered in his enormous French jail cell, four individuals stood out. One of the four, a black man named "Jean le Nègre," he revered the most.

Cummings describes Jean's arrival this way: "Even as the guards fumbled with the locks I heard the inimitable, unmistakable, divine laugh of a negro. . . . Entered a beautiful pillar of black strutting muscle topped with a tremendous display of the whitest teeth on earth. The muscle bowed politely in our direction, the grin remarked musically, *Bojour, tou' l'mond*, then came a cascade of laughter. Its effect on the spectators was instantaneous; they roared and danced with joy."[5] Jean had an even more profound impact on cummings, who fell in love with his black companion. Cummings admired Jean for his childlike innocence, for the rippling miracle of his body, for his great laughter, and for his verbal inventiveness. When Jean laughed, cummings tells us, "he laughed all over himself." What appealed to cummings in Jean le Nègre also appealed to nearly all white writers of this decade when they portrayed blacks.

In stark contrast to the savage and frightening portraits given by O'Neill and Vachel Lindsay (in his famous poem "The Congo"), cummings, Gertrude Stein, Sherwood Anderson, Carl Van Vechten, and Waldo Frank described blacks as another kind of primitive; for them, blacks were "naturals." First of all, blacks were regarded as childlike and their lives were simplistic. Nor was this a defect to these white writers, for one of the notions that runs through the 1920s is the idea of "salvation by the child," as Malcolm Cowley expressed it.[6] Another idea which gained popularity during the 1920s was "living for the moment" (or, as we would say today, "living existentially"), and with it a demand for greater creativity, for new and simpler styles of expression. A strand of sensuality also stretches across the decade, and with it a cry to imprison reason and restore the body to its rightful place. To these white writers, blacks symbolized those qualities so striking for their absence from white America.

Jean le Nègre, cummings tells us, has a "bright child of a mind" and is perfectly if not naturally adjusted to life even under the most desperate of wartime conditions. Like many other black characters, as shaped by the hands of white writers of the 1920s and 1930s (especially Eudora Welty and William Faulkner), cummings's Jean is an innocent, possessing the mind and (in this case) the body of an adolescent. He knows almost nothing about the corridors of finance and power, but he has a "natural" inheritance that more than adequately compensates. He is a naturally happy-go-lucky soul; the pleasures of the body and the unstructured life are his to enjoy. Cummings's portrait of Jean expresses, of course, much of the charm and rich playfulness with language that characterize cummings's work. But in place of a fuller portrait, cummings leans heavily on some of the traits that became stock-in-trade as white writers continued to portray blacks as "natural" primitives. Cummings's portrait points to the tendency in even fairly contemporary white writing to replace the "savage" with the "natural" as the "true" nature of black character. He also expresses the apparent longing among some white writers (Twain, Faulkner, and Mailer, among others) for a brotherhood of black and white.

Another New York writer who became fascinated with the Harlem Renaissance, and especially with Southern black life, is Waldo Frank. He founded the important literary journal *Seven Arts* in 1917 and also became close friends with the black writer Jean Toomer. Thanks to this friendship and Toomer's great insight into Southern black life, Frank produced an unusually sensitive and complex black portrait in his novel *Holiday* (1923).[7]

In early 1921 and again in 1922 Toomer and Frank travelled through the rural South together, Frank posing as a black man. He stayed with many of Toomer's friends and experienced the conditions of black life in the South. Here was a unique sharing of common materials by a black and a white writer, each filling his notebooks—Toomer, for his justly famous novel *Cane*, and Frank, for his melodramatic *Holiday*.

Waldo Frank found a vitality and earthly wholesomeness in the black homes and communities he visited, which he contrasted to the spiritual depravity of white civilization. He observed that most white readers would regard the "Alabama Negro as an illiterate, often drunk, rather vulgar creature," but to him this same farmer "drew from the soil, and the sky the grace which is refined like the grace of a flower."[8]

Although *Holiday* has severe shortcomings in character development and style, its significance is considerable. Frank's detached point of view provides a necessary distance from the attitudes and actions of his white characters to develop the consciousness of his black protagonist, a proximity that rarely occurs for white writers. It enables him to show how his white characters simplify and primitivize the real complexities of black life that he had so directly observed while traveling with Toomer.

Even more important to the Harlem Renaissance was the influence and writing of Carl Van Vechten. "Carlo," as he was called by Langston Hughes, had his own literary salon, from which he ran a one-man "know the Negro" campaign. He brought writers of both races together, striving to overcome prejudice and misunderstanding. He also helped a number of black writers find publishers for their work. His novel *Nigger Heaven* (1926) explored the seamy and primitive side of Harlem life, much to the shock of some Harlem writers, but it was perfectly packaged for that insatiable white appetite in the 1920s—for anything black and primitive.

By contrast, the Harlem Renaissance represented a serious effort by black artists and critics to interpret black life on their own terms. To be sure, works like *The Emperor Jones, Holiday, Nigger Heaven,* and Sherwood Anderson's *Dark Laughter* (1925) provided encouragement if not challenge to black writers and, as Robert Bone put it, "they created a sympathetic audience for the serious treatment of Negro subjects."[9] It was surely a two-way street, for white writers encouraged and occasionally sponsored the works of their black counterparts, but they also drew their materials and inspirations from black life, and often at its expense. In *The New Negro,* Alain Locke declared: "The popular melodrama has about played itself out, and it is time to scrap the fiction's garret and bogeys and settle down to a realistic facing of facts. The day of 'aunties' and 'uncles' and 'mammies' is equally gone; Uncle Tom and Sambo have passed on."[10]

Despite the new consciousness that was growing in Harlem and the Village, some of the traditional stereotypes of blacks persisted in white literature, and certain new ones were created. Quite consistently, whites continued throughout the 1920s, and even more recently, to look to black life as a source of primitivism.[11] No matter how complimentary the intention, the result is a quality of racial predisposition that impedes realistic depiction of black lives. In *The Big Sea* Langston Hughes commented aptly on this point. He was for a time sustained by a white patroness who was willing to support him so long as he shaped his art to her conception of black culture. She wanted him to "be primitive and know and feel the intuitions of the primitive." Although Hughes

appreciated her financial support and tries to follow her
artistic edict, it became a threat to his art and his self-
identity, and he had to sever the relationship. As he
expressed it, "I was only an American Negro—who had loved
the surface of Africa and the rhythms of Africa—but I was not
Africa. I was Chicago and Kansas City and Broadway and
Harlem."[12]

As Hughes makes clear, black artists were well aware of
the new vogue in typecasting by white patrons, editors,
artists, and publishers. Even though its intention may have
been benign, literary primitivism of this sort enslaved black
characters to their white authors' needs and preconceptions.
Despite their achievements, each of the works mentioned
here is also weakened by its particular fascination with
primitivism in black life and, as a result, by its inability to
develop black portraits in complex, diverse, and lifelike ways.
The era of "aunties," "uncles," and "mammies," of Uncle Tom
and Sambo had been discarded by most writers, but the vogue
of the primitive dominated white perceptions of blacks
during and well beyond the Harlem Renaissance.

NOTES

1. For a more detailed background on the Village Bohemians
    and/or the Harlem Renaissance, see Frederick Hoffman, *The
    Twenties: American Writing in the Postwar Decade* (New York:
    Viking Press, 1949), Robert Bone, *The Negro Novel in America*
    (New Haven, Conn.: Yale University Press, 1965), and Nathan
    Huggins, *Harlem Renaissance* (New York: Oxford University
    Press, 1971).

2. Travis Bogard, *Contour in Time: The Plays of Eugene O'Neill*
    (New York: Oxford University Press, 1971), p. 134.

3. Arthur and Barbara Gelb, *O'Neill* (New York: Harper and Row,
    1960), p. 449.

4. Langston Hughes, *The Big Sea* (New York: Knopf, 1940), p. 258.

5. e.e. cummings, *The Enormous Room* (New York: Modern
    Library, 1934), p. 270.

6.   Malcolm Cowley, *Exile's Return* (New York: Viking, 1925), p. 25.

7.   Waldo Frank, *Holiday* (New York: Boni and Liveright, 1923).

8.   Waldo Frank, *In the American Jungle* (New York: Farrar and Rinehart, 1936), p. 57.

9.   Bone, p. 60.

10. Alain Locke, *The New Negro* (New York: Boni and Liveright, 1925), p. 5.

11. See John Cooley, *Savages and Naturals: Black Portraits by White Writers in Modern American Literature* (Newark, Del.: University of Delaware Press, 1982).

12. Hughes, p. 325.

Carl Van Vechten's Black Renaissance

BRUCE KELLNER

Most of the readers—black as well as white—who made Carl Van Vechten's *Nigger Heaven* a best-selling novel in 1926 were unaware that his involvement with the work of Afro-Americans had begun before the turn of the century. Although much of his own roaring during the twenties occurred in Harlem cabarets, he had been writing essays, reviewing plays and books, evaluating music, producing program notes and dust jacket blurbs about black artists and for black artists for over a decade, and delighting in the performances of black entertainers for over thirty years. Like the blessings of other white philanthropists, Van Vechten's were undeniably mixed. The black artist both thrived and suffered, torn between well-meaning encouragement from the white race to preserve his racial identity (usually described, though not by Van Vechten, as "primitivism") and a misguided encouragement from his own race to emulate the white one. Products designed to straighten hair and lighten skin and the regular practice of black comedians wearing blackface makeup are extreme examples at opposite ends of this appalling scale. Nevertheless, the Harlem Renaissance would not have progressed so easily beyond Harlem without the intervention and support of white patronage. That it manifested itself in action which in retrospect seems patronizing is inevitable, but to deny its positive aspects is intellectually indefensible. White patronage was merely an unavoidable element in getting from the past to the present, and the roles played by several figures made a strong supporting cast. Some were bad actors; Carl Van Vechten was a better one.

The James Weldon Johnson Memorial Collection of Negro Arts and Letters at Yale University—which Carl Van Vechten founded—gives credence to this. He began it on the basis of his own vast collection of black literature and memorabilia, continued to contribute to it both materially and financially for the rest of his life, and then specified in his will that any money ever realized from reprints of his own books and thousands of photographs be donated to the Johnson endowment fund. With the present interest in black studies, students and scholars will find themselves increasingly grateful for this legacy. It is difficult to imagine books about the Harlem Renaissance or several recent black biographies (published or about to be) without it. Moreover, Van Vechten's own writings about black arts and letters are of considerable value as well.

Still, from the vantage point of the eighties, it is difficult to embrace without reservation the naiveté and paternalism of the 1920s—Van Vechten's included—as faultless. I don't presume to undermine the zeal for an independent black consciousness, but Carl Van Vechten's assistance during the painful journey most black artists in America have had to make merits our attention. During his life, particularly at the time of their composition, most of his writings—always excepting *Nigger Heaven*—probably had a modest impact: those who most needed to be informed of such riches awaiting discovery would not have been readily exposed to the sources in which his various papers appeared. When I gathered them together in *"Keep A-Inchin' Along"* (Greenwood, 1979) to introduce the present generation of readers to Van Vechten's legacy to the advancement of Afro-American literature, my greatest surprise came in discovering how much of his time and energy he had devoted to the subject.

His own involvement must have begun when he was about ten years old and heard Sissieretta Jones, "Black Patti" as she was called after the white opera singer Adelina Patti, when her opulent musical productions toured the country. By the turn of the century, he had encountered many other black entertainers, including Bert Williams, who left him "trembling between hysterical laughter and sudden tears," and whose ability to command simultaneously such contrary emotions explained the unique genius in black arts and letters, he often contended later.

Although Carl Van Vechten's initial exposure came through these only available sources—black performers often catering to the demands of white audiences—his private associations were deeply rooted. A black washerwoman and a black yardman were the first adults he knew outside his immediate family, and he was reared to address them as "Mrs. Sercy" and "Mr. Oliphant," with the same respect due any other adult. Such civility hardly strikes us as unusual today, but I am speaking here of the 1880s. His parents addressed these black employees formally as well. By the time Van Vechten left home in Iowa for college, he was already inoculated against racial prejudice to the extent it was possible in the turn-of-the-century climate in America. For three of his four years at the University of Chicago, he went with his fraternity's black housekeeper to the Quinn Chapel, where he played the piano for services and accompanied the singing. (The songs, of course, were more often Baptist hymns than the spirituals Van Vechten strove to popularize in later years.) From his journal entries and from his essays of the period, he seems to have adored that housekeeper, just as he had already preferred the company of older people during his childhood, and he saw these new acquaintances as "an intensely uncultured and uneducated race but just as intensely good hearted, humorous, . . . and even clever." They were "colored members of the human family," he concluded.[1] In the 1980s such observations may suggest condescension, but in a twenty-year-old in 1900 they do not, although the ignorance of innocence is invariably difficult to approximate once we have escaped it. Of greater

significance—given Carl Van Vechten's extraordinary
contributions to an aesthetic race consciousness—is the period
of time during which his devotion developed. It refutes his
critics' charges, particularly during the 1920s at the height of
the notoriety of *Nigger Heaven*, that his interest in the race
was necessarily superficial because it was so new.

Van Vechten's first professional writing devoted
exclusively to the subject appeared long before the sudden
craze that began with the all-black musical comedy called
Shuffle Along, bringing in the Jazz Age. In 1913, as drama
critic for the *New York Press*, he had written
enthusiastically about *My Friend from Kentucky*, part of *The
Darktown Follies*, at Harlem's Lafayette Theatre. That article,
and a review the following season of *Granny Maumee*, a play
by white writer Ridgely Torrence, with black characters
performed by white actors, and its revival with black actors
three years later, motivated Van Vechten's extended essay on
"The Negro Theatre," and it is worth noting that in 1914 he
had urged the formation of a Negro theater organization,
with black actors and black playwrights. Even earlier,
working as a cub reporter for the *Chicago American* in 1904,
he wrote about black entertainers whenever he got the
chance. In the 1920s, five years after "The Negro Theatre" was
first published, Van Vechten told black writer Eric Walrond
he thought the essay was out of date, but Walrond contended
that its ideas and points of view would still be pertinent a
decade later, and he avowed that, had he not known Van
Vechten, he would have thought the essay written by a black
because of its racial bias.[2]

During the first half of the decade "when Harlem was in
vogue,"[3] Carl Van Vechten became a popular novelist in
several cheerful fictions about "the splendid drunken
twenties" in New York, as he liked to call the period.[4] By the
time *Nigger Heaven* appeared in 1926, he had become as
well a self-proclaimed, unpaid press agent for Harlem's black
intelligentsia, and certainly for its cabarets. He had become,
he later said, "violently interested in Negroes, . . . almost an
addiction."[5] His first black literary acquaintance was Walter
White, whom he met through their mutual publisher Alfred

A. Knopf. When White introduced Van Vechten to James Weldon Johnson, that violent interest met its catalyst. They were firm believers in the idealistic theory of the "talented tenth" and became each other's entree to each other's race, each other's literary executor, each other's best friend. Also through Walter White, Van Vechten came to know Langston Hughes and Countee Cullen, and he met Wallace Thurman and Zora Neale Hurston—the latter responsible for having coined the term "niggerati" to describe Harlem's young black intellectuals and for having dubbed Van Vechten its first "Negrotarian." Soon after, he had arranged for some poems by Cullen and Hughes to appear in *Vanity Fair*, that popular fashion-setting magazine, and through his instigation Knopf published Hughes's first collection of verse, *The Weary Blues*, as well as books by black novelists Nella Larsen and Rudolph Fisher. For *Vanity Fair*, Van Vechten wrote several articles himself: about the spirituals; about the blues, indeed, the first serious consideration ever given this musical form; about black theater. Concurrently, he financed in large part the first programs of spirituals sung by Paul Robeson and another recital of similar materials by Taylor Gordon and J. Rosamond Johnson. Also, he contributed reviews to a number of publications, both black and white, for at least a dozen books by black writers and wrote blurbs for their dust jackets and copy for their advertisements. Not surprisingly, a gossip column in 1925 declared that he was getting a heavy tan, and, as he only appeared in public after dark, he had to be acquiring it in a taxi, bound for the nightclubs in Harlem.

In all candor, he devoted an inordinate amount of time to shabby pursuits—getting drunk in speakeasies, collecting Harlem sycophants about him, and having dates with steamy sepia courtesans or assignations with handsome black call boys—that were common knowledge. But his intellectual admiration was genuine. His response to black music and writing was firmly grounded in nearly a quarter of a century of serious, professional musical, and literary criticism. Moreover, his desire to share his discoveries resulted in a cultural exchange unique at the time. In their glamorous apartment in Manhattan, Carl Van Vechten and his wife, the actress Fania Marinoff, entertained frequently and lavishly, and always with fully integrated guest lists. The parties were eventually reported as a matter of course in some of the black newspapers of the city, and Walter White called their address "the mid-town office of the NAACP."[6]

And then he wrote *Nigger Heaven*. In one of his *Vanity Fair* essays, just at that time, he discussed the black artist's present reluctance to develop his unique racial qualities and the danger of white artists appropriating them for their own work. A month later, in his contribution to a symposium called "The Negro in Art: How Shall He Be Portrayed?"— actually he had ghost-written the questions for this series of articles in *The Crisis* for Jessie Fauset—Carl Van Vechten posed a counter-question: "Are Negro writers going to write about this exotic material while it is fresh or will they continue to make a free gift of it to white authors who will exploit it until not a drop of vitality remains?"[7] Given the sensational aspects of *Nigger Heaven* and the controversy they aroused, the disturbing irony is either apt or cruel, and it anticipates the accusations of many who felt that *Nigger Heaven* encouraged the worst rather than the best efforts among young black writers who followed. Novels by Claude McKay, Wallace Thurman, and Rudolph Fisher dealt far more directly with Harlem's seamy side, for example, popularizing not an articulate and educated "talented tenth," but an "untalented ninetieth." The writers were themselves black, young, and virtually unknown both north and south of 125th Street; Carl Van Vechten's long reputation as a dandy, a dilettante, and as a writer of resolutely frivolous novels did not help. For many readers of *Nigger Heaven*, the black slang word for a white person—"fay" or "ofay," pig-latin for "foe"—renewed its double meaning. For blacks familiar only with the book's title, that reaction is not surprising, but Harlem knew him as a regular customer in the cabarets, jingling his bracelets when he tipped up his sterling silver hip flask; as a white judge at the black transvestite balls at the Rockland Palace Casino; as a guest in private homes and apartments; and, finally, as Nora Holt's escort and A'Lelia

Walker's boon companion. In Rudolph Fisher's novel *The Walls of Jericho,* a black character at a Harlem party says to a white one obviously patterned after Van Vechten, "'You're the only fay I know that draws the color line on other fays.' 'It's natural,'" the white character replies fatuously. "'Downtown I'm only passing. These,' he waved grandiloquently, 'are my people.'"[8] It is not difficult to see here a Van Vechten perilously close to Ishmael Reed's viciously funny Hinckle Von Vampton in his novel *Mumbo Jumbo,* exaggerated perhaps, but inevitable.

Most of the negative criticism of *Nigger Heaven* came from reviewers who contended that Van Vechten had made use of only the "primitive" aspects of Harlem life. A surprising number of present-day critics also claim this, perhaps without having read the book themselves. By actual page count, nearly two-thirds of *Nigger Heaven* is given over to sociological and aesthetic discussions among black intellectuals and to a bloodless love affair between two dreary characters who control the story line and drag us through their passionless agonies. The other third—the lurid third— certainly does occur in cabarets and between the sheets. Any reader familiar with Van Vechten's earlier novels—all four of them as manicured as a Congreve comedy—would have had good reason to expect less of some pathetic little romance than of a world populated by numbers racketeers and elegant demimondaines and strutting pimps and plenty of sheiks and flappers doing the Charleston. Certainly its sensational elements helped *Nigger Heaven* to sell, but the same kind of elements had helped its predecessors to sell, too. *Nigger Heaven* was either admired or dismissed, but for the wrong reasons, for sensational is not necessarily primitive, and vice versa. "Primitivism"—a word Van Vechten never used— perhaps should not even be associated with any particular race or even any particular culture, Mark Helbling has suggested.[9] Rather, primitivism is an aesthetic point of view that concerns itself essentially with creativity. Picasso, for example, was not interested in Africans or in African "soul," but in their artifacts that could stimulate his own imagination. Van Vechten was no Picasso. His talents—and they were considerable—are simply not very well illustrated in *Nigger Heaven.*

None of Van Vechten's friends seem to have misunderstood the book, and he lost no friends because of it— of either color. They were aware of his genuine concern for the race but also aware of his flamboyant behavior, and they were familiar with both sides of the paradoxical coin in his writing. His acute critical perception backed by a stubborn adherence to a highly mannered style surely deterred his ever being an entirely successful novelist. He was, on the one hand, too analytical and discursive and, on the other, too arch and ornate. For many readers not personally involved with either Van Vechten's personality or his writing, *Nigger Heaven* has some serious artistic troubles not remotely connected with the Harlem Renaissance. Expressions in black dialect simply jar the reader's ear as well as eye when they are followed or preceded by obsolete or fancy vocabulary lacquered into precious locutions. In another novel and quite another context, Van Vechten causes one of his characters to reflect: "A book . . . should have the swiftness of melodrama, the lightness of a farce, to be a real contribution to thought. . . . How could anything serious be hidden more successfully than in a book which pretended to be light and gay?"[10] In *Nigger Heaven* the minor characters might have achieved this, serving up all aspects of Harlem, for the variety is considerable and probably it does offer a better cross-section of Harlem life than any other novel of the period. But the "nice" characters predominate, as they do in no other Van Vechten novel (his nice characters are almost invariably boring), and the attempt at "a real contribution to thought" gets in the way of "real contribution to thought." Van Vechten considers it important to convey observations and reflections about Harlem's intelligentsia, but I get suspicious when a character stands stage-center and recites a canned speech. We learn more from somebody who shows us rather than tells us. The earlier novels, contrarily, were not deliberately didactic, and their moral or intellectual perspective is sufficiently veiled by their cheerful carnality and outrageous good humor. When somebody asks me,

"What should I read by Carl Van Vechten?" *Nigger Heaven* is never the book I recommend. I don't think it is a very good novel, even though it created a large white readership for black writers and even though it popularized Harlem and brought plenty of business into the cabarets north of 125th Street. Whether those two influences are close enough in value to mention in the same sentence is open to question. Whatever *Nigger Heaven*'s limitations, the novel strengthened Van Vechten's ties with the race and increased his loyalty. Through the rest of his long career he devoted his energies to a wider recognition of black achievements, primarily through his photography, recording nearly every celebrated Afro-American, not to add scraps to his already rich supply, but to enhance the Johnson Collection at Yale, as well as several other collections he established around the country. If the endeavor suggested sycophancy to some suspicious few who refused to be photographed, it was nevertheless as sincere as his "violent interest" was unflagging. Van Vechten easily admitted he was star-struck all his life, from the time he first knew Bert Williams in 1906, until the last summer of his own eighty-four years in 1964 when he wrote to me: "I am in my usual state of gaping enthusiasm. (Will it never end? Probably NOT.) I heard Andre Watts at the [Lewisohn] Stadium and sans doute he is the greatest living pianist. He has everything, including good taste and he will end in glory, as he has begun."[11] Bert Williams died before Van Vechten started making photographs, and he died himself before he could get to Andre Watts, but hundreds of other subjects—white as well as black—came in between. The list of black subjects is staggering, not only in quantity but in quality, especially the number of people he photographed before their talents were generally recognized, when he sensed that same "glory" he had predicted for Andre Watts: Chester Himes at 30; Shirley Verrett at 24; Leontyne Price at 23; Lena Horne at 21; and James Baldwin, LeRoi Jones, Alvin Ailey, Diahann Carroll, Harry Belafonte, and Arthur Mitchell over thirty years ago.

With the passing of time, Carl Van Vechten's significance has been down-played, on occasion, it may be, by

design, and at best he has been given grudging
acknowledgment. All his life Van Vechten championed the
avant-garde. He wrote seriously about scores of people and
movements that came into subsequent prominence, and he
had the distinction of being the first person with sufficient
clout to draw attention to Afro-American arts and letters at
the time. By making racial integration fashionable in an
attempt to introduce his own race to the pleasures he had
discovered in another, he hoped to extend the possibilities
implicit in that theory of the "talented tenth." Hindsight
tells us that the theory was too firmly grounded in idealism
ever to survive the dream. The advocates of art as well as its
practitioners do not, alas, populate the "untalented ninetieth"
in either race.

Nevertheless, James Weldon Johnson once wrote to Carl
Van Vechten, "Has anyone ever written it down—in black
and white—that you have been one of the most vital forces in
bringing about the artistic emergence of the Negro in
America? Well, I am glad to bear witness to the fact."[12] And
George S. Schuyler, that Menckenesque editor of the
Pittsburgh Courier who was unerringly suspicious but
frequently given to overstatement, declared that "Carl Van
Vechten has done more than any single person in this
country to create the atmosphere of acceptance of the Negro."[13]

None of this addresses itself to the subtle distinction
between "patronage" and "patronizing" to which I referred
in my opening paragraph. It is doubtless easy for the one to
become the other, but it may be almost as easy for the one to
seem to become the other—blanket judgments are always
dangerous—because of black dismay over the circumstances
that led to white patronage in the first place.

NOTES

1. Carl Van Vechten Collection, Manuscript and Archives Division,
    New York Public Library, quoted with permission of Donald
    Gallup, Literary Trustee to the Van Vechten Estate; hereafter
    referred to as CVV.NYPL.

2. Letter to Van Vechten, circa 1925, CVV.NYPL.

3. Langston Hughes, "When Harlem Was in Vogue," *Town and Country*, 95, 49 (July 1940), 64–66.

4. Carl Van Vechten, *Fragments from an Unwritten Autobiography* (New Haven: Yale University Library, 1955), p. 3.

5. Carl Van Vechten, "A Rudimentary Narration," Columbia Oral History, Columbia University, New York City, 1963; hereafter referred to as CVV.Col.

6. CVV.Col.

7. Carl Van Vechten, "The Negro in Art: How Shall He Be Portrayed?" *Crisis*, 31 (March 1926), 129.

8. Rudolph Fisher, *The Walls of Jericho* (New York: Alfred A. Knopf, 1928), p. 117.

9. Mark Helbling, "Carl Van Vechten and the Harlem Renaissance," *Negro American Literature Forum*, 10 (July 1976), 46.

10. Carl Van Vechten, *The Blind Bow-Boy* (New York: Alfred A. Knopf, 1923), p. 163.

11. Carl Van Vechten to Bruce Kellner, 10 August 1964.

12. Quoted in Donald Gallup, *80 Writers Whose Books and Letters Have Been Given over the Past Twenty Years to the Yale University Library by Carl Van Vechten, Compiled in Honor of His 80th Birthday, 17 June 1960* (New Haven: Yale University Library, 1960), p. [12].

13. George S. Schuyler, quoted in Edward Lueders, *Carl Van Vechten* (New York: Twayne Publishers, 1965), p. 95.

Philadelphia's Literary Circle and the Harlem Renaissance

VINCENT JUBILEE

One of the healthiest aspects of the Harlem Renaissance was its quick growth beyond the confines of its birthplace to Afro-American literary circles of other cities in the nation. Washington, for example, aroused itself as the Renaissance gathered strength and soon was the arena for a small literary group—legitimized by its own journal, *Stylus*—centered around Howard University and closely linked to Alain Locke.[1] Afro-American literary aspirants in other cities such as Boston, Philadelphia, Baltimore, Los Angeles, and even Topeka, Kansas, responded to the "vibrant new psychology" Locke had proclaimed as the underpinnings of the "New Negro" mentality[2] by forming literary clubs, sending their efforts to *Opportunity* and *The Crisis*, and by launching, whenever possible, the requisite little literary journal.[3]

Unlike the continuing documentation of the Harlem experience of the period, however, little is written about the world in which those literary aspirants from other cities lived, the circumstances under which they produced their modest journals, or about the sociocultural environment that shaped them and affected their creative efforts.

35

Who were those aspiring authors whirling with the winds of the movement in Harlem, but settled outside the dynamics of the big city? How did they respond to the opportunities for recognition being offered in New York? What cultural instruments—publishers, patronage, and interested booksellers, for example—existed in places like Topeka and Boston for developing, nurturing, and promoting black literary talent? What factors in their own city environments helped or hindered the aspiring writers? For a fuller, more comprehensive understanding of the entire Renaissance experience, we need to know what form and impetus the dynamics of cities other than New York gave to this phenomenon, and who were the individuals, just as in Harlem, who created that direction.

One city that was particularly responsive to "New Negro" thought during the mid-1920s was New York's close neighbor, Philadelphia. The smaller city acted as something of a satellite during the period, revolving around New York, and its members took many a prize in the *Crisis* and *Opportunity* contests. But they were also busy in their own city, publishing their own literary magazine, preparing manuscripts for future publication, meeting in each other's homes, and even helping produce the New York magazine *FIRE!!.*

The circle of Afro-American writers in Philadelphia can first be located within the bindings of *Black Opals*, its little journal. *Black Opals*, a name borrowed from a poem by one of its contributors, Nellie Bright, made its debut in Spring 1927, less than a year after the short-lived *FIRE!!.* But unlike *FIRE!!*, *Black Opals* lasted through four issues, the last dated Christmas 1928.

A survey of the founders of the little magazine and of its contributors shows that the editing and contributing staff consisted mainly, if not entirely, of young people from Philadelphia's black middle class. Besides their common socioeconomic background, the group also shared a level of educational attainment and, to a great extent, professional status. All who gathered around *Black Opals* were sons and daughters of the city's Afro-American professional and entrepreneurial class. All were either college graduates or in attendance at a university—with an unusually large number at the University of Pennsylvania—or working as teachers in the city's public school system.

A significant feature of their class status is that several members of the Philadelphia literary circle were descendants of "Old Philadelphians." Their grandparents had been free blacks who had settled in the city since the early nineteenth century, perhaps among those described by Joseph Willson in his 1841 report on the lifestyle and manners of Philadelphia's "higher classes of colored society."[4] Their parents were certainly among the small sector of professionals—the teachers, clergymen, and physicians—and entrepreneurs, mainly caterers—classified by DuBois in the 1899 *The Philadelphia Negro* as "well-to-do,"[5] the 3,000 who formed "the aristocracy of the Negro population in education, wealth and general social efficiency." They were, as DuBois continued, "largely Philadelphia-born ... and [included] many mulattoes."[6]

Those older generations described by DuBois not only supported the churches, lodges, and savings associations usually found in upwardly striving black communities of that period, but also engaged in "parties and small receptions, . . . musical or social clubs,"[7] established literary and debating societies, and founded race uplift organizations such as the American Negro Historical Society, organized in the city in 1897. The majority also owned their own homes.[8]

DuBois's study is, of course, a classic in sociology. As E. Digby Baltzell, the Philadelphia sociologist, remarks in his introduction to the new 1967 edition, "There has not been a scholarly study of the American Negro in the twentieth century which has not referred to and utilized the empirical findings, the research methods, and the theoretical point of view of this seminal book."[9] But *The Philadelphia Negro* also has a value for the literary historian that has remained unrecognized until now: it holds within its pages of charts and statistics the first information about the "families of undoubted respectability earning sufficient income to live well; not engaged in menial service of any kind"; and "the respectable working-class; in comfortable circumstances with a good home, and having steady remunerative work [with the] younger children in school."[10]

These two classes of black Philadelphians in 1899 were classified by DuBois as "Grade 1 and Grade 2" under the section "Social Classes and Amusements." Unknown to DuBois at that time, those were the classes that were to produce and nurture children who would become Philadelphia's thinkers of the Renaissance period.

DuBois himself did not give many names in his study. But a few years after his publication of 1899, *The Philadelphia Colored Directory* of 1908 imbues DuBois's statistics with the light of reality. In the *Colored Directory*, published by the A.M.E. Church Press, black owners of property—perhaps DuBois's "families . . . earning sufficient income to live well"—are listed by name and address. Lawyers, doctors, teachers, and ministers, along with caterers, grocers, and beauticians, are recorded with addresses. Civic, social, charitable, and literary organizations—some of them mentioned earlier in the DuBois study—also are listed. From the pages of both DuBois's pioneer academic work and the more widely used *Colored Directory*, the family backgrounds of some of Philadelphia's black writers who participated in the Renaissance literary movement come to life.

For example, according to the *Directory*, Martin Van Buren Cowdery had a catering business—one of the most profitable and high-status occupations for blacks of past years— and a residence at 17th and DeLancey Streets.[11] The Cowdery name, however, is listed in the *Philadelphia City Directory* (the phone book) long before 1908. Its first appearance is in the 1870 edition when Martin V.B. Cowdery is shown as a waiter (phone books once listed occupations) at 1717 Addison Street. Later, Martin Cowdery has moved up and become a "caterer" at the same address. By 1890, the name Cowdery is listed at a new address, 1720 DeLancey Street.

In the first decades of the 1900s, the son of Martin Cowdery, Lemuel, begins to appear in the phone directories. In the 1902 book, Lemuel is listed as a student, living with his family at the DeLancey Street number. By 1915, Lemuel has become a clerk and—presumably married—moved to the far reaches of the city, Germantown, where he has a house at 222 West Penn Street. He was still listed there, along with wife Mary, in 1930, with the occupation "Postal Clerk."

That same Lemuel Cowdery, son of one of the city's earliest Afro-American residents and entrepreneurs, and his wife Mary, a social worker (reputedly related, like Jean Toomer, to Lt. Gov. Pinchback of Louisiana), were the parents of Mae Virginia Cowdery, a graduate of the city's Girls' High School, a promising member of the *Black Opals* group, contributor to *Opportunity*, and winner of First Prize for poetry in the 1927 *Crisis* contest. Mae Cowdery was also included in Charles S. Johnson's anthology of 1927, *Ebony and Topaz*, and one of her poems was chosen by Benjamin Brawley for inclusion in *The Negro Genius*.[12]

Pierre A. Dutrieuille and Albert E. Dutrieuille, caterers at 19th near Chestnut, were grandfather and father, respectively, of Bernice Dutrieuille Shelton, a society journalist who moved around the edges of the Renaissance period, associating with its literary aspirants. They were also relatives of Elsie Taylor Dutrieuille, contributor to both *Black Opals* and *Crisis*.[13]

The Dutrieuille name appears in *Gospill's Philadelphia Directory* as early as 1867, when Albert E. is first listed as a cook on Third Street just below Market. The more rewarding occupation of caterer appears next, but following the name Peter (later Pierre) Dutrieuille in 1876, with the business and residence given as 18th Street below Walnut. By 1890, Albert Dutrieuille has made a move, this time to 40 South 19th Street, between Market and Chestnut, a place of business he was to maintain until 1933, when he kept the property but moved into the then-fashionable area at 40th and Spring Garden.[14]

Marion Turner also came from a family of "undoubted respectability." She was a contributor to the journal *Black Opals* when she attended the University of Pennsylvania in the late 1920s. She is still living and is the daughter of the late Dr. John P. Turner, a prominent Philadelphia physician who became, in 1935, the first Afro-American member of the Philadelphia Board of Education. The family lived in a fashionable home at 1705 Jefferson Street during the 1920s.[15]

Not listed in the *Colored Directory* are several members of the *Black Opals* circle who could not be counted as authentic "Old Philadelphians," but who had settled early into the middle-class, educated levels of the city and became part of the literary vanguard. A brief sampling would include James H. Young, an *Opportunity* prizewinner, graduate of the University of Pennsylvania and a teacher with the Philadelphia public schools[16] and Nellie R. Bright, originally from Savannah, Georgia, daughter of an Episcopal minister and a graduate in 1925 with an M.A. from the University of Pennsylvania. Miss Bright helped found and contributed work to *Black Opals*, won a Third Prize in the 1927 *Opportunity* contest, and helped finance the Harlem writers' short-lived *FIRE!!.*[17]

The most outstanding writer of the Philadelphia circle and mentor of the *Black Opals* aspirants was Arthur Huff Fauset, a native of Flemington, New Jersey, but Philadelphian from the early 1900s until his death in 1983. Fauset, the half-brother of the novelist Jessie Redmon Fauset, was the son of an A.M.E. minister, Redmon Fauset, and a white mother, Bella Lehman Huff Fauset.[18]

A certain Redmon Fauset is first seen in the Philadelphia phone directory in 1867 as a tailor. In 1897, however, the Rev. Redmon Fauset is listed at a residence in North Philadelphia, and continues to be listed at least up to 1902. (His daughter, Jessie, appears in Boyd's *Combined Directory* of 1925 as a teacher living at 20th and Tasker.)

Arthur Fauset, the Rev. Redmon Fauset's son, was the leading force behind *Black Opals*, a friend of Alain Locke, and a frequent prize-winner in the *Opportunity* and *Crisis* contests of the Renaissance era. Fauset also made significant contributions to Locke's *The New Negro*, Johnson's *Ebony and Topaz*, and to *FIRE!!.* Fauset was an elementary school principal who took his M.A. from the University of Pennsylvania in 1924 and his Ph.D. in anthropology from the same university in 1942.

Altogether, then, the nucleus of Philadelphia's Afro-American literary community during the Renaissance years came either from the old, established families (some of whom had been in the city at least before the Civil War), who had prospered in business and the professions, or were late arrivals in the city and had entered the elite, educated circles of the black community by virtue of their fathers' occupations. It can be surmised, in the absence of photographs, that most (if not all) were light-skinned, as DuBois had pointed out in his remarks on the black privileged class in 1899, and many had the advantages of a higher education at the city's most prestigious school, the University of Pennsylvania.

The point is clear. Although the Harlem writers, too, were an educated, mostly middle-class group, the Philadelphia circle could hardly be thought of, in the way Saunders Redding described Hughes and MacKay, as "vagabonds, as free in the sun and dust of Georgia, in the steerage of tramp steamers, in the brothels of Lenox Avenue . . . as in the living room of Strivers Row."[19]

If not free to probe the varieties of experience Redding evokes, what did the Philadelphians find at home? A reconstruction of the tone of life that Fauset, Cowdery, Nellie Bright, and others saw around them can be attempted by using two rich sources of information that reflected Afro-American life and values during that period. These sources are the reportage of the activities of the middle class in the city's black press and the recollections of informants who were active in the mid-1920s and who were still living in the early 1980s.

During the 1920s, black Philadelphians read two weekly newspapers of wide circulation: *The Philadelphia Tribune* and *The Pittsburgh Courier*. A sampling of commentary from the social columns of the *Tribune* and the *Courier* between the years 1924 and 1930 will suggest the content of the social and intellectual ambience in which the city's black literary aspirants lived.

The *Tribune*, with a circulation of 30,000 weekly for the years examined, offered the same conventional society reportage offered by the *Courier*. The *Tribune* filled its columns with news about luncheons, dances, debutante debuts, and visits from smart out-of-towners. The *Tribune*, however, tended to be more alert than the *Courier* to cultural events. Forums and lectures were reported in the *Tribune* more frequently, as was news about books and art.

Literary topics, however, appeared infrequently in both the *Courier* and the *Tribune*, and then mainly in connection with New York writers or literary personalities. At various times, the *Courier* reported on Countee Cullen's visit to Paris, the publication of Rudolph Fisher's novel *The Walls of Jericho*, A'Leilia Walker Wilson's plans to turn over her home on West 136th Street to the National Ethiopian Art Theatre; it also offered a serialization of a story by Eric Walrond.[20] A rare column devoted to the new Afro-American literary figures once appeared below the byline of Georgia Douglas Johnson, the Washington poet, but no Philadelphia-born writers except Effie Lee Newsome were mentioned.[21]

All mentions of literary and artistic topics, when they appeared, were brief in both the *Tribune* and the *Courier*, and frequently the social aspect dominated. The Friday Evening Art Club, for example, met at the homes of various members. On one occasion, a member merited comment in the press for the repast that was equal to "a Bellevue Stratford De Luxe luncheon," served after an Art Club meeting, but what the group did with art is not discernible from the press report.[22]

Social clubs abounded in the Philadelphia Afro-American community. News about The Pequod Club, The Ugly Club, The 500 Club, The Debs, and The Frogs, a pinochle club, appeared almost every week. Several literati belonged to these clubs, though their purposes were more social than literary. The Frogs Club, for example, included among its members the school principal James H. Young, who wrote for *Black Opals*, and Allan R. Freelon, the artist and school supervisor who produced the graphic work for the little journal as well as covers for *Crisis*.[23]

The now-famous Writers' Guild dinner of March 21, 1924, was reported both in the *Courier* and the *Tribune*. The *Courier* version, written by Georgia Douglas Johnson, noted that Dr. Albert C. Barnes, the Philadelphia art collector, "gave a very charming talk on art,"[24] while the *Tribune* recorded the event as "a reception" for Jessie Fauset "by her fellow workers in the NAACP. . . ."[25] But Arthur Fauset, a published writer by 1924 who attended the dinners, was not mentioned in either account.[26] In one of Evelyn Crawford Reynolds's society columns, Bessie Calhoun Bird received a nod of recognition for her poem "A Prayer" in *Black Opals*. But her impressive new "maison" [sic] was mentioned first.[27] Mae V. Cowdery the poet—with her name misspelled— appears in a society column of February 1929, but for her presence at a dance "in a soft frock of powder blue taffeta,"[28] not for her conquest in *Crisis* or *Opportunity* or for her inclusion in *Ebony and Topaz*.

In the selection of photographs, the city's black press also neglected the literary circle. Amid the weekly photographs of political leaders, church leaders, society matrons, and debutantes, no photos appear of Mae V. Cowdery, Arthur Huff Fauset, Elsie Taylor Dutrieuille, or Nellie Bright.

Literary teas, a major form of entertainment in the black nineteenth-century society of DuBois's study, were not held frequently in black Philadelphia of the mid-1920s. The eager young writers, such as Arthur Fauset, took the train to New York to attend literary teas. Fauset says he found those gatherings to be "jovial, placid affairs . . . but enjoyed by everyone."[29]

From the accounts of informants and from a search in the black press, it appears that Philadelphia also lacked a "bohemian" haven for its black writers. I. Maximilian Martin, an astute observer of black Philadelphia, remembers that the Marion Tea Room at 20th and Bainbridge was "the only center for inter-racial literary meetings on a basis of equality. . . . Whites would come if invited."[30] Except for the Marion Tea Room, however, the black writers apparently did not have a congenial public meeting place such as a coffeehouse, bookstore, or even the living room of a Jessie

Fauset or Georgia Douglas Johnson, two of the Renaissance era's salon hostesses. In contrast, the Harlem writers had a circle of apartments that included Miss Fauset's, A'Lelia Walker's, Walter White's, James Weldon Johnson's, and Aaron Douglas's. As Arthur Huff Fauset remarked in 1977, "Mae Cowdery lived all the way up in Germantown. . . . If there had been a place to meet, we could have had a permanent literary group."[31] I. Maximilian Martin has also observed that "there was no interaction between the white and black intellectual community. You had to go to New York for that."[32]

In summary, the research on Philadelphia's black community of writers during the Renaissance reveals that the literature produced at that time came out of one isolated class, a class defined, in some cases, by the family's years of establishment in the city, by high economic status, high educational achievement, and a physical component—light skin—that was seen as an index of privilege in the black community. In addition, all the writers lived within the family circle and in residential areas that ranged from comfortable middle class to fashionable by prevailing standards of the period. Writing was not the sole occupation for any of the members of the literary circle; none chose writing as a full-time professional career. Their production did not extend beyond the literary forms of poetry, the short story, and the occasional essay; none published a novel, a play, or other kind of extended work. Furthermore, the *Black Opals* circle included no one from lower socioeconomic groups.

The research also suggests that the wider Afro-American community in Philadelphia gave little or no recognition and support to its literary aspirants. It did not provide the para-literary mechanisms—book celebrations, literary salons, charismatic leadership figures—that usually give the needed visibility to the culture of book production and add vitality and a personal identity to the hard facts of the business, making it attractive and newsworthy to the average public.

All those factors helped determine the course, the content, the quantity, and the quality of Philadelphia's contribution to the direction and ideological import of the Harlem Renaissance. If black Philadelphia's voice was not as authoritative and influential as the times required, then some of the reasons (besides the matter of real talent) might be found in the nature of the city's inherent social and cultural configurations. Alain Locke had reason to be concerned about those sociocultural influences. Writing a "greeting" to the young writers in their first issue of *Black Opals*, Locke—an "Old Philadelphian"[33] himself who had moved on to other places—warned that

> Philadelphia is the Shrine of the Old Negro. . . . But I hope Philadelphia youth will realize that the past can enslave. . . . Vital creative thinking . . . must be done, and if necessary we must turn our backs on the past to face the future. . . . If the birth of the New Negro among us halts in the shell of conservatism, . . . then the egg shell must be smashed to pieces and the living thing freed.[34]

The configurations of other cities such as Boston, Los Angeles, and Topeka may be found to be different from Philadelphia's, and research may result in a different set of conclusions. In any case, all these areas of black literary activity need to be more extensively studied. A fuller exploration of literary colonies scattered across the nation will yield findings that will help greatly in forming a picture of the characteristics of the Afro-American intellectual ambience during a vital era in black literary and social history.

NOTES

1. Lawrence Rubin, "Washington and the Negro Renaissance," *Crisis*, 78 (1971), 79–82.

2. *The New Negro* (1925; rpt. New York: Atheneum, 1970), pp. 9–10.

3. Abby Ann Arthur Johnson and Ronald M. Johnson, "Forgotten Pages: Black Literary Magazines in the 1920s," *Journal of American Studies*, 8 (1974), 363–382.

4. *Sketches of the High Classes of Colored Society in Philadelphia: By a Southerner* (1841; rpt. Philadelphia: Historic Publications, 1969).

5. W.E.B. DuBois, *The Philadelphia Negro* (1899; rpt. New York: Schocken Books, 1967), p. 172.

6. *The Philadelphia Negro*, pp. 316–318.

7. Ibid., p. 320.

8. R.R. Wright, Jr., and Ernest Smith, eds., *The Philadelphia Colored Directory* (Philadelphia: Philadelphia Colored Directory Co., 1908), p. 11.

9. Ibid., p. ix.

10. Ibid., pp. 310–311.

11. See "Caterers" and "Property Holders," *The Philadelphia Colored Directory*, 1908, pp. 57–59, pp. 81–98.

12. Biographical data on Mae V. Cowdery from interviews with Ronald Johnson, 20 March 1977; Arthur Huff Fauset, 30 March 1977, 16 April 1977, and 30 May 1977; Bernice Dutrieuille Shelton, 23 October 1979. Also from *The Philadelphia Colored Directory*, 1908, p. 58, and *Polk's Philadelphia City Directory* (Philadelphia: R.L. Polk, 1929).

13. Biographical data from Bernice Dutrieuille Shelton, 23 October 1979.

14. Interview with Bernice D. Shelton, October 1979.

15. *Polk's-Boyd's Philadelphia Directory*, 1930 (Philadelphia: R.L. Polk).

16. *Black Opals*, 1, 1 (Spring 1927), list of contributors.

17. Biographical data on Nellie R. Bright obtained through interviews with I. Maximilian Martin, 21 April 1977, 4 August 1977; with Arthur Huff Fauset, 30 July 1977; with Julia Polk Parham, 28 May 1977; and with Bernice Dutrieuille Shelton, 23 October 1979. Also in a letter from Harold Haskins of the University of Pennsylvania, dated February 26, 1981.

18. Biographical data on Arthur Huff Fauset from interviews 30 March 1977, 6 April 1977, 22 April 1977. Also Carolyn Wedin Sylvander, "Jessie Redmon Fauset, Black American Writer: Her Relationships, Biographical and Literary, with Black and White Writers, 1910–1935," Diss., University of Wisconsin-Madison 1976, pp. 51–52; Alain Locke, ed., *The New Negro* (New York: Albert and Charles Boni, 1925), p. 417; Arthur P. Davis and Michael M. Peplow, eds., *The New Negro Renaissance: An Anthology* (New York: Holt, Rinehart and Winston, 1975), pp. 285, 521–522; Ann A. Shockley and Sue P. Chandler, *Living Black American Authors* (New York: R.R. Bowker and Co., 1973), pp. 48–49; *Opportunity*, 4 (June 1926), 188–189; Benjamin Brawley, *The Negro Genius* (New York: Dodd, Mead, 1937), p. 261.

19. Saunders Redding, *To Make a Poet Black* (Chapel Hill: University of North Carolina Press, 1939), p. 103.

20. *The Pittsburgh Courier*, 6 October 1928, p. 6; 4 August 1928, p. 7; 22 March 1924, p. 9; 12 April 1924, p. 12.

21. *The Courier*, 6 October 1928, p. 6; 4 August 1928, p. 7.

22. *The Philadelphia Tribune*, 16 February 1924, p. 5.

23. Interview with I. Maximilian Martin, 4 August 1977.

24. *The Courier*, 29 March 1924, p. 3.

25. *The Tribune*, 5 April 1924, p. 7.

26. For a partial guest list of the Civic Club dinner, see Charles S. Johnson, "The Debut of the Younger School of Negro Writers," *Opportunity*, 2, 17 (1924), 143.

27. *The Tribune*, 6 December 1928, p. 4.

28. *The Tribune*, 14 February 1929, p. 4.

29. Interview with Fauset, 30 July 1977.

30. Interview with Martin, 4 August 1977.

31. Interview with Fauset, 3 March 1977.

32. Interview with Martin, 4 August 1977.

33. Directory data are from earliest extant copies available at the Van Pelt Library, University of Pennsylvania. Pliny I. Locke, Alain Locke's father, appears in the 1876 edition and until 1894, when his wife Mary appears as a "widow."

34. *Black Opals*, 1, 1 (Spring 1927), 3.

Langston Hughes and Approaches to Modernism in the Harlem Renaissance

ARNOLD RAMPERSAD

In 1936, certainly after the end of the Harlem Renaissance, one highly literate young black student, a junior at Tuskegee Institute, saw no connection between modernism and black American verse even as he recognized a link between modernism and black culture. "Somehow in my uninstructed reading of Pound and Eliot," he later wrote, "I had recognized a relationship between modern poetry and jazz music, and this led me to wonder why I was not encountering similar devices in the work of Afro-American writers." In 1936, however, the youth came across a poem by a young black Communist based in Chicago, published in *New Masses*. Although the poem "was not a masterpiece," he would write, at last "I found in it traces of the modern poetic sensibility and techniques that I had been seeking."[1]

The student was Ralph Ellison; the Communist poet, Richard Wright. The point is that Ellison, following the Harlem Renaissance, could see nothing of literary modernism in its writing, but had to depend for a glimpse of modernism in black poetry on a writer who not only had nothing to do with either Harlem or its Renaissance, but would the following year, 1937, dismiss virtually all of black writing. "Generally speaking," Wright declared (without offering an exception), "Negro writing in the past has been confined to humble novels, poems, and plays, prim and decorous ambassadors who went a-begging to white America." Wright knew well that ambassadors speak typically in archaic, sanctioned formulae; in general, they initiate nothing, make nothing new.[2]

The writers of the Harlem Renaissance apparently had not responded to Emerson's primal dictum that "the experience of each new age requires a new confession, and the world seems always waiting for its poet." Or had they? Let us resolve modernism into a series of questions aimed at these writers. Did they sense some historic shift in the world that justified Pound's famous charge to writers to "Make it new!"?[3] Did they perceive a crisis of expression, a need to, again in Pound's words, "resuscitate the dead art/Of poetry?"[4] Had blacks made a pact with Walt Whitman, as Pound had done ("I make a pact with you, Walt Whitman—/I have detested you long enough")?[5] Did they perceive the modern dominance of science and technology as requiring a self-preserving, adaptive response by art, in order to make something, in Frost's phrase, of "a diminished thing?"[6] Did they recognize a crisis in the loss of prestige by religion? Or were the black writers of the Harlem Renaissance merely, as Ellison and Wright would have us believe, dull and uninspired imitators of mediocre white writers?

I would argue that writers such as Jean Toomer, Countee Cullen, Langston Hughes, Claude McKay, Wallace Thurman, Richard Bruce Nugent, and Zora Neale Hurston were as aware as anyone else about the pressure of the modern on their lives and their art. Of course, to be aware of a situation does not mean that one acts responsibly; to act responsibly does not guarantee success. My purpose here is to look at some of the ways in which black writers engaged or failed to engage various compelling aspects of the age in which they lived. Perhaps we can thus learn something about the Renaissance, and perhaps even about modernism itself.

The movement toward the modern in black letters began, in fact, a generation before the Harlem school, when Afro-American poetry was dominated by the work, in standard English but more popularly in dialect form, of Paul Laurence Dunbar. By 1900 (he would die six years later) Dunbar's poetry enjoyed a national vogue; as a boy, for example, William Carlos Williams read the black poet as a matter of course. To Dunbar himself, however, and to at least one other black writer, James Weldon Johnson, dialect poetry, and thus Afro-American poetry, was a dead art. In it, "darkies" most often either sang, danced, ate, and stole comically, or they mourned some minor loss pathetically. Dunbar's verse led William Dean Howells to note "a precious difference of temperament between the races which it would be a great pity to lose," and to see "the range between appetite and emotion, with certain lifts far beyond and above it," as the range of the black race.[7] Such a reaction made Dunbar despair, without showing him a way out of his dilemma. "He sang of life, serenely sweet,/With, now and then, a deeper note," he wrote once about himself. "He of love when earth was young,/And Love, itself, was in his lays./But ah, the world, it turned to praise/A jingle in a broken tongue."[8]

The first step in the resuscitation of black poetry came late in the summer of 1900, when Dunbar's friend and admirer James Weldon Johnson at last read the work of a white writer who had died during the previous decade. "I was engulfed and submerged by the book, and set floundering again," Johnson later recalled in his autobiography, *Along This Way*:

> I got a sudden realization of the artificiality of conventionalized Negro dialect poetry: of its exaggerated geniality, childish optimism, forced comicality and mawkish sentiment. . . . I could see that the poet writing in the conventionalized dialect, no matter how sincere he might be, was dominated by his audience; that his audience was a section of the white American reading public; that when he wrote he was expressing what often bore little relation, sometime no relation at all, to actual Negro life; that he was really expressing only certain conceptions about Negro life that his audience was willing to accept and ready to enjoy; that, in fact, he wrote mainly for the delectation of an audience that was an outside group. And I could discern

that it was on this line that the psychological attitude of the
poets writing in the dialect and that of the folk artists faced
in different directions; because the latter, although working
in the dialect, sought only to express themselves for
themselves, and to their *own group*.[9]

Thus Johnson laid bare the central dilemma facing not
merely Dunbar but all black writers in America. The white
poet was, of course, Walt Whitman, with whom Johnson
made a pact more than a dozen years before Pound did.
Neither Johnson nor Pound, however, would have been
sensitive to Whitman had it not been for altering social and
historical conditions that first gradually, then torrentially,
made Whitman's insights into social meaning and poetic
form shine forth. For Pound, the twin factors were, perhaps,
science and technology, on one hand, and the Great War on
the other. I suspect that in 1900, when Johnson first read
Whitman, science meant relatively little to him as a threat,
and the Great War was still more than a dozen years away.
Or was it? For blacks, there was another great war, one that
saw in the 1890s (the "nadir" of Afro-American history, as
Rayford Logan has called it) racial segregation and black
disfranchisement made law by the Supreme Court and
enforced brutally by the Ku Klux Klan. In *Along This Way*,
Johnson's discussion of *Leaves of Grass* follows immediately
on his horrified recollection of the fourth major race riot in
the history of blacks in New York, occurring in 1900 and
capping a decade in which almost 1700 blacks had been
lynched, "numbers of them with a savagery that was satiated
with nothing short of torture, mutilation, and burning alive
at the stake."[10] This was for blacks the "Great War," compared
to which their involvement in the later carnage in Europe
was almost a form of affirmative action—affirmative action
with a vengeance, if you will. Every major American war
from the Revolution to Vietnam, it must be remembered, has
led to a material *advance* in the freedom of black Americans.
    That this pressure had its effect on poetic form among
blacks is independently demonstrated in the sometime
poetry of the scholar-turned-protagonist, W.E.B. DuBois. In
DuBois's verse we see rage against racism making the tropes

of traditional poetic discourse impossible, and pushing his pen, willy-nilly, toward free verse and liberated rhyme in a series of poems, such as "A Litany of Atlanta," "The Burden of Black Women," "Song of the Smoke," and "Prayers of God," published in the first two decades of this century. When the war in Europe came, it only added to the pressure toward the modern. "We darker men said," DuBois wrote in his essay "The Souls of White Folk," "This is not Europe gone mad; this is not aberration nor insanity; this *is* Europe; this seeming Terrible is the real soul of white culture,—stripped and visible today. This is where the world has arrived—these dark and awful depths and not the shining and ineffable heights of which it boasted."[11]

By this time, at least one younger black writer had taken black poetry closer to the modern. In 1912 Fenton Johnson's first book of verse, *A Little Dreaming,* was conventional and included both a long poem in blank verse and Dunbaresque dialect verse. Within two or three years, however, he had completely renovated his sense of poetry. In *Visions of Dusk* (1915) and *Songs of the Soil* (1916) he not only adopted free verse but altered his ways of viewing civilization itself. Instead of glorifying white high culture, Fenton Johnson spurned it, as Pound would do in writing of Europe as "an old bitch gone in the teeth," and "a botched civilization."[12] Unlike Pound, however, Fenton Johnson did so from an unmistakably racial perspective:

> I am tired of work; I am tired of building up some body else's civilization.
> Let us take a rest, M'Lissy Jane.
> I will go down to the Last Chance Saloon, drink a gallon or two of gin, shoot a game or two of dice and sleep the rest of the night on one of Mike's barrels.
> You will let the old shanty go to rot, the white people's clothes turn to dust, and the Cavalry Baptist Church sink to the bottomless pit. . . .
> Throw the children into the river; civilization has given us too many. It is better to die than it is to grow up and find out that you are colored.

Pluck the stars out of the heavens. The stars mark our
destiny. The stars marked my destiny.
I am tired of civilization.[13]

In "The Banjo Player," the speaker wanders the land playing
"the music of the peasant people." He is a favorite in saloons
and with little children. "But I fear that I am a failure. Last
night a woman called me a troubadour. What is a
troubadour?"[14] "The Scarlet Woman," who possesses "a white
girl's education and a face that enchanted the men of both
races," spurns classical mythic language and enters a
bordello for white men: "Now I can drink more gin than
any man for miles around. Gin is better than all the water
in Lethe."[15]

Fenton Johnson was so close to the center of the Chicago
manifestation of modernism, which is to say the center of
literary modernism except for wherever Ezra Pound
happened to be at the moment, that it is unclear how much
he owes to the more famous poets he resembles in his work—
Carl Sandburg, whose groundbreaking *Chicago and Other
Poems* appeared in 1916, and Edgar Lee Masters in his *Spoon
River Anthology* (1915). Johnson published in Harriet
Monroe's *Poetry* magazine and at least one other important
modernist outlet, *Others.* One point must be noted, however,
about the work thus far of Fenton Johnson, James Weldon
Johnson, and DuBois. For all its incipient modernism, their
verse betrays no sign of any specific innovative formal
influence by the culture, or subculture, they championed.
Indignation at the treatment of blacks moved them to change
as poets; black culture itself did not. This was the crucial
hurdle facing would-be black modernists.

Yet another poet to balk at the highest fence was Claude
McKay, the Jamaican-born writer who first gained notice in
the United States in 1917, when he published two sonnets in
Seven Arts magazine. Subsequent publications in *Pearson's,*
Max Eastman's *Liberator* (where he would serve as an
associate editor), and the leading black journals, such as the
radical socialist *Messenger* and DuBois's *Crisis,* as well as in
prestigious English publications, such as C.K. Ogden's

Cambridge Magazine, made him for a while the most respected of Afro-American versifiers. Two volumes of verse, *Spring in New Hampshire* (London, 1920), with an introduction by I.A. Richards, and *Harlem Shadows* (Harcourt, Brace, 1922) anchored his reputation. For black Americans, however, McKay's single most impressive publication was not one of his lyric evocations of nature but a sonnet published in 1919, following perhaps the bloodiest summer of anti-black riots since the end of the Civil War. In "If We Must Die," McKay implored his readers not to die "like hogs/Hunted and penned in an inglorious spot" but to "nobly die,/So that our precious blood may not be shed/In vain." Even if death is certain, "Like men we'll face the murderous, cowardly pack,/Pressed to the wall, dying, but fighting back."[16]

With McKay and "If We Must Die," we come not only directed to the Harlem school but also to one of its principal tensions—that between radicalism of political and racial thought, on the one hand, and, on the other, a bone-deep commitment to conservatism of form. As a poet, McKay was absolutely ensnared by the sonnet, which—for all the variety possible within its lines—is perhaps the most telling sign of formal conservatism in the writing of poetry in English. Perhaps no greater tension exists in a brief Afro-American text than that between the rage of "If We Must Die" and the sonnet form. McKay used the form again and again to write some of the most hostile verse in Afro-American letters, as in "To the White Fiends" ("Think you I am not a fiend and savage too?/Think you I could not arm me with a gun/And shoot down ten of you for every one/Of my black brothers murdered, burnt by you?"[17] and in "The White House," or "Tiger," where "The white man is a tiger at my throat,/Drinking my blood as my life ebbs away,/And muttering that his terrible striped coat/Is Freedom's."[18]

McKay was not alone in his commitment to conservative forms even in the postwar modernist heyday. If the work of Countee Cullen, a far younger writer, was more varied than McKay's, his formal conservatism was as powerful. Cullen's idols were John Keats ("I cannot hold my peace, John

Keats;/There never was a spring like this"), and A.E. Housman, still alive but moribund surely when one considers the distance between his blue remembered hills and the steamy streets of Harlem.[19] And unlike McKay, who wrote of both race and "universal" topics without a sense of contradiction, Cullen resented the inspiration that came from racial outrage. In a novel, *One Way to Heaven* (1932), he satirized a black woman who insists upon teaching her students verse by Langston Hughes. "While her pupils could recite like small bronze Ciceros, 'I Too Sing America'," the narrator jibes, "they never had heard of 'Old Ironsides,' 'The Blue and the Gray,' or 'The Wreck of the Hesperides.' They could identify lines from Hughes, Dunbar, Cotter, and the multitudinous Johnsons, but were unaware of the contributions of Longfellow, Whittier, and Holmes to American literature."[20] Elsewhere he ridicules a poem by a so-called "Negro poet." "Taken in a nutshell," a character explains scornfully, "it means that niggers have a hell of a time in this God-damned country. That's all Negro poets write about."[21] In perhaps his best-known couplet, Cullen lamented "this curious thing:/To make a poet black, and bid him sing!"[22]

Exactly why McKay and Cullen stuck by conservative forms in the midst of a decade of change is too complicated a question to answer here.[23] But we might take note of one or two points. If McKay was a radical socialist and an anti-modernist, he was in line with a tradition of taste among great radicals from Marx to Lenin, who fomented revolution but clung to the classics like bourgeois intellectuals. "I am unable to consider the productions of futurism, cubism, expressionism and other isms," Lenin wrote privately somewhere. "I do not understand them. I get no joy from them."[24] In addition, McKay was in line with the very philosophy of Marxism, which defines the world in a way diametrically opposed to modernism; Marxism and modernism are poles apart.

Langston Hughes, in opening his *Nation* essay in 1926, "The Negro and the Racial Mountain," bluntly attacked Cullen's dilemma without naming him. He wrote about a black friend, a writer, who wished to be known not as a Negro poet, but as a poet. "Meaning subconsciously," Hughes wrote, "'I would like to be white.'"[25] Cullen might have defended himself by quoting T.S. Eliot on tradition—or, if you permit an anachronism—by quoting Ralph Ellison, who would distinguish between (on one hand) his ancestors—T.S. Eliot and Hemingway, above all, who strongly influenced him, and (on the other) his family, such as Richard Wright and Langston Hughes, who apparently influenced him not at all. But Cullen was not Eliot nor could ever be. Eliot spoke up for the power of dead poets on aesthetic grounds, but the choice of white ancestors over black relatives cannot ever be, to say the least, a purely aesthetic matter. In addition, one must be wary of the motives of anyone, of any color, who exalts his ancestors at the expense of his family.

Let us turn from the most conservative members of the Harlem school to probably the *least* conservative according to modernist standards—Jean Toomer and Richard Bruce Nugent. Toomer's *Cane*, a pastiche of fiction, poetry, drama, and hieroglyphics published in 1923, has been hailed almost invariably as the greatest single document of the Renaissance. Bruce Nugent's published work in the 1920s was scant but very striking, especially the hallucinogenic, stream-of-consciousness story "Smoke, Lilies and Jade," which was too quickly compared by at least one review of *FIRE!!* magazine, where it first appeared in 1926, to *Ulysses*. Is it significant that Toomer and Nugent, the most modernist of the black writers, were also probably the least racial either personally or in their writing? From the start, Nugent seemed to consider race a great irrelevancy. And while Jean Toomer's *Cane* is saturated with a concern for race and the complex fate of being black in America, even as his book was appearing the extremely light-skinned Toomer was vehemently denying that he was a Negro—an attitude that only intensified over the years as his writing became more modernist and purged of the racial theme. Bruce Nugent, one black modernist, says that race doesn't matter; Toomer, another, says that race doesn't matter as long as nobody calls him black. Are we to conclude, then, that modernism and black racial feeling, with its political consequences, are incompatible?

It might be useful here to look at the work of Melvin B. Tolson, who began writing at the tail end of the Renaissance with a limited sense of the modern, but grew to be acclaimed as the first authentic black modernist poet. Tolson was the author of *A Gallery of Harlem Portraits*, posthumously published but in manuscript form by 1931; the Marxist-influenced *Rendezvous with America* (1944); and a deeply modernist *Libretto for the Republic of Liberia* (1953), among other works. Beginning with the sense of the modern derived from Edwin Arlington Robinson and Carl Sandburg, Tolson repudiated their blending of free verse, highly accessible language, and folk references in order to master the most complex version of modernism. The result was poetry beyond the ability of all but a few readers to understand, let alone enjoy. This new poetry, however, tremendously excited those privileged few, including the reformed racist Allen Tate, who in 1931 refused to attend a dinner for Langston Hughes and James Weldon Johnson in Nashville because they were black, but lived to write an introduction in 1953 to *Libretto for the Republic of Liberia*. Tolson not only showed a "first rate intelligence at work from first to last," Tate marvelled, but for "the first time, it seems to me, a Negro poet has assimilated completely the full poetic language of his time, and by implication, the language of the Anglo-American tradition."[26] As if that were not praise enough, William Carlos Williams found a place of honor for Tolson, and Allen Tate, in the fourth book of *Paterson*:

> —and to Tolson and to his ode
> and to Liberia and to Allen Tate
> (give him credit)
> and to the South generally
>
>   "Selah!"[27]

Thus encouraged, Tolson deepened his commitment to modernism with *Harlem Gallery: Book I. The Curator* (1965). In his introduction to the book, however, Karl

Shapiro questioned Tate's statement that Tolson was indebted to white modernist masters and their special language. "*Tolson writes in Negro*," Shapiro declared.[28] Let me quote some lines from the first stanza of the book:

> Lord of the House of Flies,
>   jaundiced-eyed, synapses purled,
> wries before the tumultuous canvas,
>   *The Second of May*--
>   by Goya:
>   the dagger of Madrid
>   vs.
>   the scimitar of Murat.
> In Africa, in Asia, on the Day
> of Barricades, alarm birds bedevil the Great White
> World, a Burdian's ass—not Balaam's—between oats
> and hay.[29]

Any Negro who speaks naturally like this is probably wearing a straightjacket. In its stated themes, the poem justifies Tolson's continuing sense of himself as a champion of his fellow blacks and their history; in its full language, it repudiates that sense. A while ago, Toomer and Nugent led me to *ask* whether modernism can be compatible with strong racial feeling. Tolson leads me to *understand* that complex modernism cannot be so compatible. Racial feeling, which is spurious unless accompanied by a deep sense of political wrong, demands an accessible art; the more pervasive the political wrong, the more accessible must be the art. Melvin Tolson may be on his way to Mount Olympus, but only at the expense of his people and their common poets, washed up on the shores of oblivion while the mighty modernist river rolls by.

When we drive by the scene of an accident, we feel the pain of broken bones and flowing blood. We tremble, but we drive on, unscathed and unstained. Are all of us integral victims of the accident of modernism (which followed the accident of World War I)? Or are some of us only rubbernecking? Must we assume that what is modern for the white goose is also modern for the black gander, that the dominant quality of white life in the twentieth century, as perceived by certain great white poets, is the same as the dominant temper for black? Or that the white quality is something to which blacks should have *aspired* (a tragic attitude, but one to which Jean Toomer, I think, succumbed)? Nor is this a matter of black and white alone. Robert Frost, to my mind, achieved unquestioned greatness swimming against the tide of modernism, ridiculing free verse, gentrifying run-down forms, forging out of a mixture, in which New England regionalism played a very strong part, both a critique of modernism and a body of work beyond easy category.

The major meditative poem by a black writer of the decade, Arna Bontemps's "Nocturne at Bethesda," reveals a black poet "flying low,/I thought I saw the flicker of a wing/Above the mulberry trees; but not again./Bethesda sleeps. This ancient pool that healed/A host of bearded Jews does not awake. . . ."[30] "Nocturne at Bethesda" is the black counterpart to Wallace Stevens's magnificent "Sunday Morning," in which Stevens dwells on the crisis of spirituality but denies transcendent religion in favor of a future of hedonism: "Supple and turbulent, a ring of men/Shall chant in orgy on a summer morn/Their boisterous devotion to the sun,/Not as a god, but as a god might be,/Naked among them, like a savage source,"[31] In "Nocturne at Bethesda," Arna Bontemps, who never outgrew completely the lugubriousness of his Seventh Day Adventism, nevertheless also looks to a new day beyond religion: "Yet I hope, still I long to live./If there can be returning after death/I shall come back. But it will not be here;/If you want me you must search for me/Beneath the palms of Africa."

The finest black poet of the decade, Langston Hughes, rejected metaphysics and superstition altogether; loyal to perhaps the essential modernist criterion, Hughes for the most part looked not before and after, but at what *is*. Hughes went in the only direction a black poet could go and still be great in the 1920s: he had to lead blacks, in at least one corner of their lives—in his case, through poetry—into the modern world. His genius lay in his uncanny ability to lead by following (one is tempted to invoke Eliot's image of the poet's mind as a platinum filament), to identify the black modern, recognize that it was not the same as the white modern, and to structure his art (not completely, to be sure, but to a sufficient extent for it to be historic) along the lines of that black modernism.

Modernism began for Hughes on January 1919, a month short of his seventeenth birthday, when the Cleveland Central High School *Monthly*, in which he had been publishing undistinguished verse for more than a year, announced a long poem "in free verse"—apparently the first in the history of the magazine. "A Song of the Soul of Central" ("Children of all people and all creeds/Come to you and you make them welcome") indicates that Hughes had made his individual pact with Walt Whitman.[32] With Whitman's influence came a break with the genteel tyranny of rhyme and the pieties of the Fireside poets and the majority of black versifiers. Already conscious of himself as a black, however, Hughes could not accept, much less internalize, a vision of the modern defined largely by the fate of Europe after the war. Sharing little or nothing of J. Alfred Prufrock's sense of an incurably diseased world, Hughes looked with indifference on the ruined splendors of the waste land. In practice, modernism for him would mean not Pound, Eliot, or Stevens, but Whitman, Vachel Lindsay, and, above all, Sandburg. The last became "my guiding star."[33] Hughes, however, did not remain star-struck for long; within a year or so he had emancipated himself from direct influence. In one instance, where the well-meaning Sandburg had written: "I am the nigger./Singer of Songs,/Dancer," Hughes had responded with the more dignified (though not superior) "Negro": "I am the Negro:/Black as the night is black,/Black like the depths of my Africa."[34]

The key to his release as a poet was his discovery of the significance of race, as well as other psychological factors (beyond our scope here) that amount to a final admission of his aloneness in the world, with both factors combining to make Hughes dependent on the regard of his race as

practically no other black poet has been. He responded by
consciously accepting the challenge of Whitman and
Sandburg but also by accepting as his own special task, within
the exploration of modern democratic vistas in the United
States, the search for a genuinely Afro-American poetic form.
At the center of his poetic consciousness stood the black
masses,

> Dream-singers all,
> Story-tellers,
> Dancers,
> Loud laughers in the hands of Fate—
> My people. [35]

Or, as he soon more calmly, and yet more passionately,
would express his admiration and love:

> The night is beautiful,
> So the faces of my people.
>
> The stars are beautiful,
> So the eyes of my people.
>
> Beautiful, also, is the sun
> Beautiful, also, are the souls of my people.[36]

Before he was nineteen, Hughes had written at least three of
the poems on which his revered position among black
readers would rest. The most important was "The Negro
Speaks of Rivers" ("I've known rivers:/I've known rivers
ancient as the world and older than the flow of human blood
in human veins./My soul has grown deep like the rivers.")[37]
"When Sue Wears Red" drew on the ecstatic cries of the black
church to express a tribute to black woman unprecedented in
the literature of the race.

> When Susanna Jones wears red
> Her face is like an ancient cameo
> Turned brown by the ages.
>
> Come with a blast of trumpets,
>   Jesus! . . .[38]

The third major poem of this first phase of Hughes's adult creativity was "Mother to Son," a dramatic monologue that reclaimed dialect (Dunbar's "jingle in a broken tongue") for the black poet ("Well, son, I'll tell you:/Life for me ain't been no crystal stair./It's had tacks in it,/And splinters").[39] With this poem and the resuscitation of dialect, Hughes came closer than any of the poets before him to what I have identified as the great hurdle facing the committed black poet—how to allow the race to infuse and inspire the very form of a poem, and not merely its surface contentions. Until this step could be taken, black poetry would remain antiquarian, anti-modern.

To a degree greater than that of any other young black poet, however, Hughes trained himself to be a modern poet— I am conscious here of Pound's words on the general subject, and on Eliot in particular. His high school, dominated by the children of east European immigrants, and where he was class poet and editor of the yearbook, was a training ground in cosmopolitanism. Mainly from Jewish classmates, "who were mostly interested in more than basketball and the glee club," he was introduced to basic texts of radical socialism.[40] Although at 21 he began his first ocean voyage by dumping overboard a box of his books, the detritus of his year at Columbia (he saved only one book—*Leaves of Grass*: "That one I could not throw away"), it was not out of ignorance of what they might contain.[41] "Have you read or tried to read," he wrote in 1923 to a friend, "Joyce's much discussed 'Ulysses'?"[42] By the age of 23 he could speak both French and Spanish. In 1923 he was writing poems about Pierrot (a *black* Pierrot, to be sure), after Jules Laforgue, like Edna St. Vincent Millay in *Aria da Capo*, and another young man who would soon concede that he was a poet manqué and turn to fiction to confront the gap between lowly provincialism and modernism—William Faulkner. If Hughes went to Paris and Italy without finding the Lost Generation, at least he was able in 1932 to assure Ezra Pound (who had written to him from Rappallo to complain about the lack of instruction in African culture in America) that "Many of your poems insist on remaining in my head, not the words, but the mood and the meaning, which, after all, is the heart of a poem."[43]

Hughes also shared with white modernists, to a degree far greater than might be inferred from his most popular poems, an instinct toward existentialism in its more pessimistic form. One poem, written just before his first book of poems appeared in 1926, suggests the relative ease with which he could have taken to "raceless" modernist idioms. From "A House in Taos":

> *Thunder of the Rain God*
> *And we three*
> *Smitten by beauty.*
> *Thunder of the Rain God:*
> *And we three*
> *Weary, weary.*
> *Thunder of the Rain God*
> *And you, she and I*
> *Waiting for the nothingness. . . .*[44]

Hughes, however, had already committed himself to a very different vision of poetry and the modern world, a vision rooted in the modern black experience and expressed most powerfully and definitively in the music called blues. What is the blues? Although W.C. Handy was the first musician to popularize it, notably with *St. Louis Blues*, the form is so deeply based in the chants of Afro-American slave labor, field hollers, and sorrow songs as to be ancient and comprises perhaps the greatest art of Africans in North America. Oral and improvisational by definition, the blues nevertheless has a classical regimen. Its most consistent form finds a three-line stanza, in which the second line restates the first, and the third provides a contrasting response to both. "The blues speak to us simultaneously of the tragic and the comic aspects of the human condition," Ralph Ellison has written; they must be seen "first as poetry and as ritual," and thus as "a transcendence of those conditions created within the Negro community by the denial of social justice."[45] "It was a language," Samuel Charters asserts in *The Legacy of the Blues*, "a rich, vital, expressive language that stripped away the misconception that the black society in the United States was simply a poor, discouraged version of the white. It was impossible not to hear the differences. No one could listen to the blues without realizing that there were two Americas."[46]

A long brooding on the psychology of his people, and a Whitmanesque predisposition to make the native languages of America guide his art, led Hughes early in 1923 to begin his greatest single literary endeavor: his attempt to resuscitate the dead art of an American poetry and culture by invoking the blues (exactly as George Gershwin, the following year, would try to elevate American music in his *Rhapsody in Blue*). If Pound had looked in a similar way, at one point, to the authority of the Provençal lyric of the middle ages, Hughes could still hear the blues in night clubs and on street corners, as blacks responded in art to the modern world. At the very least, Pound and Hughes (and Whitman) shared a sense that poetry and music were intimately related. To Hughes, black music at its best was the infallible metronome of racial grace: "Like the waves of the sea coming one after another, always one after another, like the earth moving around the sun, night, day—night, day—night, day—forever, so is the undertow of black music with its rhythm that never betrays you, its rooted power."[47] In the blues, in its mixture of pain and laughter, its lean affirmation of humanity in the face of circumstance, all in a secular mode (no "shantih, shantih" here; no brand plucked from the "burning!"), he found the tone, the texture, the basic language of true black modernism. A line from the epigraphic note to the volume says it all: "The mood of the *Blues* is almost always despondency, but when they are sung people laugh."[48]

Over a period of five years, starting some time around 1922, he slowly engaged the blues as a literary poet, first describing the blues from a distance, then enclosing the blues within a traditional poem, as he did in the prize-winning "The Weary Blues" ("Droning a drowsy syncopated tune,/Rocking back and forth to a mellow croon,/I heard a Negro play"), until, at last, in his most important collection, *Fine Clothes to the Jew* (1927), he proposed the blues exclusively on its own terms by writing in the form itself, alone.[49] Thus he acknowledged at last the full dignity of the people who had invented it.

Savagely attacked in black newspapers as "about 100 pages of trash [reeking] of the gutter and sewer," containing "poems that are insanitary, insipid, and repulsing," this book nevertheless was Hughes's greatest achievement in poetry, and remarkable by almost any American standard, as the literary historian Howard Mumford Jones recognized in a 1927 review.[50] "In a sense," Jones wrote of Hughes, "he has contributed a really new verse form to the English language."[51]

More important, blues offered, in a real sense, a new mode of feeling to the world (Eudora Welty has reminded us that literature teaches us how to feel) and a new life to art. To probe this point we would have to make a fresh reading of art and culture in the 1920s, for which I do not have the time or, truly, the skills. But instead of dismissively talking about the jazz age we would have to see that 1920, when the first commercial recording of a black singer, Mamie Smith's *Crazy Blues*, appeared, was perhaps as important a year for some people (certainly the millions of blacks who bought blues records in the decade, and the millions of whites down to our day who would thereafter sing and dance to the blues and its kindred forms) as was 1922, the year of Eliot's *The Waste Land*, for other people. We would see Gershwin's *Rhapsody in Blue*, premiered at Paul Whiteman's concert "An Experiment in Modern Music" in New York in 1924, as a modern American landmark that is in fact an alternative to the spirit of European modernism. We might go further, not simply to the work of other musicians such as Stravinsky and Bartok and Aaron Copland but also to the work of writers like Faulkner, whose genius was emancipated in *The Sound and the Fury*, I would suggest, by a balance between the modernism of Joyce, which dominates the first section of the novel, and the counter-modernism of the blues, which dominates the last in spite of the religious overtones there, and in spite of Faulkner's ultimate unwillingness to take on the consciousness of a black character whose life is informed by the blues. To me, it is instructive that Joycean technique facilitates the utterance of the idiot, Benjy, but that the blues temper informs the most affirmative section of the book, that dominated by black Dilsey Gibson and her people ("they endured").[52]

Far from suggesting that only Langston Hughes in the Harlem Renaissance discovered the black modern, I see the whole Harlem movement as struggling toward its uncovering. Why? Because it was inescapable; it was what the masses lived. In one sense, reductive no doubt, the Harlem Renaissance was simply an attempt by the artists to understand blues values and to communicate them to the wider modern world.

Finally, I would suggest that this question of modernism, and Hughes's place in it, needs to be seen in the context not merely of Harlem but of international cultural change in the twentieth century. By the age of twenty-one, he belonged already to an advanced guard of writers, largely from the yet unspoken world outside Europe and North America, that would eventually include Neruda of Chile, the young Borges of Argentina (who translated "The Negro Speaks of Rivers" in 1931), Garcia Lorca of Spain (see his "El Rey de Harlem"), Jacques Roumain of Haiti (see his poem "Langston Hughes"), Senghor of Senegal (who would hail Hughes in 1966 as the greatest poetic influence on the *Negritude* movement), Césaire of Martinique, Damas of French Guyana, and Guillen of Cuba (who freely asserted in 1930 that his first authentically Cuban or "Negro" poems, the eight pieces of *Motivos de Son*, were inspired by Hughes's visit to Havana that year). To these names should be added painters such as Diego Rivera, following his return from Paris in 1923, and his friends Orozco and Siquieros.

The collective aim of these writers and artists was to develop, even as they composed in the languages and styles of Europe and faced the challenge of European modernism, an aesthetic tied to a sense of myth, geography, history, and culture that was truly indigenous to their countries, rather than merely reflective of European trends, whether conservative or avant-garde. Finally, let me suggest that

Hughes's virtual precedence of place among them has less to do with his date of birth or his individual talent than with the fact that he was the poetic fruition of the Afro-American intellectual tradition, where these questions of race and culture and this challenge to civilization had long been debated, and under the harshest social conditions. In 1910, after all, when DuBois founded *Crisis* magazine, he gave it a challenging subtitle—but one he had already used for an even earlier publication. He called it "A Record of the Darker Races."

NOTES

1. Ralph Ellison, "Remembering Richard Wright," *Delta* (April 1984), 1–2.

2. Richard Wright, "Blueprint for Negro Writing," *New Challenge* 2 (Fall 1937), 53.

3. George McMichael, ed., *Anthology of American Literature: Vol. 2: Realism to the Present* (New York: Macmillan, 1974), p. 1225.

4. Ezra Pound, "E.P. Ode pour L'Election de Son Sepulchre," *Hugh Selwyn Mauberley*, in George McMichael, p. 1233.

5. Ezra Pound, "A Pact," in George McMichael, p. 1232.

6. Robert Frost, "The Oven Bird," *Complete Poems* (New York: Holt, Rinehart, and Winston, 1964), p. 150.

7. William Dean Howells, "Introduction to Lyrics of Lowly Life," in Paul Laurence Dunbar, *Complete Poems* (New York: Dodd, Mead, 1913), p. ix.

8. Paul Laurence Dunbar, "The Poet," *Complete Poems*, p. 191.

9. James Weldon Johnson, *Along This Way* (New York: Viking, 1968), pp. 158–159.

10. *Along This Way*, p. 158.

11. W.E.B. DuBois, "The Souls of White Folk," *Darkwater: Voice from Within the Veil* (New York: Schocken, 1969), p. 39.

12. Ezra Pound, "E.P. Ode," in George McMichael, p. 1237.

13. Fenton Johnson, "Tried," in James Weldon Johnson, ed., *Book of American Negro Poetry* (New York: Harcourt, Brace & World, 1931), p. 144.

14. Fenton Johnson, "The Banjo Player," *Book of American Negro Poetry*, p. 145.

15. Fenton Johnson, "The Scarlet Woman," *Book of American Negro Poetry*, pp. 145–146.

16. Claude McKay, "If We Must Die," in Wayne Cooper, ed., *The Passion of Claude McKay* (New York: Schocken, 1973), p. 124.

17. Claude McKay, "To the White Fiends," in Cooper, p. 123.

18. Claude McKay, "Tiger," *Selected Poems* (New York: Bookman, 1953), p. 47.

19. Countee Cullen, "To John Keats, Poet. At Spring Time," *Color* (New York: Harper and Brothers, 1925), p. 102.

20. Countee Cullen, *One Way to Heaven* (New York: Harper and Brothers, 1932), p. 154.

21. Countee Cullen, *One Way to Heaven* (New York: Harper and Brother, 1932), p. 162.

22. Countee Cullen, "Yet Do I Marvel," *On These I Stand*, p. 3.

23. For a suggestive treatment of Cullen's interest in traditional forms and its sources, see James W. Tuttleton's essay, "Countee Cullen at 'The Heights,'" included in this volume.

24. David Caute, *The Illusion* (New York: Harper & Row, 1972), p. 109.

25. Langston Hughes, "The Negro Artist and the Racial Mountain," *Nation* 122 (June 23, 1926), 692.

26. Melvin B. Tolson, *Libretto for the Republic of Liberia* (London: Collier-Macmillan, 1970), pp. 10–11.

27. William Carlos Williams, *Paterson* (Norfolk, Conn.: New Directions, 1963).

28. Melvin B. Tolson, *Harlem Gallery: Book I: The Curator* (London: Collier-Macmillan, 1969), p. 12.

29. Melvin B. Tolson, *Harlem Gallery*, p. 17.

30. Arna Bontemps, "Nocturne at Bethesda," in Langston Hughes and Arna Bontemps, *The Poetry of the Negro, 1946–1970* (New York: Doubleday, 1970), p. 211.

31. Wallace Stevens, "Sunday Morning," *Complete Poems* (New York: Knopf, 1968), pp. 69–70.

32. Langston Hughes, "A Song of the Soul of Central," *Central High School Monthly* 20 (January 1919), 9–10.

33. Langston Hughes, *The Big Sea* (New York: Knopf, 1940), p. 29.

34. Carl Sandburg, "Nigger," *Complete Poems* (New York: Harcourt, Brace & Jovanovich, 1970), p. 23; Hughes, "Negro," *Selected Poems* (New York: Knopf, 1959), p. 8.

35. Hughes, "My People," *Crisis* 24 (June 1922), 72.

36. Hughes, "My People," [No. 2], *Selected Poems*, p. 13.

37. Hughes, "The Negro Speaks of Rivers," *Selected Poems*, p. 4.

38. Hughes, "When Sue Wears Red," *Selected Poems*, p. 69.

39. Hughes, "Mother to Son," *Selected Poems*, p. 187.

40. Hughes, *The Big Sea*, p. 41.

41. Hughes, "The Big Sea," ms. draft; Vivian Harsh Collection, Carter G. Woodson Regional Library, Chicago.

42. Langston Hughes to Alain Locke, n.d. [1923]; Alain Leroy Locke Papers, Moorland-Spingarn Research Center, Howard University.

43. Langston Hughes to Ezra Pound, 22 April 1932; Langston Hughes Papers, Beinecke Rare Book and Manuscript Library, Yale University.

44. Hughes, "A House in Taos," *The Big Sea*, p. 260.

45. Ralph Ellison, *Shadow and Act* (New York: New American Library, 1966), p. 249.

46. Samuel Charters, *The Legacy of the Blues* (New York: Da Capo, 1977), p. 22.

47. Hughes, *The Big Sea*, p. 209.

48. Hughes, *Fine Clothes to the Jew* (New York: Knopf, 1927), n.p.

49. Hughes, "The Weary Blues," *Selected Poems*, p. 33.

50. *New York Amsterdam News*, 5 February 1927; *Chicago Whip*, 26 February 1927.

51. *Chicago Daily News*, 29 June 1927.

52. William Faulkner, "Appendix," *The Sound and the Fury & As I Lay Dying* (New York: Modern Library, 1957), p. 22.

Sterling A. Brown:
Outsider in the Harlem Renaissance?

ROBERT B. STEPTO

One of the most useful activities Afro-Americanist literary historians have been engaged in recently is reassessing the Harlem or New Negro Renaissance. This work has been useful both in terms of shedding new light on the Renaissance and in terms of revealing the subtle processes involved in composing historiography. Let me offer several examples.

In deciding whether to call the Renaissance the "Harlem," "Negro," "New Negro," or "Black" Renaissance, and in choosing whether to employ the term "Renaissance" or "Movement," historians are making major decisions about the Renaissance's literal and symbolic geographical siting. "Harlem" denotes a community, a city that can be alternately referred to, largely for rhetorical purposes, as a "metropolis" or a "mecca." "Negro" and "New Negro" expand the geographical limits further, suggesting something of a national scale, perhaps the Negro nation within the American nation, a nation that is paradoxically as substantial demographically as it is elusive geographically. "Black" is the least used of these terms, principally because it was used least by Renaissance participants. But the phrase "Black Renaissance" helps make an essential point that others at this symposium are exploring: the Renaissance was international in scale both in terms of where its contributors came from and in terms of its being merely the North American component of something larger and grander that embraced the *Negritude* and *Negrismo* movements as well.[1]

In choosing to employ one or more of these terms, historians are also making a choice about the extent to which they wish to portray the Renaissance as a cultural and/or political phenomenon, this being in part an assertion of how interdisciplinary they and we must be in researching, teaching, and writing about the Renaissance. "Harlem," "Negro," "New Negro," "Black," Renaissance," and "Movement" are all interdisciplinary terms, but some conventions are being established and the terms are no longer interchangeable. Addison Gayle, for example, has felt the need to yoke "Renaissance" and "Movement" together in order to stress that the activities were both cultural and political, sometimes simultaneously so. (This, of course, allows him to assert more easily than he might otherwise that the Renaissance is epitomized by both Jean Toomer and Marcus Garvey).[2] In contrast, Robert Bone years ago established the phrase, "Negro Renaissance," mainly, I believe, to channel our historiography in the direction of placing the Renaissance in a series of other, primarily literary, American renaissances, beginning with that of the American 1840s and including the New Orleans renaissance of the 1890s, among others.[3]

Within the ranks of historians emphasizing literary activities, periodizing the Renaissance has been more important than naming it. Of greatest interest here has been the role that literary genre has played in steering scholars to their respective formulations. Among the historians of fiction, for example, Robert Bone, Amritjit Singh, and Addison Gayle illustrate the range of opinion that can be seen. Writing thirty years ago, Bone, in his *Negro Novel in America*, adopts what is essentially a non-literary formulation of the period, focuses exclusively on writing of the 1920s, and sees everything ending not with the publication of a certain text or some other literary event, but with the stock market crash of 1929.[4] Singh also adheres to the idea that the Renaissance was roughly a decade, but creates a literary decade, not a cultural-historical one, arguing basically that something began in 1923 with the publication of Jean Toomer's *Cane* and ended in 1933 (years *after* the market crash) with the printing of Jessie Redmon Fauset's *Comedy: American Style* and Claude McKay's *Banana Bottom*.[5] Addison Gayle, is, to say the least, the most expansive in his formulation. He argues, in *The Way of the New World*, that you have to see the period beginning in the 1890s with the militant fictions of Sutton Elbert Griggs, and ending with those of the later 1930s and early 1940s of Richard Wright, the latter including especially *Native Son*. This argument is especially useful to Gayle, since it allows him to historicize the Renaissance while writing history "according to Wright," which is often his goal.[6]

All of these period definitions have their merits, but part of what is fascinating about them is that historians of Afro-American poetry, for example, would probably find them unuseful. The later French Afro-Americanist, Jean Wagner, is, for instance, greatly interested in Toomer's *Cane* but not as the point of departure for Renaissance poetry, and he certainly has little use for the poorly written though politically interesting novels of Sutton Griggs. For him, the Renaissance begins in 1906 with the death of Paul Laurence Dunbar and the completion of DuBois's "Litany at Atlanta" and reaches its zenith in the 1920s *and* 1930s, with the publication of three books, Langston Hughes's *The Weary Blues*, Weldon Johnson's *God's Trombones*, and Sterling Brown's *Southern Road*.[7] Albeit to different ends, the American Gloria Hull also has little interest in the definitions of the fiction historians, her argument being that all such definitions that emphasize one genre or another tend to exclude women writers, and that any focus on Harlem results in the exclusion of all writers outside Harlem, but especially those women poets such as Georgia Douglas Johnson who were active in workshops and writing circles in cities including Chicago, Cleveland, and Washington, D.C.[8]

It seems clear that our understanding and definition of the Harlem or New Negro Renaissance are very much in flux, partly because we are beginning to realize just how much scholarly interests and emphases affect the formulation of its history, and partly because figures as various as Claude McKay, Jean Toomer, Zora Neale Hurston, Georgia Douglas Johnson, and perhaps especially Sterling Brown, both do and do not fit in even the most contemporary assessments of the Renaissance. Brown is a special problem, chiefly because he has asked in a variety of ways to be left out of *Harlem* Renaissance histories. This he has done in conversation, as when he responds to the charge that he wasn't on the "Renaissance boat" by saying, "I didn't go down to the pier." And he has done so in print, as when he questions the *Harlem* Renaissance in his essay, "The New Negro in Literature, 1925–1955," arguing:

> The New Negro is not to me a group of writers centered in Harlem during the second half of the twenties. Most of the writers were not Harlemites; much of the best writing was not about Harlem, which was the show window, the cashier's till, but no more Negro America than New York is America.[9]

There are several ways to receive this pronouncement. One is to conclude that Brown is simply valorizing the term "New Negro" over that of "Harlem," as other historians have done. Another is to appreciate how Brown, before Gayle, Singh, and Hill, was creating space in literary history for writers much like himself who did not confine themselves to Harlem or to Harlem subjects. A third matter here is Brown's assessment, however slight, that the Renaissance was, in terms of literature, more of a publisher's "happening" (congruent, more than we would like to think, with the "happenings" in galleries and "happy hours" in bars and clubs) than an actual renaissance—the "cashier's till" being perhaps the same one that chimed in the 1960s with the "discovery" of black male writers and that rings today now that black women writers have been "unearthed." We don't have to choose; all three responses to Brown's statement are valid. With them in mind we can better understand the place of Brown's work in Renaissance writing, and not surprisingly, we can find poems which suggest that he found a middle ground, one in which he contributed mightily to the Renaissance while going his own way.

I see Brown inside the Renaissance in these terms. To begin with, he is easily as much a part of the Renaissance as is an uncontested figure like Zora Neale Hurston, chiefly because his early published works, like Hurston's, were published in New York during the 1920s and were contextualized in the Renaissance, especially when they received awards from chief Renaissance publishing outlets such as *Opportunity* magazine. (Recall here that Brown's first published poem, "When de Saint Go Ma'chin' Home," was printed by *Opportunity* in 1927 and received its poetry prize for 1928.)[10] Moreover, while Brown's poems do not appear in the pages of Alain Locke's *The New Negro*, which is too often seen as *the* anthology of Renaissance writing, they do appear in Countee Cullen's *Caroling Dusk* (1927), Charles S. Johnson's *Ebony and Topaz* (1927), and V.F. Calverton's Modern Library volume, *The Anthology of Negro American Literature* (1929). When one adds to this the fact that Brown reviewed about a half dozen books for *Opportunity* in the late 1920s (including novels by Julia Peterkin, Roark Bradford, DuBose Heyward, Howard Odum, and Langston Hughes— Brown's review of *Not Without Laughter* actually appeared in October, 1930), it is clear that Brown was part of the Renaissance literary scene, no matter how infrequent his "stopovers" (his term) in New York actually were.

But a more substantive point can be made. Brown *wrote* himself into the Renaissance, in his contribution to blues poetry and in his two major sequences of what I am persuaded to call Renaissance poetry.[11] In the field of blues poetry, Brown matched Langston Hughes step by step, or, innovation by innovation, when he duplicated classic blues forms in poems such as "Tin Roof Blues," and when he successfully simulated entire, communally contextualized blues performances in poems including "Ma Rainey." Where

he went beyond Hughes was in his singular creations of
blues quatrains.

Hughes, for the most part, was content to take the first
and third lines of a classic blues stanza (the opening and
closing lines), to break each line into two at its caesura, and
to call the whole a quatrain. This may be illustrated as
follows. The opening stanza of "Sylvester's Dying Bed," in
classic blues stanzaic form, is probably something like:

> I woke up this mornin', 'Bout half-past three,
> Woke up this mornin', mama, 'bout half-past three,
> All the womens in town was gathered round me.

Hughes's variation is

> I woke up this mornin',
> 'Bout half-past three.
> All the womens in town
> Was gathered round me.[12]

With this he has a quatrain, formed upon the first and third
lines, one that is effective but which, as the late George Kent
would argue, does not constitute the "real opportunity" for the
Afro-American writer.[13] In contrast to Hughes, Brown seeks
the "real opportunity" in more poems than one.

Consider, for example, the opening and closing stanzas
of "Riverbank Blues," which are blues quatrains of new order.

> A man git his feet set in a sticky mudbank,
> A man git dis yellow water in his blood,
> No need for hopin,' no need for doin,'
> Muddy streams keep him fixed for good.
>
> *"Man got his sea too lak de Mississippi*
> *Ain't got so long for a whole lot longer way,*
> *Man better move some, better not git rooted*
> *Muddy water fool you, ef you stay. . . ."*[14]

The lines are blues lines, certainly in mood, virtually in
meter; the stanzas are especially remarkable in that they

exhibit anticipated blues features of repetition and call-and response (see especially the first stanza) while modifying those features (in the second stanza, for example, the repeating line is the third line, not the second, and this breaking of blues form in and of itself communicates that one should move on and out of "muddy-water"—away from blues situations and circumstances).

While it can be said that Brown was outside the Renaissance in that he was in college at Williams when it began and either teaching at Negro colleges or in graduate school at Harvard later on, he was really only outside in the sense that his experiences in the South were more important to him and to his art than those he had in the North. It was in the South that he heard the folk expressions and cadences, the tales and the humor, that pervade his poetry; it was there that he met unforgettable figures like Big Boy Davis and Sister Lou, who are forcefully and lovingly portrayed in poems such as "Odyssey of Big Boy," "Long Done," "Sister Lou," and "Virginia Portrait." Brown's Southern odyssey, like Jean Toomer's for him, was a turning point in his life. But we should not overemphasize the place of the resulting poems in Brown's canon any more than we should read just the Southern sections of Toomer's *Cane.* Indeed, *Southern Road* and *No Hidin' Place,* like *Cane,* offer a careful orchestration of rural and urban images, and Brown's urban settings, unlike Toomer's, include Harlem.

Brown was inside the Renaissance in that he, like Hughes, declared, "I, too, sing America," and outside in that, unlike Hughes, he really meant what he said. How he went his own way is best seen in the fact that this art was far more affected by the flood of 1927 than by cabaret life or Marcus Garvey (though he wrote of cabarets and Garvey, too). In this regard, he was more like Ma Rainey and Bessie Smith than like the average Renaissance writer, and that probably was to his benefit.

The Renaissance gains in stature when our definitions of it allow a place for Sterling Brown, and if our definitions do not offer him a place then they need to be changed. Brown's blues poems are superior to Hughes's; his *Southern Road* rivals Toomer's *Cane* as a presentation of Negro American geography; his portraits of the folk, rural and urban, and his renderings of their speech, have no match.

NOTES

1. I refer principally to the two panels (III and Vb) on "Negritude: African and Caribbean Connections"; for one of the better discussions already in print, see Melvin Dixon, "Rivers Remembering Their Source: Comparative Studies in Black Literary History—Langston Hughes, Jacques Roumain, and Negritude," in Dexter Fisher and Robert B. Stepto, eds., *Afro-American Literature: The Reconstruction of Instruction* (New York: MLA, 1979), pp. 25–43.

2. Addison Gayle, Jr., *The Way of the New World* (New York: Doubleday, 1975), pp. 180–181.

3. Robert Bone, *The Negro Novel in America* (New Haven: Yale University Press, 1955), *passim*.

4. Ibid., p. 107. Let me stress here that this is where Bone's work was thirty years ago; he has recently explored other, less purely historical, periodizations of the Renaissance period.

5. Amritjit Singh, *The Novels of the Harlem Renaissance* (University Park, Pa.: The Pennsylvania State University Press, 1976), *passim*. Although Singh's book is a study of 21 novels published between 1923 and 1933, he views the Harlem Renaissance in his opening chapter in a broader historical framework.

6. Gayle, pp. 180–181.

7. Jean Wagner, *Black Poets of the United States* (*Les Poètes Nègres des Etats-Unis*, 1962), trans. by Kenneth Douglas (Urbana: University of Illinois Press, 1973), pp.149–193.

8. Based upon remarks Prof. Hull delivered at the MLA/NEH Summer Seminar, "Afro-American Literature: From Criticism to Course Design," Yale University, June 1977.

9. Sterling A. Brown, "The New Negro in Literature, 1925–1955," in Rayford W. Logan, ed., *The New Negro Thirty Years Afterwards* (Washington: Howard University Press, 1955), p. 57.

10. Altogether, *Opportunity* printed at least three of Brown's poems ("When de Saint Go Ma'chin Home," "Thoughts of Death," and "Riverbank Blues") as well as the sketch, "Roland Hayes," in the 1920s.

11. See "Tin Roof Blues," Part Three of *Southern Road*, and "Harlem Stopover," Part One of *No Hidin' Place*; both appear in *The Collected Poems of Sterling Brown* (New York: Harper & Row, 1980), pp. 92-103, 155-166. These sequences include poems such as "Mecca," "Cabaret," "Harlem Happiness," and "Negro Improvement League."

12. Langston Hughes, *Selected Poems of Langston Hughes* (1959; rpt. New York: Vintage, 1974), p. 38.

13. George Kent, *Blackness and the Adventure of Western Culture* (Chicago: Third World Press, 1972), p. 60.

14. *Collected Poems of Sterling Brown*, p. 90.

Langston Hughes and
the Blues He Couldn't Lose

RICHARD K. BARKSDALE

My old man's a white man
And my old mother's black.
If ever I cursed my white old man,
I take my curses back.

If ever I cursed my black old mother
And wished she were in hell,
I am sorry for that evil wish
And now I wish her well.

My old man died in a fine big house
My ma died in a shack.
I woner where I'm gonna die,
Being neither white nor black?

Langston Hughes wrote this short but emotionally powerful poem in 1925, the year in which he won his first literary prize in the competition sponsored by *Opportunity* magazine. Significantly, this poem, which he entitled "Cross," was not the poem that brought him first honors; his "The Weary Blues" was the prizewinner. According to Faith Berry, Hughes thought that "Cross" had merit and submitted it for consideration in the first Amy Spingarn Contest in Literature and Art in August 1925.[1] The chief judge in that contest, William Stanley Braithwaite, however, did not think Hughes's submission was poetically meritorious and awarded it only a third prize. Countee Cullen, who apparently wrote poetry more attuned to Braithwaite's "talented tenth" sensibilities, won first prize. Undaunted, Hughes submitted his "third class" poem to *The Crisis*, where it was accepted and published in December 1925. Since that time, "Cross" has been one of the poet's widely reprinted poems; it was included in Hughes's first volume, *The Weary Blues*, and in the 1959 volume of *Selected Poems* and has been widely anthologized ever since.

Evidently, Hughes entitled the poem "Cross" because of the *double entendre* suggested by that word. One meaning is that mulattoes were "cross-bred" or "little mules" in the original meaning of the Spanish term. A second meaning was that the mulatto heritage was slavery's bitterest memory and thus, in the poet's opinion, the heaviest cross that blacks had to bear. Later, in a poem entitled "Black Seed," Hughes softened the mulatto image: in this poem mulattoes were likened to scattered flowers of many hues spread throughout the diaspora like "Hybrid plants/In another's garden/Flowers . . . /Cut by the shears/Of the white-faced gardeners."

However, Hughes captured the full drama of the tragic mulatto's status in a poem entitled "Mulatto," which he wrote in the summer of 1926. In his autobiography *The Big Sea*, the poet recalls that "I worked harder on that poem than any other that I have ever written." He reports further that he felt more than amply rewarded when, at a poetry reading session at James Weldon Johnson's house, the poem received warm applause.[2] Like "Cross," "Mulatto" has been reprinted many times—in *Fine Clothes to the Jew* and in *The Saturday Review of Literature* in 1927, in *Selected Poems* in 1959, and in many anthologies.

In "Mulatto," the ironic tone found in "Cross" is intensified and the generalized comment on the cultural and psychological dilemma of the mulatto described in the earlier poem is changed into a highly dramatic confrontation between a white father and his

unacknowledged bastard mulatto son. Although throughout
the poem the spotlight remains on "the little yellow bastard
boy" who cries, "I am your son, white man!," the poet uses
several lines to describe the background of a sensual South
where defenseless black women were powerless to resist the
raping and seduction that forced them into concubinage.

> The moon over the turpentine woods
> The southern night
> Full of stars
> Great big yellow stars.
> What's a body but a toy?
>   Juicy bodies
>   Of nigger wenches
>   Blue black
>   Against black fences
>   O, you little bastard boy
> What's a body but a toy?
> The scent of pine woods stings the soft
>   night air
>   *What's the body of your mother?*
> Sharp pine scent in the evening air.
>   A nigger night
>   A nigger joy
>   A little yellow
>   Bastard boy.

This dynamically assertive poetic statement, written when
Hughes was 24 years old, later became the basis of a short
story, "Father and Son," in the poet's first collection of short
stories, *The Ways of White Folks*, written upon his return
from the Soviet Union in 1933. And, as Arthur P. Davis has
indicated, Hughes's preoccupation with the mulatto theme led
him to write two more short stories on the subject ("Passing"
in *Ways of White Folks* and "African Morning" in
Laughing to Keep from Crying); a play, *Mulatto*, which
enjoyed a successful Broadway run in 1935--1936; and an
opera, *The Barrier*, which the poet wrote in collaboration
with Jan Meyerowitz.[3]

There are at least three conclusions which can be drawn
from Hughes's preoccupation with the tragic mulatto theme.

First, his ability to write on this subject in four different genres indicates a literary virtuosity that few of his contemporaries, white or black, could rival. Among his black literary friends, Bontemps, McKay, and Cullen had each turned from poetry to fiction; and Cullen did come out of literary retirement in the early 1940s to collaborate with Bontemps on *St. Louis Woman*; but none of Hughes's contemporaries in the Renaissance period demonstrated a comparable range and versatility. A second conclusion—that Hughes's preoccupation with the tragic mulatto theme flew in the face of Renaissance literary trends and tastes—has significant and challenging implications. Similarly challenging is a third conclusion—namely that there was something psychologically engrossing about the poet's seemingly obsessive preoccupation with the mulatto theme— that he had a deeply rooted personal involvement with the mulatto theme—a blues he could not lose, however debonairly he sought to "Play it cool/And dig all jive" in the never-ending struggle to "stay alive."

Although one cannot agree with Jean Wagner's assertion that the tragic mulatto theme in Hughes's poetry was "irrelevant" for American blacks,[4] it is true that it was by no means a popular theme with the writers of the Harlem Renaissance. Indeed, one can justifiably ask, how could a literary and cultural movement led by mulattoes concentrate its literary energies on excoriating mulattoes? For the composite "New Negro" whom Locke and others sought to define had, in searching for new literary and cultural perspectives, long since turned away from the tragic mulatto or tragic octoroon themes once so popular in Reconstruction times. Few if any of Hughes's associates remembered Harper's *Iola LeRoy* or William Wells Brown's *Clotel*. Rather, young black writers, like young white writers, of the gin-drinking 1920s, were dedicated in their struggle to counter the Establishment and shake the tree of cultural orthodoxy. If there was a concern about mulattoes and their heritage among black writers, it was positive and not negative and manifested itself in a prideful awareness of the fact that mulattoes were probably more integration worthy than other blacks because of their education and cultural attainments. At least, that seemed to be the message of Jessie Fauset's *There Is Confusion* (1924), which was hailed by literary Harlem with the first of the decade's gala literary banquets. Fauset wrote her novel in response to white author T.S. Stribling's race novel, *Birthright.* She sought to prove that the mulatto mainliners of Philadelphia lived just as well, dressed just as well, and socialized just as elegantly as Philadelphia's upper middle-class whites. Indeed, as one critic has written:

> *There Is Confusion* was Stribling's *Birthright* rewritten to the approved literary canons of the Talented Tenth, a saga of the sophisticated in which French, and occasionally German, tripped from the protagonists' tongues as readily as precise English; a novel about people with good blood lines. . . .[5]

Apparently, all literary Harlem rejoiced over the appearance of its first authentic mulatto novel, including a somewhat misanthropic George Schuyler and the elitist W.E.B. DuBois, who wanted works of fiction to be propaganda tracts first and literature only secondarily.

Fauset's 1924 novel was followed by three more novels, all with mulatto protagonists who were sometimes illegitimate but always socially proper. Undoubtedly, Fauset's success stimulated Nella Larsen to write *Quicksand,* a novel which was also enthusiastically accepted and reviewed by DuBois when it appeared in 1928, even though its mulatto heroine, Helga Crane, was, by the end of the novel, sucked into a quicksand of self-destructive eroticism, evidently caused, the novelist strongly implies, by the heroine's black genes.

So Langston Hughes's persistent involvement with the tragic mulatto theme was for the period's literary and cultural arbiters a preoccupation that appeared to deny what they fervently believed in—mainly the existence of a psychologically secure and stable mulatto-colored "talented tenth" whose members were firmly and deservedly in control of the black man's present and future cultural and literary destiny. They were not, as Hughes seemed to suggest, appalled by their illegitimate backgrounds and sometimes

incestual family trees; nor were they traumatized by racial
memories of cruel rapings and bastard beginnings.

Although Hughes was never specifically attacked for his
emphasis on the tragic mulatto's dilemma, he knew that the
Talented Tenth neither understood nor sympathized with
his emphasis on the subject. In a sense, his response is
contained in his 1926 essay, "The Negro Artist and the Racial
Mountain," in which he inveighs against black writers
whose mulatto dispositions and "urge for whiteness" dictated
a primary concern for what he termed "Nordic faces, Nordic
art, and Episcopal Heaven."

Finally, there is no doubt that Langston Hughes's
emphasis on the tragic mulatto theme reflected a deeply
rooted personal concern about his own mulatto heritage. Both
his maternal and paternal great grandparents had white
male progenitors. His father, James Nathaniel Hughes, had
white grandparents on both his maternal and paternal sides;
and the poet's mother, Carolyn Langston Hughes, had as her
paternal grandfather a wealthy Virginia planter named
Ralph Quarles. The latter's three children by Lucy Langston,
Quarles's half-Indian, half-Negro housekeeper, included
John Mercer Langston, the first black Oberlin graduate and
a distinguished Reconstruction educator and statesman.
Charles Langston, the poet's maternal grandparent, did not
become as famous as his younger brother John, but he did
complete two years at Oberlin and was so active in the affairs
of the Ohio Antislavery Society that he was jailed and fined
for helping a fugitive slave escape to Canada in 1851.

Notwithstanding the achievements of some of his
immediate ancestors, Hughes was apparently less than
enamored with his mulatto background. An incident which
he recorded in *The Big Sea* gives a hint about his attitude. In
1923, after a less-than-fulfilling academic year at Columbia
in 1921–1922, the poet shipped out as a mess boy on a
merchant ship, the S.S. *Malone*, bound for Africa. In his
autobiography, he recalls his feelings as he first glimpsed
the African shoreline:

> When I saw the dust-green hills in the sunlight something
> took hold of me inside. My Africa, Motherland of the
> Negro peoples! And me a Negro! Africa! The real thing to
> be touched and seen. . . .[6]

But his exultation about returning to his motherland was
quickly tempered when he went ashore and found that
African natives considered him to be a white man. "They
looked at my copper-brown skin and straight black hair . . .
and they said 'You white man.'" His racial status in Africa
was confirmed when, desiring to attend a juju ceremony in
a Nigerian village, he was told, "White man never go see Ju-
Ju."

His experiences at ports of call on Africa's West Coast
reflected mere surface concerns, however. Of much deeper
import were his relations with his mulatto father from
whom he was estranged after 1922. The intensity of the
confrontational dialogue between white father and mulatto
son both in the story "Father and Son" and in *Mulatto*, the
play, suggests that by the time of the composition of these two
works, the poet was convinced that he was indeed a "little
yellow bastard boy" who had been cruelly abandoned by an
uncaring "white" father. For prior to his two-year visit with
his father in Toluca, Mexico, after his high school
graduation, Hughes had seen his father only twice—once
when he accompanied his mother to Mexico in 1908 on her
fruitless quest for a marital reconciliation and once when he
spent an unhappy summer in a visit between his junior and
senior years in high school. The poet relates that on all of
these visits, his relations with his father were always
strained. Gradually, he came to view his father as a
businessman and capitalist who was, in his attitude and
bearing, more white than black. Indeed, the young poet
found that because of his father's success as a Yankee
entrepreneur in Mexico, he had developed great scorn and
disdain for his erstwhile black American brothers who, in
the latter's opinion, were mired in the muck of their own
racial inertia. So, after 1922, when the poet became fully
estranged from a father who, having abandoned him as an
infant, now lived in another country, spoke another

language, and had married another woman, it was as though a door in his life had closed, which in reality had never quite opened.

One does not sense the extent of the alienation and psychological damage wrought on the son's psyche by the image of the unopened door until one reads the scenes in "Father and Son" and in *Mulatto* in which Bert, the unacknowledged mulatto son, swept by a towering Oedipal rage, slowly chokes his white father to death. Significantly, the murder occurs just inside the closed front door of the father's plantation mansion—a door that had always been closed to the "little yellow bastard boy." It is a compelling dramatic scene that provides chilling evidence that, in his preoccupation with the mulatto theme, Langston Hughes truly had the blues he could not lose.

NOTES

1. Faith Berry, *Langston Hughes: Before and Beyond Harlem* (New York: Lawrence Hill, 1983), pp. 62–63.

2. *The Big Sea* (1940; New York: Hill & Wang, 1963), p. 262.

3. Davis, "The Tragic Mulatto Theme in Six Works of Langston Hughes," *Phylon*, 15, 2 (1955), 195–204.

4. Jean Wagner, *Black Poets of the United States*, trans. Kenneth Douglas (Chicago: University of Illinois Press, 1973), p. 455.

5. David Levering Lewis, *When Harlem Was in Vogue* (New York: Knopf, 1981), p. 124.

6. *The Big Sea*, p. 107.

Sterling Brown, Poet,
His Place in Afro-American Literary History

CHARLES H. NICHOLS

A renaissance is a rebirth. It is also a celebration, a flowering of the creative arts. The New Negro poetry of the 1920s and the 1930s was one such flowering. No writer of our generation has given us a deeper sense of the continuity of Afro-American poetry than Sterling Brown. Born on the Howard University campus, he grew up in the company of leading black intellectuals, studied with the most respected scholars at Williams and Harvard, and steeped himself in the cultural ferment of the Harlem Renaissance. "At Harvard I went into careful study of American poetry. I learned from Edwin Arlington Robinson's *Tilbury Town*, where he took up the undistinguished, the failures, and showed the extraordinary in ordinary lives. I learned Robert Frost. I learned from my own; the man I was brought up on was Dunbar. I learned from Claude McKay. I participated in what I called the New Negro Renaissance."[1] Brown is a conscious heir to the mainstream of British and American literature, a child of Walt Whitman, Thoreau, and Mark Twain. In the South, Sterling Brown tells us, "I learned the strength of my people. I learned the fortitude. I learned the humor. I learned the tragedy."[2] In his own poetry, Brown found a range of authentic voices by which he expressed the intensity,

the pain, the fierce endurance and pride of Afro-Americans.
The legacy of work-songs, folk melody, of blues and jazz
provided the basis for his portraits of the wronged, the
disinherited, the hopeless, the proud, the defiant and the
triumphant ones. There is fine art and supreme design in
the terseness, irony, and aptness of expression in these
poems. As Sterling Stuckey writes: "I wondered . . . how a
Williams College Phi Beta Kappa, Harvard man, a college
professor and eminent writer, could have a voice with so
much of earth and sky and sunlight and dark clouds about it;
a voice unafraid, an instrument Blues-tinged."[3]

I propose to analyze here some of the expressive forms of
Sterling Brown's poetry—the personae (the voices), the tone,
the central images, and the meanings of his verse. Such an
interpretation of these elements will reveal how vitally they
employ traditional modes of folk poetry and how they feature
in the work of our contemporary black poets. The stark
realism of poems like "Southern Road," "Old Man Buzzard,"
and "Johnny Thomas" is achieved by terse language, irony,
and passionate intensity. Brown's souls are shackled by an
oppressive world. Consider the "Harlem Street Walkers":

> Why do they walk so tragical.
> Oh never mind.
> When they are in
> The grateful grave, each whitened skull
> Will grin. . . .[4]

Southern Road was published in 1932. It reflects the
desperate condition of the Southern farmer. For most black
people, the ebullience of the jazz age has passed. Lynching,
peonage, poverty, and black segregation were rampant. A
poem like "Ole King Cotton" reflects the weary struggle of
the sharecropper:

> Ole King Cotton
> Ole King Cotton
> Keeps us slavin'
> Tell we'se dead an' rotten
>
> . . . .

Starves us with bumper crops,
Starves us wid po'
Chains de lean wolf
At our do'
. . . .
Cotton, Cotton
All we know;
Plant cotton, hoe it,
Baig it to grow;
What good it do to us
Gawd only know!

(pp. 64–65)

Sterling Brown began his teaching career in the South. He became the editor on Negro Affairs in the Federal Writers Project of the W.P.A. and did research for the Gunnar Myrdal Study which was published as *An American Dilemma*. He wrote the first scholarly survey of black poetry, *Negro Poetry and Drama* (1937), and edited with Arthur P. Davis and Ulysses Lee the first major anthology of Afro-American Literature, *The Negro Caravan*.

Brown uses the pattern and spirit of the blues effectively. "The blues . . . are a music and a poetry of confrontation," writes Stephen Henderson, "with the self, with the family and loved ones, with the oppressive forces of society, with nature and, on the heaviest level, with fate and the universe itself."[5] As Ralph Ellison has written, "The blues is an impulse to keep the painful details and episodes of a brutal experience alive in one's aching consciousness, to finger its jagged grain, and to transcend it, not by the consolation of philosophy but by squeezing from it a near-tragic, near-comic lyricism."[6]

Although a great many of Sterling Brown's poems employ the tone and feeling of the blues, even the classic repetitive form of the blues, it is important to notice how he has enriched and deepened meanings in his blues-ballads. "Memphis Blues," for example, operates on three levels: In Part I, Nineveh, Tyre, and Babylon invoke the glories of the past; Part II deals with the present-day Memphis which,

under the judgment of God, is threatened by fire; Part III
affirms the spiritual triumph of the black man's style and art.

> All dese cities
> Ashes and rust
> De win' sing sperrichals
> Through deir dus'
>
> (p. 61)

Part II of the poem makes especially felicitous use of the blues
form with its incremental repetition and the call and
response of the traditional black church.

> Whatcha gonna do when Memphis on fire,
> Memphis on fire, Mistah Preachin' Man?
> Gonna pray to Jesus, loud as I can,
> Gonna pray to Jesus, loud as I can,
> Gonna pray to Jesus, oh my lawd!
>
> (p. 60)

The five remaining stanzas put the same question to the
"Lovin' Man," the "Music Man," the "Workin' Man," the
"Drinkin' Man," and the "Gamblin' Man." Each will ply his
trade with renewed vigor:

> Memphis go by flood or flame
> Nigger won't worry
> All the same—
>
> (p. 61)

The poem "Ma Rainey" is a triumphant affirmation of the joy
of life, a song sung against the background of "aches and
miseries." As Stephen Henderson says, "It is . . . a
consummate dramatization of the spirit and power of the
blues and their historic role as ritual in Black life."[7]

O Ma Rainey
Sing yo' song;
Now you's back
Whah you belong
Get way inside us,
Keep us strong. . . .

(p. 62)

The poem "Cabaret," with its setting in "Black and Tan Chicago," recalls the floods of 1927, even while "the jazz band unleashes its frenzy" and the fat overlords enjoy the Creole beauties who dance about them. The waiters and the dancers are serving their masters to the feverish beat of the drums. It is very likely that Sterling Brown is here mocking the Cotton Club atmosphere of a Harlem that exists to amuse "Rich, flashy, puppy-faced Hebrew and Anglo Saxon . . . overlords. . . ." The sardonic tone and clash of motley sound is unsettling. And Brown is not mesmerized by the amoral hedonism of the Harlem Renaissance.

Sterling Brown and Langston Hughes are justly celebrated for their use of the rhythm and melody of the blues and jazz, for their conversational tone, and for their capacity to enrich the language and feeling of ordinary people. Brown is especially remarkable for his uses of dialect. Here is the man who knows the dialect voices of Joel Chandler Harris, Irwin Russell, and Paul Laurence Dunbar. But he knows how to transcend the stereotypes, the burlesque, and the patronizing sentimentality and crassness of these mentors. Above all, there is in Sterling Brown's verse a living, pulsing quality of felt experience and intimacy born of an unpretentious human feeling.

Some of Sterling Brown's finest efforts are in his portraits, for which he is justly famous. No one who had read them can forget "Sporting Beasley," "Slim Greer," "Old Lem," or Joe Meek. Humor, irony, and sarcasm give them life. These are ordinary men, marginal, often despised men, clinging to some rag of honor, surviving by their wits, yet even in their desperate circumstances they conduct themselves with style and grace.

It is said that "Sporting Beasley" was a well-known Washington dandy, renowned for his sartorial splendor. On one occasion he boarded a public bus and sat down next to a white woman who made it obvious that she objected to a black man's presumption in sharing her seat. She rose in a huff. With an elaborate gesture, Beasley took out his white silk handkerchief, wiped off the seat she had been occupying, and moved over into it after dropping the handkerchief out of the window. The poem uses the voice of the knowledgeable street man:

> Good glory, give a look at Sporting Beasley
> Strutting, oh my Lord. . . .
> Tophat cocked one side his bulldog head,
> Striped four-in-hand, and in his buttonhole
> A red carnation; Prince Albert coat
> Form-fitting, corset like; vest snugly filled,
> Grey morning trousers, spotless and full flowing,
> White spats and a cane.
> Step it, Mr. Beasley, oh step it till the sun goes down
> . . . .
> Oh, Jesus, when this brother's bill falls due,
> When he steps off the chariot
> And flicks the dust from his patent leathers with his
>   silk handkerchief
> When he stands in front of the jasper gates, patting his
>   tie,
> And then paces in
> Cane and knees working like well-oiled, slow-timed
>   pistons;
> Lord help us, give a look at him.
> Don't make him dress up in no night gown, Lord
> . . . .
> Let him know it's heaven. . . .
>   (p. 99)

The detailed description rivets our attention and the observer's voice keeps our eye focused, our imagination inflamed.

The Slim poems achieve an intimate portrait of the character and satirize the South most memorably. Slim in Atlanta makes fun of discriminatory laws:

> Down in Atlanta
> De Whitefolks got laws
> For to keep all de niggers
> From laughin' outdoors
> Hope to Gawd I may die
> If I ain't speakin truth
> Make de niggers do their laughin'
> In a telefoam booth. . . .
>
> (p. 81)

Slim, a waiter, tells a tale of

> How he in Arkansaw
> Passed for white,
> An' he no lighter
> Than a dark midnight.
>
> (p. 77)

When Slim goes to heaven, St. Peter sends him to hell to "see all that's doin/And report to me." Hell reminds Slim of Dixie, and St. Peter exclaims: "Where in hell/D'ja think hell *was* anyhow?"[8]

Many of the poems make plain the presence of the past. There is the "Memo: for the Race Orators," recalling the traitors of the group. There is "Strange Legacies," which celebrates Jack Johnson, John Henry, and the crowd of farmers, sharecroppers, and laborers who endured calamity after calamity, muttering:

> Guess we'll give it one mo' try.
> Guess we'll give it one mo' try.
>
> (p. 87)

And there are travellers in Dixie who are remembering Nat Turner.

Long-suffering endurance is only part of the historic achievement of black Americans. There is also bold courage

and faith and art. "Old Lem," "Strong Men," and "Transfer"
combine the spirit of protest with stubborn hope. The well-
tuned ear, the sharp eye, the ironic perception of Sterling
Brown are combined with a warm and generous humanity.
No writer of the 1930s approaches his conversational tone, his
authentic voice, and his sharp, ironic unmasking of
pretension, hypocrisy, and brutality. His work reveals the
numerous ways in which as a people we have been redeemed
by art and enlarged by suffering.

In 1955 Arna Bontemps wrote Langston Hughes,
"[Charles S. Johnson] tells me he was on a panel in D.C. last
Friday night and that the subject was the Harlem
Renaissance. Sterling [Brown], he said, was the most vocal
heckler from the floor denying that there *was* any such
movement."[9] In "The New Negro in Literature, 1925–55"
Sterling Brown wrote, "The New Negro is not to me a group
of writers centered in Harlem during the second half of the
Twenties. Most of the writers were not Harlemites; much of
the best writing was not about Harlem, which was the show
window, the cashier's till, but no more Negro America than
New York is America."[10] For Sterling Brown, the flowering
of Negro talent in the 1920s and 1930s was, in its deeper
essentials, a part of a long development in American letters,
not a provincial, flashy sensation or a part of the Van
Vechten Vogue. With his broad humanity, detachment, and
identification with the sharecropper, the street walker, the
convict, the jazz musician—the people—he recoiled from the
celebration of an artistic elite. As in the great tradition of our
major writers and aware of the essential tragedy of life,
Sterling Brown is most deeply concerned with the spirit of
men struggling to realize itself in a vast and indifferent
universe:

> The devil is a rider
> In slouch hat and boots
> Gun by his side
> Bull whip in his hand
> The devil is a rider;
> The rider is a devil
> Riding his buck stallion

> Over the land
> The poor-white and nigger sinners
>
> Are low-down in The Valley,
> The rider is a devil
> And there's hell to pay;
> The devil is a rider,
> God may be the owner,
> But he's rich and forgetful,
> And far away.
>
> ("Arkansas Chant," pp. 167–168)

Plainly the life of man is a long march through the night. The "Revelations" brings a sober truth:

> Always now with me
> The halfwit's text
> Sour truth for my wits
> Poor, perplexed
>
> If a man's life goes
> Beyond the bone
> Man must go lonely
> And alone,
> Unhelped unhindered
> On his own. . . ."
>
> (pp. 88–89)

NOTES

1. Michael S. Harper and Robert B. Stepto, eds., *Chant of Saints* (Chicago: University of Illinois Press, 1979), pp. 16–17.

2. Ibid., p. 17.

3. Stuckey, "Introduction" to *Collected Poems of Sterling A. Brown,* selected by Michael S. Harper (New York: Harper & Row, 1981), p. 9.

4. *Collected Poems of Sterling A. Brown,* p. 98. All quotations from Brown's poems are from this edition, unless otherwise indicated.

Page numbers for subsequent citations have been indicated in the text.

5. Henderson, "The Heavy Blues of Sterling Brown: A Study of Craft and Tradition," *Black American Literature Forum*, 14, 1 (Spring 1980), 32.

6. *Shadow and Act* (New York: Random House, 1964), p. 78.

7. Henderson, p. 37.

8. From "Slim in Hell," included in Abraham Chapman, ed., *Black Voices* (New York: New American Library, 1968), p. 410.

9. Charles H. Nichols, ed., *Arna Bontemps–Langston Hughes Letters, 1925–1967* (New York: Dodd Mead, 1980), p. 332.

10. Rayford W. Logan, ed., *The New Negro Thirty Years Afterwards* (Washington, D.C.: Howard University Press, 1955), p. 57.

Countee Cullen at "The Heights"

JAMES W. TUTTLETON

The present work undertakes to describe the undergraduate career of Countee Cullen at New York University between 1922 and 1925 and to present an edited text of his most significant surviving piece of undergraduate critical prose, the senior honors thesis he presented to the Department of English on May 1, 1925: "The Poetry of Edna St. Vincent Millay: An Appreciation." In both biographical and critical treatments of Cullen, these years have received scant attention, although they were immensely formative in his experience as a poet. In fact, the thesis that is presented here has never been published and is largely unknown to Cullen's readers or to students of the Harlem Renaissance.

The mind of a poet, the poetic influences to which he is exposed at an impressionable moment in his life, the critical context in which these influences are received, and the personalities of those having a decisive effect on the shaping of his perceptions and values—all of these are essential in understanding his originality, his development, and his reception. In the case of Countee Cullen, an adequate account of these influences—including the impact of Millay's love lyrics and ballad forms—would require a full-length biography, one devoted with greater rigor to the facts and their critical meaning, moreover, than is evident in

Blanche E. Ferguson's *Countee Cullen and the Negro Renaissance* (1966). In the space available here, no such full account is possible. But something of a start may be made by presenting his essay on Millay and by bringing to light some of the facts—hitherto unknown or forgotten—of this remarkable poet's education at New York University.

As will be evident to anyone reading this thesis, Countee Cullen, though only twenty-one years old when he wrote the work, was an accomplished and subtle student of poetry. The essay reflects a sensitive understanding of the varied generic and metrical gifts of Millay. And it is passionately responsive to her sense of the fragility and transience of beauty and love in a world where all must change and die. Students of Cullen's poetry have sometimes noted, without demonstrating at any length, the impact on him of Millay's lyric verse. (An exception is Margaret Perry's suggestive comparison, in the work cited below, of "The Shroud of Color" with Millay's "Renascence.") The present thesis offers, I believe, the critical ground on which a fuller influence study and a more informed comparative evaluation can be based. For here, in Cullen's "appreciation," will be found a description of the thematic and technical features of Millay's art that Cullen most admired, as well as a commentary on those defects of her performance of which he was most critical.

I am not of course the first to note the relation of Cullen's art to that of Millay. Walter White, for example, linked Cullen to a poetic tradition "of which A.E. Housman and Edna St. Vincent Millay are the bright stars" (quoted in Margaret Perry, *A Bio-Bibliography of Countee P. Cullen, 1903–1946*, Westport: Greenwood Press, 1971, p. 29). Perry herself has remarked that "Countee Cullen's poetry also bears a close resemblance to both the poetry of Edward Arlington Robinson (whom Cullen considered to be America's finest poet) and of Edna St. Vincent Millay" (ibid., pp. 28–30). But Perry was apparently not aware that Cullen had written this thesis—it is not listed among the "Unpublished Works" in her bibliography—so that the ground for a more extensive comparison was not available to her.

I shall perhaps go further than White and Perry. I will argue that, if in 1930 Cullen gave to Robinson the laurel as the best American poet, in 1925—when he wrote his thesis and published *Color*—Millay was foremost in his mind. Further, while granting that some of the following themes may also be found in Houseman and Keats, I will argue that common to both Cullen and Millay are these thematic elements: 1) A profound recognition of the transience of life; 2) a sense of the world as the vale of inexplicable agony and suffering; 3) an awareness of the inadequacy of the usual Christian explanation of why God permits, if he does not authorize, human suffering; 4) the impulse, therefore, to seize the day, to indulge in and celebrate poetically the pleasures of life—especially love in its erotic character and sensuous beauty in all of its forms. I would call this a frank aesthetic and sexual paganism, typical of the disillusioned youth of the 1920s; 5) nevertheless, a recognition that love is transient and sexual pleasure is fleeting—a recognition conveyed in both poets in wry, flip, cynical, and anguished tones; 6) yet the implied wish that it might be otherwise, that the order of existence might fulfill the heart's desire, especially in relation to love and sexuality, together with an occasional affirmation, sometimes like resignation, that there *is* a providential ordering, somehow, of human affairs. All this is just perhaps another way of saying what Countee Cullen himself said in a headnote in *Caroling Dusk* (New York: Harper, 1927), namely, that one of his chief difficulties had always been "reconciling a Christian upbringing with a pagan inclination" (p. 179). This aesthetic and sexual hedonism, or paganism, in Millay was one of the chief appeals of her work. To these six thematic elements that link Millay and Cullen I would add a seventh, technical parallel: both poets' preference for the conventional forms of the poetic tradition—in relation to rhythms, rhyme schemes, stanzaic structures, and genres—especially the sonnet and the ballad.

Perhaps, however, it is best now to let the thesis speak for itself. At its conclusion, however, I shall try to set it in the fuller context of Cullen's life and work as an undergraduate at New York University. "The Poetry of Edna St. Vincent

Millay" exists in a typescript of nine numbered pages, plus an unnumbered title page and an unnumbered final page listing Cullen's references and bibliography. It is contained in a brown cardboard cover marked in black ink "Cullen" and "1925" (perhaps in Cullen's hand). Stamped on the title page is "Library/N.Y. Univ." Between 1925 and 1972, this thesis was shelved in the English House Library at University College in the Bronx. When this college at The Heights was merged with Washington Square College in Greenwich Village, Cullen's thesis was transported, with others, to the downtown English Department storage room, where after a flood in the building in 1976, the present editor identified and salvaged it. The thesis now reposes in the Cullen papers of the New York University Archives. Xerox copies of it have also been recently deposited in the Fales Collection of the Elmer Holmes Bobst Library at New York University, in the Cullen papers on deposit at Fisk University, and at the Amistad Research Center at Tulane University in New Orleans. A copy of the thesis was also presented to the late Mrs. Ida Mae Cullen, who graciously granted permission to publish it here.

The essay is typed on plain white bond, 8 1/2 x 11-inch typing paper, now yellowed, with the watermark "Whiting's Mutual Bond," and a logo of a capital W within which rests an acorn. The title page, now marked with smudged fingerprints, lists title and author as well as Professor Rollins's evaluation, about which I shall say more in due course. The exact wording of the title pages prefaces the text of this essay (Cullen repeated the title at the top of p. 1; that repetition is not reproduced here). The nine-page typescript of the text has margins of about 1 3/4 inches on the left and one inch on the top, right, and bottom. The text is paginated in type at top center. The footnotes, entered in black ink at the bottom, are not numbered consecutively throughout the paper, but begin on each new page with "(1)"; they are also entered by hand in the text. The brand of typewriter is unknown to me; hence it cannot be calculated precisely whether the text is double-spaced or set at 1 1/2 line spaces. By modern standards, it has the look of the latter.

Throughout, evident typing errors are sometimes corrected in black ink in Cullen's hand or through typewriter strikeovers. The present editor makes no effort to present a facsimile of the text. Strikeovers, hand-corrections, misspacings, misspellings, and other features of imperfect student typing and orthography are here silently corrected. Cullen's occasional errors in the transcription of Millay's poetry are also corrected. (It is possible that he quoted from memory or used a corrupt popular reprint of Millay's poems rather than the standard edition.)

Professor Hyder E. Rollins, to whom Cullen submitted the paper, did not assign the paper a letter grade. Instead, his handwritten evaluative comment appears on the title page: "Approved (after some mental reservations!) Hyder E. Rollins, May 6, 1925." His mental reservations are specified only in his underlining the word *immortal* in the sentence of Cullen's essay beginning "But in 'The Poet and His Book' Miss Millay rises to immortal heights. . . ."

The Poetry of Edna St. Vincent Millay
An Appreciation
by
Countee Cullen

We are forever searching for the hand behind the picture, for the physical embodiment that wrought the mighty symphony and the majestic poem; and we are forever being disappointed and disillusioned. Curiosity is, however, a mortal ailment, and idols must continue to fall. I remember absenting myself from classes one day last summer, and dispensing with my last dollar, unterrified by certain retribution in the form of a lunchless week, in order to hear Edna St. Vincent Millay read her poems at Union Theological Seminary! My idol did not fall, but surely she wobbled dangerously. After the manner of the great, she was tardy. She made a *grande entree*, half an hour after her scheduled time, amid a flutter of applause, half-resentful, half-joyfully anticipatory. She was attired, most conspicuously, in a brilliant yellow-and-red Spanish shawl, the effect of which she must have appreciated, since she consumed a full five minutes in languidly divesting herself of it. She read in a calm, even voice; she deprecated our applause, and her grey-green eyes had a far away look that usurped one's attention from her poetry. Once when a poem was called for from the floor, she had to consider whether she had written it. I thought this rather astounding, but admissible under the caption of "temperament", an indispensable concomitant of artistic endowment.

To this rather shadowy picture of Edna Millay may be appended, with more clarifying results, this portrait by the anonymous person who sketched her for the BOOKMAN's "Literary Spotlight":[1] "Edna St. Vincent Millay is a slim

1. "The Literary Spotlight," Doran, 1924, p. 77.

young person with chestnut-brown hair shot with glints of
bronze and copper, so that sometimes it seems auburn and
sometimes golden; a slightly snub nose, and freckles; a
child mouth; a cool, grave voice; and grey-green eyes".*

"With these materials she achieves a startling variety of
appearances. When she is reading her poetry, she will seem
to the awed spectator a fragile little girl with apple blossom
face. When she is picnicking in the country she will be, with
her snub nose, freckles, carroty hair, and boyish grin, an
Irish 'newsy'. When she is meeting the bourgeoisie in its
lairs, she is likely to be a highly artificial and very affected
young lady with an exaggerated Vassar accent and
abominably overdone manners. In the basement of the
Brevoort, or in the Cafe de la Rotonde in Paris, or in the
Cafe Royal in London, she will appear a languid creature of
a decadent civilization, looking wearily out of ambiguous
eyes and smiling faintly with her doll's mouth, exquisite
and morbid. A New England nun; a chorus girl on a
holiday; the Botticelli Venus of the Uffizi gallery. . . ."

Most people, faithful to the faulty memory of
humankind, will remember Edna Millay's "Renascence" as
a poem which was submitted in a prize-poem contest, and
published, among other poems, in the "Lyric Year" for 1912;
so far, so good, but in the light of succeeding days, they will
also be prone to remember that the poem won the prize. In
fact, this poem, which is now one of the marvels of present-
day poetry, received none of the three awards. It excited a
measure of interest and admiration in the breasts of a few
of the more discerning critics and poetry-lovers. But,
according to Louis Untermeyer:[1] "Its author, totally

1. "American Poetry Since 1900," Louis Untermeyer,
Henry Holt, 1923.

Editor's note. This portrait of Millay was first published in "Edna St.
Vincent Millay," *Bookman*, 56 (January 1922), 272–278, and was
reprinted in *The Literary Spotlight*, ed. John C. Farrar (George H.
Doran, 1924). There is some dispute as to its authorship. Norman A.
Brittin, in *Edna St. Vincent Millay* (New York, 1967), identifies the
author as Floyd Dell. But John J. Patton, in "A Comprehensive
Bibliography of Edna St. Vincent Millay," published in *The Serif*,
argues that Farrar is the author.

unknown at the time, was little more than a child living on
the sea-coast of Maine, and it was not until her first book
was published five years later that it became possible to
appraise the work of Edna St. Vincent Millay".

With the publication of "Renascence" by Mitchell
Kennerley in 1917, Edna Millay took her place as one of the
giants of Parnassus. She did not, however, immediately
create the Edna St. Vincent Millay vogue, nor establish the
legend which now surrounds her. That is another story. Yet
"Renascence", which still continues to be the most favored
of her books, contains, to a greater or less degree, all the
ear-marks which accentuate or limit her powers. One finds
in it her marked inclination toward form, her superb
mastery of word-marriage,her simplicity, which, in less
capable hands, would degenerate into banality, her sudden
flourishes of frivolity which mar many fine poems worthy
of a happier termination. "Renascence" is too well known
and too much of a unit in its mystic grandeur to permit
dissection; but mighty as it is, and as extensive as is its
scope, the briefer "God's World", with its heart-break and its
anguish at the revelation of beauty, is no less expressive,
and lends itself more readily to quotation:

GOD'S WORLD
O world, I cannot hold thee close enough!
        Thy winds, thy wide grey skies!
        Thy mists, that roll and rise!
Thy woods, this autumn day, that ache and sag
And all but cry with colour! That gaunt crag
To crush! To lift the lean of that black bluff!
World, World I cannot get thee close enough!
Long have I known a glory in it all,
        But never knew I this:
        Here such a passion is
As stretcheth me apart,—Lord, I do fear
Thou'st made the world too beautiful this year;
My soul is all but out of me,—let fall
No burning leaf; prithee, let no bird call.

Louis Untermeyer, in speaking of Miss Millay's lyric
genius in "Renascence", says,[1] "This lyrical mastery is

1. "The New Era in American Poetry," Louis Untermeyer,
Henry Holt, 1919.

manifest on all except a few pages (such as 'Interim' and 'Ashes of Life' which lisp as uncertainly as the hundreds of poems to which they are too closely related)". One must respect expert criticism; but it seems to me that "Ashes of Life" is one of Miss Millay's best lyrics, exemplifying a simplicity which is at once so acute and yet so expressive that it approaches legerdemain, and which in its last stanza executes an audacity of monotony that only a genius would have dared perpetrate. What other poet, having written so effective a stanza as this, with its courageous third line, would have allowed it to stand:

Love has gone and left me,—and the neighbours
    knock and borrow,
And life goes on forever like the gnawing of a
    mouse,—
And tomorrow and tomorrow and tomorrow and tomorrow,
There's this little street and this little house?

Although Miss Millay's first book contained only six sonnets, these were enough to mark her as a master-craftsman in that form. Under her command the medium accomplishes a Shakespearean rejuvenation; octave and sestet are no longer compromised; each has its beginning and its ending, and their mating is the sonnet as it has rarely been written before, and as no one else writes it today. One critic writes of her,[1] "Her sonnets, with the phrasing cut down to the glowing core, exhibit the same sensitive parsimony that one finds in the best of the Imagist poets, plus a far richer sense of human values".* That such an encomium is justified is borne out by a survey of almost any one of her sonnets. The manner in which she adds image to image unto the perfect whole, the rush with which her words flow on, with no one word able to be dispensed with, is an astonishing feat, to put it mildly. With her there is no padding for the sake of rhyme or rhythm, truly nothing but the "glowing core". Let the following octave be a more vivid testament than I:

Editor's Note: Although Cullen quotes and provides a footnote number in the text, he neglected to identify his source.

Time does not bring relief; you all have lied
Who told me time would ease me of my pain!
I miss him in the weeping of the rain;
I want him at the shrinking of the tide;
The old snows melt from every mountain-side,
And last year's leaves are smoke in every land;
But last year's bitter loving must remain
Heaped on my heart, and my old thoughts abide.

Or consider the perfect unity of this:

Pity me not because the light of day
At close of day no longer walks the sky;
Pity me not for beauties passed away
From field and thicket as the year goes by;
Pity me not the waning of the moon,
Nor that the ebbing tide goes out to sea,
Nor that a man's desire is hushed so soon,
And you no longer look with love on me.

Miss Millay's anonymous biographer in "The Literary
Spotlight" says, "In the last few years there has grown up an
Edna St. Vincent Millay legend, a sort of Byronic legend,
which the younger generation is pleased to believe in. . . .
The Edna St. Vincent Millay legend is based on her
poems—, or, to speak more exactly, upon one particular
book of poems, the one entitled 'A Few Figs From
Thistles'.* With the publication of 'Figs From Thistles'
(Frank Shay, 1920), she became the poet laureate of the
younger generation".

And why should the younger generation not pin its
faith on a poet who writes:

My candle burns at both ends;
        It will not last the night;
But ah, my foes, and oh, my friends—
        It gives a lovely light!

Editor's Note: Cullen silently deletes here these intervening sentences
in the text being quoted: "Its title gives an indication of its cynical
optimism. Previous to this volume she had been known as the author
of 'Renascence', and had gained the devout admiration of a few poetry
lovers, but no popular audience".

Does she not say, with a more articulate clarity, what youth has cried out since the world began, when she sings:

Safe upon the solid rock the ugly houses stand:
Come and see my shining palace built upon the sand!

Some persons who have passed the rainbow romantic stage complain that with these poems Miss Millay has exchanged her birthright for a mess of pottage. But her young admirers are of a different opinion; for they love her for these kindred utterances, as many of the Rev. Robert Herrick's parishioners must have loved him less for his sermons than for his worldly advice to gather rosebuds while they might.

In 1921, when she published "Second April" through Mitchell Kennerley, Miss Millay showed that she could eat her mess of pottage, and yet retrieve her birthright. A treasure-trove of beauty—"Second April". Death, the grave concern of most young poets, plays an important part in this book, and is the butt of the poet's many moods. In "Spring", overwhelmed with the vitality of little leaves opening stickily," and of "the spikes of the crocus," she is intrigued into the belief that "it is apparent that there is not death". But recollection brings this reaction:

But what does that signify?
Not only under ground are the brains of men
Eaten by maggots.
Life in itself
Is nothing,
An empty cup, a flight of uncarpeted stairs.
It is not enough that yearly, down this hill,
April
Comes like an idiot, babbling and strewing flowers.

In "Passer Mortuus Est" she speaks of death's finality in all things, in love as well as in life, with a resignation that is also flippant:

Death devours all lovely things:
        Lesbia with her sparrow
Shares the darkness,—presently
        Every bed is narrow.
* * * * * * * * * * * * * * * *

After all, my erstwhile dear,
        My no longer cherished,
Need we say it was not love,
        Just because it perished?

In "Alms" she accepts the death of love with a listlessness that is extremely bitter in its passivity:

There was a time I stood and watched
        The small, ill-natured sparrows' fray;
I loved the beggar that I fed,
        I cared for what he had to say, . . .
But it is winter with your love;
        I scatter crumbs upon the sill,
And close the window,—and the birds
        May take or leave them, as they will.

"Mariposa" accepts the fact of death neither bitterly nor flippantly, but as an inevitability that makes it logical to say:

Suffer me to take you hand.
Suffer me to cherish you
Till the dawn is in the sky.
Whether I be false or true,
Death comes in a day or two.

But in "The Poet and His Book" Miss Millay rises to immortal heights,* and, relying on the strength of her work, cries out:

Down, you mongrel, Death!
        Back into your kennel!
I have stolen breath
        In a stalk of fennel!
You shall scratch and you shall whine
        Many a night, and you shall worry
        Many a bone, before you bury
One sweet bone of mine!

Editor's Note: Professor Hyder E. Rollins has underlined the word "immortal" and posed a question mark in the right margin.

And surely while love of beauty and sincerity persist, "The Poet and His Book" shall give the lie to death.

"The Ballad of the Harp Weaver and Other Poems" (Harper and Brothers, 1923) is a combination of the finer artist and her legendary self, with the legendary too much in evidence. It is this book which makes evident the force of the following remark by Carl Van Doren: "What sets Miss Millay's poems apart from all those written in English by women is the full pulse which . . . beats through them. . . . Rarely has a woman since Sappho written as outspokenly as this."* Indeed, this is a book of the utmost candor, almost to the point of indiscretion. There are persons who, knowing nothing else that Miss Millay has written, can quote with startling accuracy her sonnet beginning:

> I, being born a woman and distressed
> By all the needs and notions of my kind,

and whose opinion of her takes such a sonnet as its guide. Yet, another poem equally confessional, can be expressed so lyrically that one accepts the circumstance as vindicated by the poem:

> What my lips have kissed, and where, and why,
> I have forgotten, and what arms have lain
> Under my head till morning; but the rain
> Is full of ghosts tonight, that tap and sigh
> Upon the glass and listen for reply,
> And in my heart there stirs a quiet pain
> For unremembered lads that not again
> Will turn to me at midnight with a cry.

The title poem of this last volume, telling the tragic story of maternal sacrifice, is one of the finest literary ballads in the language, an actual *tour de force*. But the author's efforts to tell a story in sonnet form in her "Sonnets From an Ungrafted Tree" are less happy. Not even she is

---

*Editor's Note: No footnote is provided, nor is Van Doren listed in the "References" at the end of the essay. Cullen's source was either Van Doren's "Youth and Wings," *Century*, 106 (June 1923), 310–316, or his book *Many Minds* (New York: Knopf, 1924, which reprints the article.

able to make a form which is so complete in itself the means of narrative continuation. And her substitution of a hexameter last line in these sonnets for the accustomed pentameter line jars because of its unexpectedness, which was probably meant to be its virtue. Moreover, the language of this sequence is less Miss Millay's than the cryptic word arrangement of Edwin Arlington Robinson, without his peculiar magic.

No appraisal of Miss Millay's poetry can omit to mention her two most important plays: "The Lamp and the Bell" (Frank Shay, 1921), and "Aria da Capo" (Mitchell Kennerley). Both plays show her marvelous control over the stringent, uncompromising blank-verse form. Most poets have recognized, not losing sight of its beauty and serenity, the restrictions of blank-verse, and have chafed under the restraint. But generally, where they have come out in open rebellion, their quarrel has been too boisterous; the reader finds himself stumbling, tripping upon miscast beats, and foundering upon extra syllables maladroitly placed. But Edna Millay is a tamer of words; beneath the soft sleeking of her hands the most recalcitrant becomes docile and dutiful. Some poets ply Pegasus with lash and spur, and are nine days in falling from their perch; but she talks to him, flatters him, cajoles him, and subdues him with her patience. When we come to that sardonic tragedy "Aria da Capo," to the premier appearance of which an entire edition of Harold Munro's CHAPBOOK was devoted, and which is now an inevitable part of the repertoire of every Little Theatre movement in the country, we see the fruition of her patience and the triumph of her subtlety in such a passage as this:

> I find no jewels . . . . . but I wonder what
> The root of this black weed would do to a man
> If he should taste it . . . . . I have seen a sheep die,
> With half the stalk still drooling from its mouth.
> 'Twould be a speedy remedy, I should think,
> For a festered pride and a feverish ambition.
> It has a curious root. I think I'll hack it
> In little pieces . . . . . First I'll get me a drink;
> And then I'll hack that root in little pieces
> As small as dust, and see what the color is
> Inside.

In such a passage we find the noblest vehicle of English versification not made ignoble in being shorn of its rhetoric, nor rendered unpleasing to the ear because its arbitrary cadences have been shifted and modified to meet the exigencies of situation and the demands of genius. "Aria da Capo" and "The Lamp and the Bell" afford numerous instances of such control. The latter play also contains three of Miss Millay's most exquisite lyrics, significant for their beauty and expressive of their maker's attitude toward life. Those to whom she is high priestess surely bring richer homage to her altars, when they find their sluggish blood rekindled by lines like these:

Oh, little rose tree, bloom!
Summer is nearly over.
The dahlias bleed, and the phlox is seed.
Nothing's left of the clover,
And the path of the poppy no one knows.
I would blossom if I were a rose.

Such a gospel needs must win its adherents, as surely as the plainness of the following bit of truth needs must assume a sad significance conducive to a "Carpe diem"! reaction, when couched in terms so simple and direct:

Beat me a crown of bluer metal;
Fret it with stones of a foreign style:
The heart grows weary after a little
Of what if loved for a little while.

Few poets writing today seem more destined than she to escape the treachery of the world's unremembering mind. Time is the truest connoisseur of wisdom and beauty; constrained to careful selection lest any new endeavor suffer in comparison with what has already been voted "immortal", the years will perhaps reject the legendary Edna Millay, who gestures prettily, snaps her fingers at convention, and laughs at life and death and love; they may pass her candor by as a lamentable indiscretion, but surely they will find a separate, enduring niche for her exaltation and for the golden felicity of language which is hers. "Renascence", "God's World", "The Ballad of the Harp Weaver", many of her sonnets,—all are reasons enough for this poignant utterance, too true to savor of conceit, in "The Poet and His Book":

> Sexton, play your trade!
>   In a shower of gravel
> Stamp upon your spade!
>   Many a rose shall ravel,
>
> Many a metal wreath shall rust
>   In the rain, and I go singing
> Through the lots where you are flinging
>   Yellow Clay on dust!

Countee Cullen
May 1, 1925

References

"The New Era in American Poetry", Louis Untermeyer, Holt, 1919.

"Miss Millay's Poems", Padraic Column in the "Freeman" for November 2, 1921.

"Taking the Literary Pulse", Joseph Collins, Doran, 1924.

"The Literary Spotlight", Doran, 1924.

"American Poetry Since 1900", Louis Untermeyer, Holt, 1923.

Bibliography

"Renascence", Mitchell Kennerley, 1917.

"A Few Figs From Thistles", Frank Shay, 1920.

"The Lamp and the Bell", Frank Shay, 1921.

"Aria da Capo", Mitchell Kennerley, 1921.

"The Harp-Weaver and Other Poems", Harper and Brothers, 1923.

Now let us set this senior honors thesis in the context of Countee Cullen's undergraduate studies at New York University. Cullen matriculated at University College of Arts and Pure Science in February of 1922 and was graduated on June 10, 1925, with a B.A. degree. This college, familiarly called "The Heights," was one of two undergraduate liberal arts colleges of New York University at that time; it was located at University Heights, overlooking the Harlem River in the Bronx. There Cullen majored in English and took a First Minor in French and a Second Minor in Philosophy. Since there has been, as yet, no detailed account of Cullen's educational development, and since he was a poet, it will perhaps be of value to future students of his life and art if I discuss his coursework at The Heights. However, as a biographical preliminary, I wish to present some information, derived from his University College transcript, that will perhaps serve to clarify other aspects of his background and development.

First, since there is some uncertainty as to his place of birth, it is worth noting that his natal data are given as "5/30/03 Louisville, Ky." If, as seems likely, Cullen filled out his own application forms in 1922, he was giving his birthplace as Louisville rather than New York. His religious denomination is listed as "Protestant." Pencilled in above these data is the registrar's handwritten notation "Negro." Such notations were common in American colleges of the time, usually as a way of determining quotas of admission for minority applicants—whether black, Jewish, Hispanic—or of otherwise singling them out. I have been unable to confirm that there was such a quota for admission of blacks at New York University in the 1920s. But a review of the yearbooks during Cullen's undergraduate period suggests that a black student was indeed a rarity at The Heights. Still, it should be remarked that New York University was open to ethnic, immigrant, and working-class minorities; and there is no evidence that Cullen experienced significant prejudice at the college. In fact, the memoirs of his white classmates acknowledge Cullen with admiration and affection.

In the transcript, Frederick Asbury Cullen, his adoptive father, is given as his parent, and his address is listed as "234 West 131st Street, NYC." This is of course the parsonage of the African Methodist Episcopal Church in Harlem, where the Rev. Cullen served for forty-two years as pastor. Countee Cullen was admitted without entrance conditions, by diploma, as a graduate of De Witt Clinton High School. He is noted as having matriculated on 2/2/22 in the class of 1925. It would appear that he had a state scholarship in 1924–1925. His special adviser was listed as Professor Thorne, but this name is then crossed out and "Borgman" replaces it. (This change doubtless occurred when Cullen declared an English major, for Albert S. Borgman was a member of the English Department.) The registrar's handwritten entries indicate that Cullen was elected to Phi Beta Kappa in March of 1925. The records of his election by the Phi Beta Kappa association at The Heights indicate that Cullen stood thirteenth in a class of 102 students, with an average of 88.2 Although only nine seniors were elected, some of those with higher averages did not receive the necessary three-fourths approval of the voting faculty members. Cullen did, and so was inducted into Phi Beta Kappa on 11 March 1925. He is recorded as having requested copies of this transcript on 17 October 1924; on 23 June 1925 (for his application to graduate study at Harvard); on 5 November 1927 (for a Guggenheim Fellowship application); and in September of 1928.

The transcript itself indicates that Cullen began his classwork in the spring of 1922 and took a summer program that year so as to catch up with the other freshmen. (Thereafter, he did not attend summer school.) In the first two years, his curriculum involved a wide array of courses in introductory English, French, Latin (always with *cum laude* grades), math, physics, geology, philosophy, Greek, physical science, and (as a holdover from the World War I years) military science. As an upperclassman, he concentrated on intermediate and advanced English and French, picked up German, and took additional courses in history and philosophy. And, as a senior, he took a number of courses in education that prepared him for certification as a teacher in the public school system of New York City, in which he served with great distinction in after years.

Cullen's program of studies and his manifest distinction as a student, then, indicate that he received a solid liberal arts education with a strong emphasis on languages and literature, history and philosophy. He was well-prepared for graduate study at Harvard in either English or French, both of which he later taught in New York City. But even more importantly, for our purposes, this undergraduate education—although just the foundation of his career as a poet—made him acquainted with a wide range of literary forms, styles, and techniques; it educated him about the culture of writers in several national traditions; and it helped him to understand the literary heritage in its historical and philosophical contexts. This much, of course, can be inferred from the poems alone, for his engagement with the literary heritage is implicit in all his characteristic themes and subjects, in his literary allusions, and in his strategies of versification and language use.

When one studies the transcript information against the college bulletins for the years 1922–1925, one particular facet of Cullen's program appears remarkable. Although the English Department boasted a faculty of between fifteen and twenty professors during these years—including local eminences like Dean Archibald L. Bouton, Francis Henry Stoddard, Vernon Loggins, Arthur Huntington Nason, and Homer Watt—almost all of Cullen's English coursework was taken with one man, Professor Hyder E. Rollins.

The major required that Cullen take the prerequisite English 10-20, *Rhetoric and Composition*; this multi-section course was taught by Professors Rollins, Allen, Borgman, et al. It cannot be determined that Rollins was his instructor here, but it is possible. Certainly in English 30-40, *Advanced Composition*, Rollins was his teacher. Professor Borgman taught the required introductory course, English 31-41, *History of English Literature*. But thereafter, all of Cullen's English courses were taught by Rollins: English 52-62, *English Poetry of the Nineteenth Century*; and English 53-63, *English Prose Fiction*. Cullen could have taken a wide array of other courses—*Shakespeare, American Literature, Types of Literature,* etc. But he appears to have elected only those courses that Rollins offered, even though, as the transcript makes plain, Rollins was a hard grader who gave him quite a number of B grades. I shall later return to the influence of Rollins on Countee Cullen's development. But it should be noted that Cullen's apprenticeship as a poet was not limited to the classrooms at The Heights. For he was deeply involved in the extracurricular literary life of the university—in ways that are not evident in the published biographies and bibliographies of his work.

For one thing, Cullen was published in the university literary magazines as early as 1922; and in his junior and senior years, Cullen was in fact the poetry editor of *The Arch: The Literary Magazine of New York University.* The issues of November 1924, and January, March, and May 1925 list him on the masthead. In this role, Cullen corresponded and conferred with other student writers, selected verse for publication, and oversaw the printing of this department of the magazine, which incidentally served students of every college of the university. Even more important, Cullen's own verse appeared in *The Arch.* Neither his poetry editorship nor his publications in *The Arch* have been noted in previous bibliographies of his work. This is worth stressing because critical treatments of volumes like *Color* (1925) and *Copper Sun* (1927) sometimes suggest that the poems in these volumes appeared only in national publications like *Harper's, The Nation, Poetry, Vanity Fair,* etc. However, some verses in these volumes first appeared in *The Arch.* For the sake of clarifying the record, therefore, some attention to his extracurricular work in *The Arch* and its relation to other sites of publication seems warranted.

In Volume I, Number 8 of *The Arch* (June 1922), p. 13, there appears a "Triolet" beginning "I did not know she'd take it so"; this "Triolet" had first appeared in *the Magpie* (Christmas 1921), the literary magazine of the De Witt Clinton High School. It was renamed "Under the Mistletoe" and republished in *Copper Sun.*

In Volume II (misprinted Volume I), Number 1 of *The Arch* (November 1923), p. 8, appear two poems. The first is "To ——," beginning "Whatever I have loved has wounded me"; this poem is retitled "A Poem Once Significant, Now Happily Not," and is reprinted in *Copper Sun.* The second is "Triolet," beginning "I have wrapped my dreams in a silken cloth"; this poem, retitled "For a Poet," was dedicated to John Gaston Edgar and was republished in *Harper's* (December 1924) and in *Color.*

In Volume II, Number 2 of *The Arch* (January 1924), pp. 40–42, appears one of Cullen's most well-known poems, "The Ballad of the Brown Girl." This was of course the Second Prize poem in the Witter Bynner Intercollegiate Poetry Contest. Bynner thought it should have won, and advised Cullen to send it for republication to *Palms*, where it appeared in the Early Summer Issue of 1924. Finally, it was republished in book form by Harper and Brothers in 1927.

In Volume II, Number 3 of *The Arch* (March 1924), p. 88, appeared "The Love Tree," which was reprinted in *Copper Sun.* And in Volume II, Number 4 (May 1924), p. 122, appeared "Sacrament," which was reprinted in *Color.*

Finally, in Volume III, Number 1 of *The Arch* (November 1924), p. 17, appeared "Variations on a Theme," which was reprinted in *Copper Sun*; and in the March 1925 issue appeared "The Poet" (p. 14), also reprinted in *Copper Sun.* (This very early poem first appeared in *The Magpie* in November of 1920.)

This record of Cullen's student publications in *The Arch* suggests several things: first, that some of the poems appearing in national periodicals were first tried out in *the Arch*; second, that a number of his other poems in the published volumes first appeared in the NYU student literary magazine; and third, that some of the poems reprinted in *Copper Sun* as "juvenilia" were indeed the work of either his high school or undergraduate years, poems that he had not deemed worth including in *Color.* The pressure to publish his second volume led him to recycle them in order to expand *Copper Sun* to a proper book length.

Let us turn now to Cullen's senior honors thesis and set it in the context of his academic program. In addition to required and elective courses in the English major, the regulations of University College between 1894 and 1925 required that each student submit to the college faculty a "satisfactory thesis" related to the student's major. After 1925 this college requirement for graduation was abandoned, but several humanities disciplines immediately instituted departmental honors programs. To be graduated with Honors in English required, in addition to an overall grade of B, with an even higher average in the major, the submission of an acceptable thesis. It would appear that, since Cullen graduated in the year that the college thesis requirement was abandoned, his essay is a senior honors thesis, submitted to the Department of English. It was hand-dated and signed "Countee Cullen May 1, 1925."

The genteel English Department faculty naturally stressed the classic writers, most of whom were safely dead. But Professor Hyder E. Rollins (to whom Cullen submitted the thesis for reading) was perhaps exceptional: he was not averse to essay topics involving living writers. Most of his colleagues would probably have looked askance at Millay, but such was the personal authority of Rollins that his acquiescence in the subject carried the day.

The English Department's tolerance for the subject of Edna St. Vincent Millay, however, is surprising in view of her scandalous reputation in 1925. Although Millay was only ten years older than Cullen, she had already incurred a notoriety, in the eyes of the older generation, owing to her highly publicized sexual escapades, about which she wrote with unaccustomed frankness. However liberated her behavior, though, Millay's distinction as a lyric poet and ballad writer had become widely acknowledged; it was confirmed by the award of a Pulitzer Prize just two years previously, in 1923. And, since 1925 saw "Flaming Youth" in full rebellion against the oldsters' genteel values, the New York University English Department seems to have allowed their talented majors to pay attention to literary incarnations of this revolution. Still, as the essay makes plain, Countee

Cullen felt an obligation to his instructor, Professor Rollins, to rescue Millay from the excesses of her own behavior in order to salvage her reputation.

As I have noted above, Countee Cullen took at least three and perhaps as many as four of his five two-term English courses with Rollins: possibly *Rhetoric and Composition*; and certainly *Advanced Composition, English Prose Fiction,* and *English Poetry of the Nineteenth Century.* What was the magic appeal of this particular instructor? Because I believe Hyder Rollins to have been a major influence on Countee Cullen's development, some attention to this extraordinary scholar and teacher seems warranted here.

Hyder E. Rollins (1889–1958), a Texan by birth, had been educated at Southwestern University and Harvard, where he took his doctorate in 1917, under the supervision of George Lyman Kittredge, one of the greatest American scholars of the Middle Ages and Renaissance. Upon completing his doctorate, Rollins was recommended to NYU by Kittredge but, World War I intervening, Rollins entered the U.S. Army as a lieutenant in the 313th Field Signal Batallion of the AEF and served in France until the Armistice. After demobilization, he spent 1919 in London at the British Museum, where he began amassing a collection of unpublished English and Scottish broadside ballads of the Renaissance. During this research year his salary was renegotiated upward with Dean A.L. Bouton so that he could return to England each summer in order to collect more ballads. In a letter to Bouton of 13 October 1919, he writes, "I meet a new Harvard Ph.D. every day [at the British Museum]: not War, Pestilence, or Sudden Death can stop them." Even so, that research year was, for Rollins, a difficult one. On 12 February 1920, he wrote to the Dean: "England is starving me to death, and withal I'm working too hard." Nonetheless, out of this work came his magisterial first book, an edition called *Old English Ballads, 1555–1625* (1920).

During World War I, the enrollment in the German Department at The Heights had collapsed, and German professors were assigned to English Department courses. Consequently, Rollins was offered a program that was not his specialty. To Dean Bouton he expressed the wish that he could be assigned a ballad course or one in the Restoration drama; and he complained that the short story was not his field. It appears, he wrote to Dean Bouton on 12 February 1920, that "everything I really know—everything for which I am competent—has been staked out already; and as a new-comer I do *not* want to arouse commotion and prejudice by infringing on the fields of colleagues." If he was to be assigned something outside of his field, "if it must be poetry, please drag in Keats and Tennyson!—and I shall do my best with them. It will be a splendid thing for me to be obliged to study something 'out of my line.' I have been in nothing but a line, or perhaps it's a trench, for many a day."[1]

Once he had arrived on campus, Rollins quickly distinguished himself as one of the most erudite and challenging professors on the faculty. Accepting an assistant professorship in 1920, he rose rapidly through the ranks to full professor in just four years. In 1926 he left NYU to accept a professorship at Harvard, where he taught until his retirement in 1956. Although Rollins's professional career is nowadays wholly identified with the Harvard English Department, where (following Kittredge in the Guerney Professorship of English Literature) he is remembered for his great scholarly distinction, Rollins actually attained international recognition while yet at University College. His meteoric rise in university teaching is largely owing to definitive publications like *A Pepysian Garland* (1922), *Cavalier and Puritan: Ballads and Broadsides* (1924), *A Handful of Pleasant Delights* (1924), and *An Analytical Index of Ballad-Entries in the Registers of the Company of Stationers in London* (1924)—all books appearing during Cullen's undergraduate years.[2]

In one respect, the assignment of a course in which Keats was "dragged in" had a permanent influence on Rollins's future career—as on Cullen's as well. For Rollins became enchanted with Keats and devoted to his life and work. Out of this ardor came, after Cullen's graduation, several of Rollins's major publications: *Keats' Reputation in America to 1848* (1946), the two-volume *The Keats Circle: Letters and*

Papers, 1816–1878 (1948), *Keats and the Bostonians* (1951), *More Letters and Poems of the Keats Circle* (1955), and the magisterial two-volume edition of *The Letters of John Keats, 1814–1821* (1958). In my judgment, the many Keatsian thematic and technical characteristics of Cullen's verse—not to speak of the encomia in "To John Keats, Poet. At Springtime" and "To Endymion"—are directly attributable to Rollins's impassioned lectures on Keats in *English Poets of the Nineteenth Century* during Cullen's junior year, 1923–1924.[3]

Rollins's devotion to Keats and the departmental processes by which essay topics were devised by the English Department staff are suggested by a letter in the NYU Archives in which Rollins writes to Dean Bouton about the subjects to be assigned for a prize essay. The topics Rollins proposes are "Permanent Qualities of the Poetry of John Keats," "John Keats and John Gould Fletcher: A Study of Imagery," and "The Sensuous Appeal of Keats' Poetry." Then, as if this too much reflected his own ardor for Keats, he adds "Originality in the Love Songs of Sara Teasdale," "Portrait-Painting in the Poems of Edgar Lee Masters," "The Narrative Art of John Masefield's Poems," "A Study of Thomas Hardy's *Dynasts*," and "Drinkwater's *Abraham Lincoln* and Shakespeare's *Henry IV*: A Study in the Technique and Matter of the Historical Play." These last topics, involving modern writers, suggest that Rollins was perhaps exceptional among the English staff in inviting attention to modern writers, such as Millay, about whom Cullen eventually wrote his thesis. To Dean Bouton, Rollins remarked that he found the subjects for the English prize essay "very difficult to decide on, for my mind runs along the line of 'problems.'" He noted that "All these subjects, save the first three, are ultra-modern. Possibly it might be wiser simply to assign as a subject 'The Poetry of John Keats.' The average undergraduate needs something broad. But whatever subject is assigned, I shall do my best to get my own students interested in it."[4] Needless to say, Countee Cullen was not an average undergraduate. Although he came to revere Keats as Rollins did, he selected his own topic for the senior honors thesis, an ultra-modern writer conspicuously absent from Rollins's list for Dean Bouton.

Setting aside Keats for the moment, Rollins's mind was also profoundly oriented toward the Renaissance, where his research involved the compilation of an immense collection of popular broadside ballads. On these ballads he worked assiduously during Cullen's undergraduate years. There must have been many occasions when Cullen went to Rollins's office, perhaps to discuss a paper or an assignment, and noted piles of photocopied ballad manuscripts, just arrived from the British Museum or another repository. Rollins worked over these manuscripts meticulously, comparing them with variant ballads in the Scottish, Irish, and other north European literatures, readying his next edition. Cullen left no account of this teacher, to my knowledge, but a letter in the NYU Archives from Chancellor Elmer Ellsworth Brown to the Guggenheim Foundation describes Rollins as "a comparatively silent man, and works night and day, week in and week out. Nevertheless, he is personally liked by his classes."[5] This seems to have been the case, for in one of Rollins's letters to the Chancellor (15 January 1924)—in which Rollins appropriately boasts that three of his books have been published in one month—Rollins goes on: "Meanwhile, two admiring classes have given me a huge quantity of cigarettes—and with this tangible honor to boast of, I think it certain that research isn't injuring my teaching!"[6] Sitting there in that office, perhaps with a magnifying glass, perhaps even a green eyeshade, Rollins must have communicated his immense enthusiasm for the old popular ballads to his young black student.

But if Rollins communicated enthusiasm for ballads to Countee Cullen, behind Rollins—forming a link with Cullen—was Rollins's own mentor, George Lyman Kittredge, who lectured on the ballad form at Harvard and inspired students like Rollins to carry on the work. Kittredge was a man of formidable erudition whose knowledge of the English ballad was founded on the work of *his* Harvard master, F.J. Child. The five-volume *The English and Scottish Popular Ballads,* edited by Francis James Child (to which the young Kittredge had supplied notes and annotations), was the groundwork upon which the work of Kittredge and thereafter Rollins was based. Ultimately, it was also the source of Cullen's ballad poems. Kittredge's one-volume edition of *The English and Scottish Popular Ballads* (1904) also served as the introduction to these poems for generations of Harvard students such as Rollins. But Rollins went even beyond his mentor Kittredge and rivalled Child's monumental work in preparing the original collections I have already named, as well as others published after Cullen's graduation.

Is it any wonder, then, that Cullen's first three volumes, *Color* (1925), *Copper Sun* (1927), and *The Ballad of the Brown Girl* (1927), are full of ballad settings, characters, and stylistic features? Or that he wrote his thesis on a woman poet who, in "The Ballad of the Harp Weaver," had established her claim to eminence with a Pulitzer Prize? Such lines as Cullen's "He rode across like a cavalier,/Spurs clicking hard and loud" ("Two Who Crossed a Line"), are unimaginable except under the influence of Rollins's *Cavalier and Puritan: Ballads and Broadsides.* . . . Cullen's portrait of his parents in "Fruit of the Flower" is a reflection of Rollins's influence: "My mother's life is puritan,/No hint of cavalier. . . ." Such narrative poems as "Judas Iscariot," as well as Cullen's recurrent use of the *abcb* quatrain, culminate in "The Ballad of the Brown Girl," published in *the Arch* in 1924. This is not the place to offer a full critique of that remarkable poem, which grew directly out of Millay's experiments and out of Rollins's lectures on the ballad tradition and his editing of four volumes of ballads during Cullen's undergraduate years. Yet some observations and clarifications of fact may perhaps be offered here. First, it is very unlikely that Cullen found the source for the ballad in *The Oxford Book of Ballads* or *The Ballad Book*, as Alan R. Shucard has suggested in *Countee Cullen.*[7] In view of Rollins's intimate involvement with Kittredge, with whom he continually corresponded about his ballad work, and in view of Kittredge's connection to F.J. Child, it is more likely that Rollins steered Cullen to the source in Child's edition of

"Lord Thomas and Fair Annet" and its variants like "The Nut-Brown Bride," "The Brown Bride and Lord Thomas," "Lord Thomas and Fair Elinor," or "Sweet Willie and Fair Annie."[8] These Child versions of the ballad give the full dramatis personae of Cullen's poem, as the abbreviated versions in the *Oxford* and *The Ballad Book* collections do not. Further, it is beside the point to criticize Cullen for verboseness in expanding the ballad from ten (*Oxford* version) or fifteen (*Ballad Book*) stanzas to fifty.[9] Cullen's poem is only slightly longer than the "E" version of the ballad ("Sweet Willie and Fair Annie"), which runs to forty-two stanzas. Nor is there any point in faulting Cullen, as Houston A. Baker, Jr., does in *A Many-Colored Coat of Dreams: The Poetry of Countee Cullen*, for making Lord Thomas dependent on his mother, since this aspect of Lord Thomas is found in the originals.[10]

Blanche E. Ferguson has reported that it was only after Cullen had written *The Ballad of the Brown Girl* that he discovered that her color did not refer to race: "The term was merely used to identify her as a peasant."[11] I do not know the source of Ferguson's remark here. But it will be evident to anyone reading the originals that the nut-brown maid was dark complexioned and, in view of her wealth, no common peasant. I doubt seriously that Cullen, who worked so extensively with Rollins, would not have known precisely what a nut-brown maid, as a recurrent type-character, meant in these old ballads.

Alan Shucard has also called "a surprising piece of information"[12] the report that Blanche E. Ferguson gives of Kittredge's reaction to the poem. Ferguson remarks that the ballad "also prompted the writing of one of the most highly prized letters that Countee had ever received. This letter came from the outstanding authority on ballads, Professor Lyman Kittredge of Harvard. Countee found it hard to believe Dr. Kittredge had written that 'Ballad of the Brown Girl' was the finest literary ballad he had ever read."[13]

This *is* surprising, and I cannot find the published source of this claim. However, in the Amistad Research Center collection of Cullen correspondence is a Hyder Rollins letter to Cullen, dated 7 December 1923, thanking Cullen for a copy of "The Ballad of the Brown Girl" (probably in *The Arch* version). "Your ballad seems to me charming—even if, in spots, a bit too literary to be a genuine ballad. Many thanks for the copy, which I forwarded to Mr. Kittredge (the G.L.K. whose initials appear below). I shall let you see Mr. Kittredge's acknowledgment. Meanwhile, it occurs to me that even this bare note will interest you." Attached to Rollins's letter is a note from Kittredge: "Dear Rollins, I see that a Negro student at N.Y.U. has won a prize for a ballad. May I have a copy? Yours ever, G.L.K." Kittredge received the copy Rollins sent him and responded directly to Cullen on 8 December 1923: "Professor Rollins, in response to my request, has kindly sent me a copy of your 'Brown Girl,' which I am very glad to have. It will stand me in good stead as an unusually successful example of poetical composition in the style of the 'popular ballad.' Allow me to congratulate you on your achievement."[14] However commendatory, this letter does not suggest that Kittredge thought the poem to be "the finest literary ballad he had ever read," as Ferguson suggests. It is, however, a literary ballad of great distinction.

In 1925, the year that *Color* was published and Cullen submitted his senior honors thesis to Professor Rollins, the NYU faculty and students showered Cullen with compliments. Rollins, for example, wrote, "We are proud of you, we New York University people, and we hope that Harvard, with its erudition, won't ruin you."[15] Even the chancellor of NYU, Dr. Elmer Ellsworth Brown, sent Cullen this handwritten note: "I happened on a copy of your book, *Color,* at the University book store down town to-day, brought it home, and have read it this evening. I want to tell you how deeply I am stirred by the terrible singing sincerity of your words."[16] Chancellor Brown is even recorded as having committed "For Joseph Conrad" to memory and quoting it in the august precincts of the Century Club of New York City.[17] Later, Brown recommended Cullen for the Guggenheim Fellowship he won, as did Dean Bouton at University College. In a gesture of thanks, Cullen sent Bouton *The Black Christ, and Other Poems.* Bouton responded on 28 October

1929 that it was "a profoundly significant piece of work" that would continue "to be heard from after the printing press is dry and your first edition is long exhausted." Dean Bouton told Cullen: "I certainly foresee splendid things ahead of you and am glad to have been present, even if only in a very slight way, at the time when you were in the making, so to speak. It is particularly gratifying that the Guggenheim Foundation should be so broad in the interpretation of its functions that they have seen their way clear to give you a fellowship for creative work. That, of course, is rather a novel thing in American education and you are doing much for the future, I think, of many deserving young men by what you are now accomplishing under the fellowship which you hold."[18]

This praise from Cullen's professors was matched by the comments of some of his classmates. The undergraduate poet Charles Norman, when he came to write of their college days in retrospect, in *Poets and People* (1972), remarked: ". . . I think I can honestly say that the only poet I ever envied was Countee Cullen, who had been my schoolmate. One day, when I praised his work, he told me that there was nothing of his already published work that he could not have improved if he wanted to. I received an impression of immense talent which I would be unable to overtake or match. He said it without vanity, without self-consciousness, in his soft, sincere, melodious voice."[19] Perhaps for this reason, Norman turned his attention to biography and is remembered for his lives of Ezra Pound and e.e. cummings.

This sense of undergraduate rivalry among the NYU college poets is rather softened, however, in Martin Russak's recollection in the NYU literary publication, *The Critical Review*, for March 1928: "When Countee Cullen was a junior at New York University, I was a freshman and therefore came into contact with him only rarely. But I remember how proud we all were that he was our school-mate. That was a banner year for our campus; Charles Norman was there, and there was a whole group of young poets. Though we were all good friends, there were, of course, minor jealousies; but Cullen had our complete admiration and was our chief pride.

Always a quiet, modest, retiring fellow, he could nevertheless seldom be seen walking across the campus without two or three of us chattering and gesticulating around him. It was not his poems or his inter-collegiate poetry prize that captured our imaginations; it was the air about him and his name—the air of one who is unmistakably marked out for achievement, the indefinable air of one who carries within him, deliberately, some very precious burden entrusted to his particular safekeeping." For Russak, *Color* and *Copper Sun* fulfilled the bright promise of Cullen's undergraduate years, justifying their faith in him so that "Today [1928] Countee Cullen stands as without a doubt the most important and distinguished young poet before the public."[20]

In 1926 Professor A.H. Nason, a member of "The Heights" English Department and the Director of the NYU Press, had accepted Hyder Rollins's recommendation that the press publish *Some Recent New York University Verse*, edited by David L. Blum. In the collection, Cullen's "Heritage," "To John Keats, Poet. At Springtime," "Love in Ruins," and "The Poet" were reprinted. In his introduction, James B. Munn, Dean of the Washington Square College, remarked: "What will be the future achievement of these young poets, we cannot tell. Some may lose the vision; others may seek a different medium of artistic expression. Will there be one or two who will pursue the search until the end? If so, what will the search bring? There is always a chance that such a volume may presage some great achievement." Munn felt that "all those whose work appears here have been subjected to academic influence and have apparently withstood whatever effects it may have to eradicate individualism." This is an odd remark, but it points to issues implicated in Cullen's alleged failure to fulfill his promise as a poet. Was his individualism, as a black, "eradicated" by the program of English studies he undertook with Rollins and others? Was it inhibited by his turning to the wrong models—to Keats, Millay, Housman, Robinson, the ballad, the white English literary tradition—rather than to the literature of rising black consciousness, represented by Dunbar, McKay, Hughes, and others in Harlem? Or should his models have been the literary modernists then bursting on the scene—Pound, Eliot, cummings, and Hart Crane?[21] Whatever the case, Dean Munn improbably remarked that "If the poetry of youth be ardently sincere, its promise frequently makes its very imperfections insignificant. Let the young poet not fear the critic who, Jeffrey-like, says 'This will never do.'"[22]

One New York University critic who was not afraid to say what would not do was Professor Eda Lou Walton, who taught English at the Washington Square Campus. (I have found no information on whether Cullen knew the playwright and future novelist Thomas Wolfe, who also taught at the Square.) She and Cullen sometimes read or listened to other poets. In *The Critical Review* issue in which Martin Russak fondly remembered his freshman awe of Cullen, Professor Walton undertook to criticize the negative effects on individualism of the "Teasdale-Millay school" then so popular in colleges. In view of the defensive tone of Cullen's thesis on Millay, Walton's comments in "The Undergraduate Poet" deserve serious attention. Speaking of the impact of Teasdale and Millay on youthful writers, Walton remarked: "These young poets upon first falling in love begin to sing sweetly and tritely of their hearts and souls, of longing and yearning, and burning. If they confuse their hearts and souls with trees and stars, with moons and seas, so much the better. They lift and fall with the tides; they are swept by storms, they are lonely as clouds. They are safe in the uniqueness of their emotion and blind, for the most part, to its amusing commonplaceness. Then comes the first disillusionment. They begin 'burning the candle at both ends' and pretending that 'it makes a lovely light,' although often they do not believe a word of it. They turn a bit cleverly cynical and can never end a lyric without some ironical fillip. They announce stridently the uselessness and stupidity of the opposite sex. They try to pick out figs, but are more intent on thistles."[23] For Walton, the "Teasdale-Millays" had little to say, in contrast to another camp of undergraduate poets, whom she identified as the "Cerebrals," whose masters were T.S. Eliot, Hart Crane, e.e. cummings, and Marianne

Moore. In characterizing these two camps, Walton was of course implicitly highlighting—and condemning—the conventional academic romanticism of the kind of poetry Cullen was writing, although she never mentions Cullen by name. Cullen's indifference to those currents of poetic modernism, developing on the campus as well as in the international literary culture, has indeed been a constant factor in the definition of his work as "minor."

Whatever one may claim to have been the proper model for Cullen's art, there is no doubt that for Hyder Rollins the English tradition from the Middle Ages onward was the right foundation for a poet. His hope that Harvard's erudition would not ruin Cullen was largely facetious, an in-joke, for Rollins himself was on the eve of departure for Harvard, where he joined Kittredge on the English faulty. On 15 May 1926, Rollins wrote to Cullen: "No doubt you already know that I am going abroad on June 12, thanks to a Guggenheim Fellowship, and that, accordingly, I shan't reach Harvard until September, 1927. That means you'll have to stay on for two more years! I shall certainly hope to see you in either Cambridge or New York."[24] In fact, Cullen did not study with Rollins at Harvard; he completed his M.A. work in one year, studying instead with Irving Babbitt, Bliss Perry, Robert Hillyer, Kittredge, and others. Nevertheless, Rollins and Cullen continued to correspond throughout the 1920s. When Cullen sent his mentor a copy of *The Black Christ*, Rollins replied on 28 October 1929 that he had "read it with genuine interest and enjoyment. There's no denying that you're a poet, and a good one, and I am proud of your successes and achievements." He commended Cullen's choice of Paris for Cullen's Guggenheim year and remarked that "the weather of London is so devilish that, after three winters' experience of it [collecting ballads], I fear I shall never be courageous enough to face it again." In a final allusion to their time together at NYU, Rollins concluded: "Life seems rather dull on the Charles. Next week I'm going to N.Y.U. to see if it is also dull on the Harlem or whether *I'm* the dull one!" And he closed, "Every good wish forever. Your sincere friend."[25]

This overview of Countee Cullen's undergraduate years at "The Heights" suggests several conclusions. First, Cullen was a highly popular and academically successful student who attained an impressive celebrity with his classmates and professors. Trained in a conventional academic program that emphasized the classic writers of the white English tradition, Cullen naturally gravitated to the work of Keats, Robinson, Millay, Masters, and the old ballad writers. Essentially shaped by Hyder E. Rollins, an international scholar with a deep affinity for Keats and the ballad forms, Cullen supplemented his studies by extracurricular activities like publishing in the student literary periodical, *The Arch*, even editing the magazine in his last two years, and by attending and giving readings of poetry on campus and throughout the country. His achievement was thus an inspiration to other young poets. Some have suggested that Harvard, with its erudition, may have "ruined" Cullen for the task of elevating the quality of down-home, right-on black poetry in the twentieth century. But for better or for worse, Cullen's direction was set well before he got to Harvard: the route was fixed at The Heights.

There is no doubt that his work would have benefited from deeper immersion in the modernist poets then attaining fame—writers like Eliot, Pound, Stevens, and Williams. And it is highly probable that the application of modernist techniques to problems of racial identity and experience would have deepened the impact of poems like "Heritage," "The Black Christ," and others that express his sense of the meaning of blackness in white America, thereby allying him more intimately with the poetic projects of Claude McKay, Langston Hughes, and other figures of the Harlem Renaissance. But Cullen was the product of the forces that shaped him and of the choices and models that he elected. Within those terms and limits, he attained exceptional distinction as a lyric poet with an impassioned romantic sensibility. If he failed to scale the highest point of Parnassus, he did reach the lesser heights.

NOTES

1. Letter of Hyder E. Rollins to Dean A.L. Bouton, 11 February 1920. NYU Archives.

2. For an account of Rollins's Harvard career, see Herschel Baker's *Hyder Edward Rollins: A Bibliography* (Cambridge: Harvard University Press, 1960).

3. Keats's influence on Countee Cullen is often mentioned but rarely treated in depth. Yet see Margaret Perry's *A Bio-Bibliography of Countee P. Cullen, 1903–1946* (Westport: Greenwood Press, 1971), pp. 28–30.

4. Hyder E. Rollins to A.L. Bouton, 28 February 1921. NYU Archives.

5. Chancellor Elmer Ellsworth Brown to Henry Allen Moe, Guggenheim Foundation, 21 October 1925. NYU Archives.

6. Hyder E. Rollins to E.E. Brown, 15 January 1924. NYU Archives.

7. Alan R. Shucard rightly remarks that "it is to Cullen's credit that, whatever the version or versions of the frequently reprinted old ballad he was familiar with, his treatment is more dramatic than those presented, for example, in two standard collections, *The Oxford Book of Ballads* and *The Ballad Book.*" *Countee Cullen* (Boston: Twayne, 1984), p. 110.

8. *The English and Scottish Popular Ballads*, ed. Francis James Child (New York: Dover, 1965), II, pp. 179–199.

9. Shucard, p. 110.

10. Houston A. Baker, Jr., *A Many-Colored Coat of Dreams: The Poetry of Countee Cullen* (Detroit: Broadside Press, 1974), p. 45.

11. Blanche E. Ferguson, *Countee Cullen and the Negro Renaissance* (New York: Dodd, Mead, 1966), p. 39.

12. Shucard, p. 125, n18.

13. Ferguson, p. 39.

14. G.L. Kittredge to Countee Cullen, 8 December 1923. Amistad Collection, Tulane University. Cf. *Guide to the Microfilm Edition of the Countee Cullen Papers, 1921–1969*, compiled by Florence E. Borders (New Orleans: Amistad Research Center, 1975).

15. H.E. Rollins to Countee Cullen, 9 January 1926. Amistad Collection.

16. Cancellor E.E. Brown to Countee Cullen, 20 October 1925. Amistad Collection.

17. E.E. Brown to Countee Cullen, 17 March 1926. Amistad Collection.

18. A.L. Bouton to Countee Cullen, 28 October 1929. Amistad Collection.

19. Charles Norman, *Poets and People* (Indianapolis and New York: Bobbs-Merrill, 1972), p. x.

20. Martin Russak,"Countee Cullen," *The Critical Review* (NYU literary publication), March 1928, p. 7.

21. For representative opinions on Cullen's verse in relation to the black tradition and to poetic modernism, see Shucard, pp. 111– 114; Mercer Cook and Stephen E. Henderson, *The Militant Black Writer in Africa and the United States* (Madison: University of Wisconsin Press, 1969), p. 116; and David Littlejohn, *Black on White: A Critical Survey of Writing by American Negroes* (New York: Grossman Publishers, 1966), pp. 55–56.

22. James B. Munn, "Introduction," *Some Recent New York University Verse,* ed. David L. Blum (New York: New York University Press, 1926), pp. vii–viii.

23. Eda Lou Walton, "The Undergraduate Poet," *The Critical Review,* March 1928, p. 7.

24. H.E. Rollins to Countee Cullen, 15 May 1926. Amistad Collection.

25. H.E. Rollins to Countee Cullen, 28 October 1929. Amistad Collection.

———————

For permission to publish the senior honors thesis of Countee Cullen, the editor wishes to thank the poet's widow, the late Mrs. Ida Cullen. Thanks are also due to Tom Frusciano, curator of the New York University Archives, for permission to quote from *The Critical Review,* as well as from letters and documents housed in the Records of the Dean, University College, New York University Archives (RG 18.0.2), and the Records of the Chancellor (Elmer Ellsworth Brown), Series I, Box 61, Folder 10 (RG 3.0.4). I also wish to thank the New York University Press for permission to quote from *Some Recent New York University Verse.* Thanks are also due to Herschel Baker, literary executor of Hyder Rollins, and to The Countee Cullen Papers, Amistad Research Center, Tulane University, for permission to quote from the letters of Hyder Rollins. The editor also gratefully acknowledges the permission of Elizabeth Barnett, Literary Executor, to reprint Cullen's excerpts from *Collected Poems* by Edna St. Vincent Millay (Harper & Row, copyrights 1916, 1921, 1922, 1923, 1945, 1948, 1950, 1951, by Edna St. Vincent Millay and Norma Millay Ellis); and from *Aria da Capo* and *The Bell,* by Edna St. Vincent Millay (copyright 1920, 1922, 1948, and 1950, by Edna St. Vincent Millay). Reprinted by permission.

Vindication as a Thematic Principle in Alain Locke's Writings on the Music of Black Americans

PAUL JOSEPH BURGETT

This essay focuses attention on one aspect of a blossoming intellectual exercise whose rubric concerns the aesthetic theories regarding Afro-American art and culture. This exercise, which has received some degree of systematic scholarly attention, owes much to early scholars such as W.E.B. DuBois and Alain Locke as well as more recent scholars such as Hoyt Fuller, Addison Gayle, Jr., and others, all of whom have encouraged and contributed to disciplined theories leading toward a black aesthetic. My main concern here is with the music of black Americans and, more specifically, with the aesthetic theories of Alain Locke in his treatment of this music.

Relatively early in my research, critical issues considered in aesthetic theories of Afro-American music seemed to me to center on the creative act, the aesthetic object, aesthetic expression, aesthetic judgment, and the function of art—all of which comprise a theoretical model of problems in aesthetics which has been proposed by Eliseo Vivas and Murray Krieger.[1] These problems seemed useful in my efforts to negotiate the questions of what Afro-American music is and what its definable characteristics are—seminal questions in the early 1970s and ones which have served as the focus of a continuing dialectic.

A logical solution in the search for answers seemed to lie in identifying and examining aesthetic theories that treated the music of black Americans within specific ideological frameworks and, more specifically, that explored the writings of black scholars who had developed systems of thought which were theoretically consistent and logical. My search of the literature yielded the work of two writers whose efforts satisfied those criteria. One is Alain Locke; the other Amiri Baraka.

Essential to understanding Locke's aesthetic perspective on black art is an understanding of the philosophical orientation that informed his views. Horace Meyer Kallen observes that Locke's philosophical orientation had initially been monist or universal. This philosophy, which has enjoyed widespread Western currency, holds to the principle of the "primacy of totalitarian unity . . . and its supremacy in the consummation of all existence."[2] Further, while conceding the pervasiveness of variety and difference, the monistic creed denies their existence and subscribes to a concept that recognizes only the One, and not the Many, as real. Kallen cites the example of Man the one versus Man the many; that is, men, in all their variety, come and go, but Man goes on forever.[3] Kallen states that the dominant trend among philosophers is always to prove unity and to work at unifications—to assert *one* humanity, *one* universe, *one* system of values and ideals that somehow argues away as unimportant the actualities of penalizing one for being oneself.[4]

These totalitarian or absolutist doctrines incorporated social and cultural implications that eventually were to have a deep effect on Locke. One can immediately recognize the conflicts they posed for social and cultural interaction. A more powerful absolutist philosophy would necessarily be able to accommodate differing philosophies only on its own terms, which would mean the rejection or at least the subordination of those philosophies. In other words, social or cultural reciprocity, on an equal basis, among cultures of varying ideologies, all existing within an essentially monistic framework, is a contradiction.

Considering Locke's academic background, it is readily apparent how he came to espouse the prevailing monistic doctrine. Western European culture, which is essentially monistic, was the philosophical backbone of his academic training. Clare Crane notes a particularly revealing observation made by Van Wyck Brooks, a contemporary of Locke at Harvard.

> It was to England and Europe . . . that virtually all the Harvard professors looked as the centers of culture, observing with "smiling contempt" America's lack of native art and literature.[5]

Crane goes on to say,

> Brooks recalled that he and other Harvard men eagerly rushed abroad after their graduation to touch the sources of art and literature in Italy, France and England. Locke himself spent four years abroad.[6]

Because of what Kallen calls Locke's exposure to the "exigent harshness of experience," that is, the unpleasant social imperatives inevitable in the lives of most black Americans, Locke gradually moved away, however unwillingly, from a monistic philosophy to a philosophy of cultural pluralism.

Ironically, it was while he was a student at Harvard that Locke became acquainted with the concept of cultural pluralism. This philosophy recognizes and accepts the fact that very real differences exist among people and ideas; that these differences are to be considered "equal," not only in the sense of meaning "like" or "similar" but also parity of the unequal.[7] Kallen states:

> [Locke] would have preferred reality to be basically a One and not a Many, and human reality to be expressive of this Oneness. His preference interposed an active reservation to

the actuality of the plural. It long kept him from completely committing himself.[8]

Once committed, however, Locke pursued this ideal relentlessly in his own philosophical writings and in his advice to the many black artists and writers to whom he was a mentor.

Locke believed that pluralism and its concomitants, social and cultural reciprocity, as well as the relativity of values, could prosper most efficaciously in the congenial atmosphere of what he called "intellectual democracy." In such a setting, dogmatism, bigotry, and arbitrary orthodoxy as they apply to religious, ideological, and cultural values could not long survive.[9] Such a belief led Locke to the conviction that cultural pluralism was capable of functioning successfully within the framework of the American democratic system. While he believed that the system was faulty, that American society was mired in a pervasive provincialism that was inspired by the cultural hegemony of Europe and that discouraged identity, autonomy, and growth among minority groups, Locke firmly believed in the potential of the system, the American dream, and he argued his theories persuasively in many of his philosophical essays and other writings.

The concept of vindication is a persistent theme in Locke's writings about the music of black Americans and an examination of this theme is instructive of certain early thinking on the issue of a Black Aesthetic.

An initial observation in this matter holds that the Negro intelligentsia, from the Civil War through the Negro Renaissance, according to Crane, were essentially elitist in relation to the black population.[10] The individuals comprising the Negro Renaissance, by virtue of their education and cosmopolitanism—many of them had spent time abroad and their interactions at home were expanded to include a wide-ranging interracial spectrum of people— made up a new class of persons who did not have, to use Nathan Huggins's words, "a grass roots attachment." This elitism remained an intact principle despite certain philosophical differences among disparate perspectives—for example, DuBois's devotion to a referential or propaganda theory of art in contrast to Locke's espousal of a more absolutist perspective, i.e., art for art's sake.

Despite such differences, there clearly was a tendency among the black intelligentsia that sought the cultural transformation of black folk culture into a formal or high culture. Huggins points out that most "aspired to *high* culture as opposed to that of the common man, which they hoped to mine for novels, poems, plays, and symphonies."[11] Huggins observes further that, except for the poet Langston Hughes, none of the Harlem intellectuals took jazz seriously. While people like James Weldon Johnson and Alain Locke respected jazz as an example of folk music, their greatest expectations lay in its transformation into serious music of high culture by some race genius in the tradition of a Dvorak or a Smetana.

The theme of vindication in Locke's thinking can perhaps best be seen and understood by looking briefly at Afro-American music as he saw it and by analyzing the philosophical perspective that emerges from that framework. The framework, developed by Locke, and reported, essentially, in his book *The Negro and His Music*, is embodied in three categories of musical history, all derived from folk origin, which embrace both sacred and secular types.

The first is folk music. Produced without formal musical training or intention, Negro folk music is fundamentally a product of emotional creation. This type, according to Locke, ". . . has produced the most characteristic Negro musical idiom,—sad but not somber, intense but buoyant, tragic but ecstatic . . . a unique and paradoxical combination of emotional elements."[12] The second type is derived from original folk music. It is, however, a diluted form, "imitatively exploited by both white and Negro musicians, [which] has become the principal source and ingredient of American popular music."[13] The third type, according to Locke, is strictly a formal or classical type of music, which can be "properly styled Negro music only when obviously derived from folk music idioms or strongly influenced by them."[14]

Incidental to these three categories is another type of music composed by blacks, which Locke mentions only in passing. It is what he calls music in the universal mode without trace of folk idiom or influence. It is, to use Locke's words, "in the general mainstream of cosmopolitan or classical music." According to Locke, music of this sort, composed by Negro musicians, can in no sense be called "Negro music."[15]

It is the original black folk music, the spirituals and the secular songs, which Locke uses as a base in developing his views of Afro-American musical development. Several observations about his views of black folk music deserve further development here.

First of all, despite Locke's insistence on the general worth of this music, one senses that its value for him was directly related to its potential for some "higher" development. In other words, folk music is valuable at a specific level. Its value, however, increases when elements of this music can be used to influence the music of some higher level. For example, Locke makes the statement that the spirituals received the "highest possible recognition" when they were used as thematic material for symphonic music in Dvorak's symphony *From the New World.* Specifically, he points to the theme of the slow movement as expressing the true atmosphere of a "Negro spiritual," and he says of the Scherzo movement that it was "nose close to jazz, for Dvorak took his rhythms and tone intervals from the shout type of Negro dance."[16] Locke asserts that Dvorak chose spirituals to represent the atmosphere of America. Because of this symphony, Locke goes on to say,

> . . . the spiritual and even the secular Negro folk melodies and their harmonic style have been regarded by most musicians as the purest and most valuable musical ore in America; the raw materials of a native American music. So gradually ever since, their folk quality and purity of style have been emphasized by real musicians.[17]

It is important to pursue this particular example because the findings establish important implications for Locke's theories about black music.

Despite claims by Locke and others that Negro folk tunes as well as American Indian tunes were used in the symphony to represent American atmosphere, Dvorak himself indicated that this was untrue. In a letter to a friend, he states:

> I send you Kretzschmar's analysis of the symphony but omit that nonsense about my having made use of "Indian" and "Negro" themes—that is a lie. I tried to write in the spirit of those American folk melodies.[18]

Furthermore, and again by Dvorak's own admission, any suggestion of the Negro spiritual idiom in the symphony is actually original material created by the composer.[19]

There is no doubt that Dvorak heard and was influenced by spirituals. Harry T. Burleigh, a black singer and student at the National Conservatory of Music in New York at the time Dvorak was its director, was known to have sung spirituals for Dvorak on several occasions.[20]

A curious and somewhat ironic aside which concerns Burleigh is Locke's condemnation of black composers' abuse of the spirituals by affecting their settings with too much influence from formal European idioms and mannerisms. He cites Burleigh as one composer responsible for such abuses.[21]

At this point, a look at specific parts of the symphony involving questions of Dvorak's use of spirituals will be helpful. In the first movement, the second theme, in G major, is played by solo flute:[22]

The first four measures of this theme have been likened to the spiritual melody, "Swing Low Sweet Chariot." Actually, the shape of Dvorak's melody would encompass roughly only the words of the spiritual," chariot, coming for to carry me home." The first phrase of the spiritual melody is shown below.[23] The asterisks identify the melodic intervals that appear in the Dvorak symphony.

The English horn melody of the Largo movement is another salient example.[24]

Several sources suggest that this melody was inspired by Dvorak's interest in Longfellow's "Song of Hiawatha" and that the Largo theme describes the burial of Minnehaha in the forest. Clapham and Evans cite the Longfellow inspiration; but both concede that the melody has an unmistakable Negro flavor about it.[25] Clapham goes on to suggest, on the basis of clearly speculative evidence, that the reason Dvorak may have chosen the English horn as solo instrument was that it resembled the quality of Burleigh's singing.[26]

This writer could find no evidence either in other sources or from his own examination of the music to support

Locke's thesis that the Scherzo movement is "nose close to jazz" in its rhythms. In fact, Edwin Evans observes:

> We may dismiss the suggestions that the Scherzo is an Indian dance associated with Hiawatha, or that its rhythmic insistence has Negro affinities for neither has much relation to its true character, which is, as fundamentally Slavonic as that of most of Dvorak's Scherzi.[27]

These are probably the most obvious examples involving the issue of Dvorak's use of black folk music materials. Despite the fact that the composer used no specifically Afro-American melodies, his own or the original, there can be no doubt that the black folk idiom, at times, permeates the symphony very subtly.

In view of these facts, it seems to me that to subscribe to Locke's suggestion of the presence in the Dvorak symphony, *From the New World,* of the spiritual "Swing Low Sweet Chariot" or his sense of an inspiring Afro-American influence in the English horn melody of the second movement, or insisting as he does on the presence of jazz rhythms in the scherzo is to belabor what are, at best, tenuous theories.

Disproving the theories of Locke and others in this instance is, however, not the central issue. Had Dvorak literally employed Negro spirituals in the symphony, the issue would be no less obscured. The real issue seems to involve an attitude about black music. In this instance, that attitude is reflected in Locke's attempts to vindicate the value of black folk music, especially the spirituals, by pointing out their use in a musical form not endemic to the spiritual's culture of origin but, rather, in a highly valued form of Western European culture, i.e., the symphony, by a renowned and respected composer.

There are two other points to be made in relation to Locke's ideas about black folk music. One senses that, for him, the Negro spirituals hold a position of superior value over the secular music. Locke describes the former as

. . . the most characteristic product of Negro genius to date.
The spirituals are its great folk-gift, and rate among the
classic folk expressions in the whole word because of their
moving simplicity, their characteristic originality, and their
universal appeal.[28]

Locke does assign the secular folk songs the status of folk
classics but he refers to them as being "second . . . to the
spirituals" (p. 28).

The second point relates to the musicians mentioned in
Locke's discussion of the Dvorak symphony. He asserts that
"most musicians" regard black folk music as the purest and
most valuable musical ore in America. Further, he
maintains that the folk quality and purity of style of black folk
music have been emphasized since the twentieth century by
"real musicians." The musicians of whom he speaks are
clearly not those engaged in the creation of folk music.

The second category of black music which Locke treats is
derived from original folk music. He calls it a diluted form,
"the petty dialect," as opposed to the great dialect of the
spirituals. It is this second type of black music that served as
the principal ingredient of American popular music
including minstrelsy, ragtime, and jazz (p. 9). For Locke,
this type of black music spanned a significant period of
history—from about 1850 to 1936, the year *The Negro and His
Music* was published.

It is in his treatment of jazz, especially, that one obtains a
clearer picture of the vindication theme in Locke's treatment
of the music of this second category. He asserts that jazz
eventually took up more or less permanent residence in two
places. "Chicago became the reservoir of the rowdy, hectic,
swaggering style of jazz that has since become known as 'hot
jazz'" (p. 84). Locke devotes relatively little attention in his
writings to the "hot jazz" of Chicago.

"New York (and Paris and London)," on the other hand,
"has furnished the mixing bowls for the cosmopolitan style of
jazz notable for stressing melody and flowing harmony
known as 'sweet jazz'" (p. 84). Locke clearly places much
greater emphasis on this style. Of the early New York school
of jazz (1905–1915), he singles out four Negro musicians for

special consideration. The four, Ford Dabney, James Reese Europe, Will Marion Cook, and W.C. Handy, are called "arrangers of genius" by Locke, because they "organized Negro music out of broken, musically illiterate dialect and made it a national and international music with its own peculiar idioms of harmony, instrumentation, and technical style of playing" (p. 66).

As Locke saw it, the chief common contribution of these men was the "vindication" of black music. These four men were the "ambassadors who carried jazz to Europe and the haughty citadels of serious music" (p. 85). Because New York jazz was polished and sophisticated in contrast to its Chicago counterpart, which was comparatively crude, Locke felt that it was more appropriate and fortunate that the New Yorkers' "smoother, more mellow jazz was the first to become world famous and to have international influence" (p. 85). Further contributions of these men included the "vindication" of black music as the preferred dance vogue on the American stage (pp. 66–67).

The activities of the early New York jazz people culminated in an event of significant historical proportions. In May 1912 a concert was held at Carnegie Hall in which a jazz orchestra of 125 black musicians under the direction of James Reese Europe presented a concert of black music. Locke's comments about this event are worth reporting:

> The formal coming-out party was at Carnegie Hall, the audience, the musical elite of New York, the atmosphere and the comparison challenged that of any concert of "Classical music," and the compositions conducted by their own composers or arrangers . . . that night the Cinderella of Negro folk music found royal favor and recognition and under the wand of Negro musicians put off her kitchen rags. At that time ragtime grew up to full musical rank and the golden age of jazz really began.
>
> (p. 68)

Locke's perspective on the role of white jazz performers is especially important here. In his view, the musical techniques of early jazz, rooted as they were in a distinctive

black style of technical performance, were capable of being
imitated, making jazz the property of a universal audience.
To quote Locke:

> . . . white performers and arrangers and conductors had
> learned the new tricks and were feverishly and successfully
> competing in carrying jazz style to a rapid perfection.
>
> (p. 82)

> . . . the white musicians studied jazz, and from a handicap
> of first feeble imitation and patient hours in Negro cabarets
> listening to the originators finally became masters of jazz,
> not only rivaling their Negro competitors musically but
> rising more and more to commerical dominance of the new
> industry.
>
> (p. 82)

Locke observes finally that although jazz is basically Negro,
"fortunately, it is also human enough to be universal in
appeal and expressiveness" (p. 72). Such an extraordinary
statement and those which precede it establish Locke's
democratic views regarding aesthetic experience; that in the
matter of black musical materials, he allowed for no
distinctions in perception based on race.

The third of Locke's three categories of black music is
what he calls strictly formal or classical type. This category
actually includes three types: jazz classics, classical jazz, and
modern American music. The first two types are what Locke
calls "worthwhile jazz as distinguished from the trashy
variety" (p. 96). The latter refers primarily to the commercial
efforts of Tin Pan Alley. A jazz classic is a work which,
"rising from the level of ordinary popular music, usually in
the limited dance and song-ballad forms, achieves creative
musical excellence" (p. 96). The jazz classics were products of
the jazz orchestras that were emerging in the late 1920s.
Locke admits as principal figures in the creation of these
classics such big-time black figures as Fletcher Henderson,
Earl Hines, Luis Russell, Claude Hopkins, "Fats" Waller, Cab
Calloway, Louis Armstrong, Don Redman, Jimmie
Lunceford, and, of course, Duke Ellington. White bands

singled out for recognition include those of Jean Goldkette, Paul Whiteman, Ben Pollack, Red Nichols, Ted Lewis, The Casa Loma Orchestra, Jimmy Dorsey, and Benny Goodman (p. 98).

Locke saw one of the major efforts, indeed responsibilities, of these musicians as the exploitation of black folk materials. In the hands of these skilled musicians, jazz was to be "harnessed and seriously guided . . . to new conquests" (p. 97). It was the black musicians, especially, who had the greater responsibility. Jazz, says Locke, is the spirit child of the black musician, and its artistic vindication rests in its sound development by these musicians (p. 101).

It was Duke Ellington whom Locke viewed with greatest critical admiration. Of Ellington, Locke says:

> . . . in addition to being one of the great exponents of pure jazz, Duke Ellington is the pioneer of super-jazz and one of the persons most likely to create the classical jazz toward which so many are striving. He plans a symphonic suite and an African opera, both of which will prove a test of his ability to carry native jazz through to this higher level.
>
> (p. 99)

Locke saw the work of Ellington as especially important to the placing of intuitive music under control, as restraining and refining crude materials. In Locke's words, "Someone had to devise a technique for harnessing this shooting geyser, taming this wild well" (p. 100).

In making his distinction between jazz classics and the "trashy variety" of popular music, Locke had decisively steered black music out of the progressive stages of a maturing folk music onto the early plane of what he would call "art" music, the universal and timeless quintessence of the composer's creative efforts.

Classical jazz, the second type of Locke's third category, is music "which successfully transposes the elements of folk music, in this case jazz idioms, to the more sophisticated and traditional musical forms" (p. 96). Classical jazz and modern American music are related types, if not the same thing. They represent yet a further development upward of black music. The most obvious medium for the development of classical jazz was what Locke refers to as symphonic jazz—a form derived from but ultimately divorced from dance jazz and popular song ballads (p. 112).

It is not altogether easy to understand clearly just what symphonic or classical jazz is. By his own admission, Locke calls it "a somewhat unstable and anaemic hybrid" (p. 112). It does seem to be inclusive of all sorts of symphonic music. The works Locke discusses include Gershwin's "Rhapsody in Blue," "Porgy and Bess," William Grant Still's "Afro-American Symphony," Edmund Jenkins's "Charlestonia: A Negro Rhapsody for Full Orchestra," and William Dawson's "Negro Folk Symphony" (pp. 110–112). Locke saw the work of these composers as pioneering efforts in elevating jazz to the level of the classics.

There is a curious comment which Locke makes regarding such cultural elevation in the work of the black composer, Florence E. Price. Concerning her symphony in E minor and her piano concerto, Locke says:

> In the straight classical idiom and form, Mrs. Price's work vindicates the Negro composer's right, at choice, to go up Parnassus by the broad high road of classicism rather than the narrower, more hazardous, but often more rewarding path of racialism. At the pinnacle, the paths converge, and the attainment becomes, in the last analysis, neither racial nor national, but universal music.
>
> (p. 115)

Locke does not offer many clues about what he means but he concludes his discussion of black music with some observations about the ultimate achievement of black music.

He suggests first that "Negro idioms will never become great music nor representative national music over the least common denominators of popular jazz or popular ballads that are in common circulation today" (p. 130). Locke goes on to say that "neither America nor the Negro can rest content as long as it can be said: 'Jazz is America's outstanding contribution, so far, to world music'" (p. 130).

He speculates that classical jazz may indeed itself be no more than a transitional stage of American musical development. "Eventually," says Locke, "the art music and the folk-music must be fused in a vital but superior product" (p. 130). Locke was not specific about what this superior product would be because he himself did not know. He did point to appropriate prototypes elsewhere in the world that have successfully blended the folk with the formal.

Locke cites Russian, Hungarian, and Bohemian composers who were confronted with this problem and who

> . . . widened the localisms of their native music to a universal speech; they were careful, in breaking the dialect, to reflect the characteristic folk spirit and preserve its unique flavor. What Glinka and his successors did for Russian music, Liszt and Brahms for Hungarian music, and Dvorak and Smetana for Czech music, can and must be done for Negro music.[29]

Because of his desire for cultural reciprocity, it is clear that Locke sought to fashion an aesthetic alliance between European culture and black American culture. Central to this alliance was the vindication of black musical materials. Essential to vindication was the use of these materials as inspiration in European musical monuments such as the symphony, opera, and ballet.

It is difficult to understand fully what Locke's real motivation was in urging these efforts at vindication. On the one hand, his language suggests a psychological undercurrent of cultural inferiority about black music. His statement, "fortunately, [jazz] is also human enough to be universal in appeal and expressiveness," raises serious questions about how Locke really felt about the value of jazz. His observations about the use of black materials in the Dvorak E minor symphony reveal a pitiable straining for respectability. Locke's reliance on white arbiters of taste are revealing when he cites the following critics of "jazz of the better sort" as names "certainly authoritative enough": Kreisler, Rachmaninoff, Koussevitsky, and Stokowski. Other white critics of jazz whom Locke cites as among the most

authoritative include Henri Prunières and Robert Goffin of
Paris, Constant Lambert of England, and Hughes Panassie,
author of *Le Jazz Hot* (1934).

Locke's aesthetic perspective invites comparison with the
efforts of the late nineteenth-century nationalist composers
but it was in fact quite different. It was affected to some extent
by a vindication syndrome. In fact, the disturbing thread of
cultural inadequacy implied in Locke's language about black
folk music suggests the strong influence on him of Western
monism, which, despite its uncompromisingly racist posture,
simply may have been too irresistible in the end.

An alternative interpretation, however, treats the issue of
vindication from another perspective. Perhaps Locke was
absolutely convinced of the value and greatness of black music
and was equally convinced of the efficacy of its integration, on
an equal basis, within the white cultural mainstream.
However, music of the Negro, as well as black culture
generally, was viewed by the white and much of middle-class
black American culture as inferior. Considering the strong
anti-black sentiment that prevailed within the American
mainstream about black folk music materials, the use of these
materials or even the suggestion of their use, for example, by
so eminent a composer as Dvorak, must have seemed to Locke
a significant step forward toward the goal of greater
recognition and use by "serious" composers, black and white.
It may have been that vindication was essential—not in the
sense that black folk music needed such exploitation to prove
its worth but rather to suggest that such use was the only way
the worth of this music would ever be recognized. In other
words, Locke's perspective may have been politically
motivated. He understood only too well the powerful
hegemony of Western European tradition over American
culture. He also understood the racist posture of American
culture, and that as a black American and philosopher, he
could not expose himself to the indignities of the
dehumanization, the pain, and suffering wrought by
Western monistic thought. In the words of Kallen,

> As a human being with an individuality of his own, [Locke]
> knew that no commitment or obligation could be laid on
> him heavier than anybody else's, and that the necessities of
> vindicating his integrity and realizing his own potentialities
> in his own way had the first claim and the last.[30]

In the end, then, it would seem that Alain Locke was a
victim of conflicting forces. On the one hand, there were
powerful influences of his education: twice a Harvard
graduate (magna cum laude and Phi Beta Kappa honors,
1907; Ph.D., philosophy, 1918), where, in his own words, he

> . . . was exposed to the Golden Age of liberalism and,
> deeply influenced by Barrett Wendell, Copland, Briggs, and
> Baker, shed the Tory restraints for urbanity and humanism,
> and under the spell of Royce, James, Palmer, and
> Santayana, gave up Puritan provincialism for critical-
> mindedness and cosmopolitanism.[31]

He was the first black Rhodes scholar to Oxford and was a
student of philosophy at the University of Berlin, where he
studied under Brentano and Meinong, and under Bergson
in Paris. On the other hand, there loomed the exigent
harshness of the racial experience in America. This
towering intellect would have preferred to embrace a monist
or universal perspective. His educational background and
training disposed him favorably to its elegant logic and, as
Kallen points out, this preference interposed an active
reservation to the actuality of the plural, and long kept Locke
from completely committing himself to the philosophy of
cultural pluralism.

From the perspective of the 1980s, there may be a
tendency to be confused by this conflict and to criticize the
efforts of Locke as naive, myopic, elitist, and bourgeois. One
needs, however, to understand Locke's efforts in their proper
context. The Negro Renaissance was a phenomenon of
another time. In order to be understood fairly and correctly,
Locke must be viewed not from the perspective of the 1980s but
from the perspective of his own time. To that end, as Huggins
has observed, the historical analyst's task, when negotiating

the efforts of the men and women of that era, requires "a humanism, that will modulate . . . his own ego and self-consciousness enough to perceive theirs."[32]

The thinking of Alain Locke and other members of the Negro Renaissance was, in its day, startlingly new and considered even radical by many. Within this context, the theme of vindication, whatever criticism it might sustain, was supported by its own special and not uncomplicated logic, and was an appropriate response to conditions of the time. In whatever light this thinking may be viewed today, criticism of Locke's efforts needs to be tempered by the humanity of which Huggins writes.

NOTES

1. Eliseo Vivas and Murray Krieger, eds., *The Problems of Aesthetics* (New York: Rinehart and Company, 1953), pp. 5–10.

2. Horace Meyer Kallen, "Alain Locke and Cultural Pluralism," *The Journal of Philosophy*, 54 (February 1957), 119–120.

3. Ibid., p. 120.

4. Ibid., p. 122.

5. Clare Bloodgood Crane, "Alain Locke and the Negro Renaissance" (Ph.D. dissertation, University of California, San Diego, 1971), p. 28.

6. Ibid.

7. Ibid., p. 120.

8. Ibid., p. 123.

9. Alain Locke, "Pluralism and Intellectual Democracy," in *Conference on Science, Philosophy, and Religion, Second Symposium* (New York: The Conference, 1942), p. 201.

10. Crane, "Alain Locke and the Negro Renaissance," p. 28.

11. Nathan Irvin Huggins, *Harlem Renaissance* (London: Oxford University Press, 1971), p. 5.

12. Alain Locke, *The Negro and His Music* (Washington, D.C.: Associates in Negro Folk Education, 1936; rpt. New York: Arno Press and the New York Times, 1969), p. 8.

13. Ibid.

14. Ibid., p. 9.

15. Ibid.

16. Ibid., p. 106.

17. Ibid., pp. 20–21.

18. Notes on record jacket (Antonin Dvorak, Symphony No. 9, *From the New World*, Columbia 31809).

19. John Clapham, *Antonin Dvorak* (New York: St. Martin's Press, 1966), p. 87.

20. Ibid.

21. Locke, *The Negro and His Music*, p. 23.

22. Score. Antonin Dvorak, Symphony No. 5 in E minor, *New World*, op. 95 (Scarsdale, N.Y.: E.F. Kalmus Orchestra Scores).

23. Frederick J. Work, ed., *Folk Songs of the American Negro* (Nashville, Tenn.: John W. Work and Frederick J. Work, n.d.), p. 21.

24. Score. Dvorak, Symphony No. 5 in E minor.

25. Clapham, *Antonin Dvorak*, p. 88; Edwin Evans, "The Symphonies and Concertos," in *Antonin Dvorak*, ed. Viktor Fischl (Westport, Conn.: Greenwood Press, 1970), p. 87.

26. Clapham, *Antonin Dvorak*, p. 90.

27. Evans, "The Symphonies and Concertos," p. 87.

28. Locke, *The Negro and His Music*, p. 18.

29. Margaret Just Butcher, *The Negro in American Culture*, 2nd ed. (New York: Knopf, 1972), p. 91.

30. Kallen, "Alain Locke and Cultural Pluralism," p. 123.

31. Stanley J. Kunitz and Howard Haycraft, ed., *Twentieth Century Authors* (New York: H.W. Wilson Co., 1942), p. 837.

32. Huggins, *Harlem Renaissance*, p. 6.

Controversial Sounds:
Jazz Performance
as Theme and Language
in the Harlem Renaissance

KATHY J. OGREN

The Salvation Army of Cincinnati obtained a temporary injunction today to prevent the erection of a moving picture theatre adjoining the Catharine Booth Home for Girls, on the ground that music emanating from the theatre would implant "jazz emotions" in the babies at the home. The plaintiffs realize that they live in a jazz age, declared the suit, . . . "but we are loathe to believe that babies born in the maternity hospital are to be legally subjected to the implanting of jazz emotions by such enforced proximity to a theatre and jazz palace."

New York Times, 1926

Readers of the *New York Times* in the 1920s would not have been surprised by this news item, dateline, Cincinnati, Ohio. Throughout the decade, the *Times* as well as other newspapers recorded a growing controversy concerning the influence of jazz music. Reports came from cities across the nation and in Europe. Most of them documented fears about the spread of this new form of popular music. As the Cincinnati Salvation Army admitted, jazz was not only a popular craze of the 1920s, but was often the music that described the ambiance or mood of the decade. Indeed, this description remains a common one in present-day accounts of the 1920s.

The centrality of jazz in our historical memory is neither an accident nor a convention derived from the "roaring twenties" stereotype. Although the injunction requested by the Cincinnati Salvation Army sounds slightly comical today, it should not be dismissed lightly. Americans chose this powerful new music—characterized by improvised melodies, syncopated rhythms and a strong beat—to represent fundamental cultural changes they experienced in the early twentieth century. Detractors criticized both its musical characteristics and its origins in lower-class black culture. Jazz-lovers hailed it as everything from exciting entertainment to an antidote for repressive industrial society. In either case, Americans found jazz symbolic of fundamental changes they identified in postwar life. Participation in jazz performance provided an opportunity to experience, celebrate, and perhaps cope with change.[1]

One aspect of the jazz controversy that has not received sufficient attention is the debate concerning popular music— especially blues and jazz—that took place among prominent Harlem Renaissance participants. Jazz musicians were among the many migrant artists who moved to New York in the mid-1910s and 1920s in search of improved job opportunities and national exposure via radio and recording contracts. Some musicians were counted among the creative artists of the Harlem Renaissance, but most of them were not jazz musicians. The musicians themselves do not seem to have paid much attention to the manifestos of artistic pride that characterized this outpouring of Afro-American arts and letters. Participants in the Harlem Renaissance, however, certainly heard—and debated—jazz.[2]

Many Harlem Renaissance scholars point out that leaders of this cultural movement devalued blues and jazz, preferring the spirituals as a source of artistic inspiration. Some leaders also ignored jazz because of its identification with vice and crime or its association with the cult of primitivism.[3] Nathan Huggins neatly summarizes this position:

> Harlem intellectuals promoted Negro Art, but one thing is very curious, except for Langston Hughes, none of them took jazz—the new music—seriously. Of course, they all mentioned it as background, as descriptive of Harlem life. All said it was important in the definition of the New Negro. But none thought enough about it to try and figure out what was happening. . . . The promoters of the Harlem Renaissance were so fixed on a vision of *high* culture that they did not look very hard or well at jazz.[4]

Huggins attributes this neglect of jazz to the Harlem Renaissance leaders' belief that blacks would prove their artistic ability by measuring up to white cultural standards and impressing white patrons. Presumably, these leaders assumed jazz could serve neither need.

More recent studies of Harlem in the 1920s also emphasize the opposition of the intelligentsia to jazz. David Levering Lewis concludes that the "talented tenth"'s encouragement of the arts was a political strategy of "civil rights by copyright." Their endorsement of assimilationist values led them to reject most jazz and blues as disreputable music. Fletcher Henderson's Rainbow Orchestra gained their approval, according to Lewis, because "the funkiness and raucousness of jazz dissipated" under his direction, and he gained support from white audiences.[5]

Although these historians have effectively explained the biases against jazz shown by some Harlem Renaissance leaders, other participants in the Harlem Renaissance found jazz a provocative challenge to their analysis of Afro-American culture and a positive stimulus to their imagination. Harlem Renaissance critics studied the striking musical features of jazz, in particular its innovative rhythms and improvisation. They noted that jazz was created in live performance, and that performer-audience interactions, particularly in the black community, helped perpetuate the participatory and spontaneous qualities of jazz.

In their estimation, the music provided a valuable record of the Afro-American experience.

In addition to exploring the communicative and historical meaning of jazz, Harlem Renaissance writers pointed to jazz and blues as evidence of the Afro-American creative potential crucial to the developing renaissance. For example, even though James Weldon Johnson, Joel A. Rogers, and Alain Locke all dreamed of "more dignified" symphonic expressions of jazz, each applauded the popularity of jazz and tried to explain its salient characteristics. Literary artists such as Claude McKay, Langston Hughes, and Zora Neale Hurston used jazz and blues not only for settings and themes in their novels and poems, but also as a language expressing their particular artistic vision and containing the potential for a more general Afro-American aesthetic.

Jazz performance became not only a subject of analysis and discussion in the Harlem Renaissance; it informed debates about the Harlem Renaissance itself. This is especially clear from discussions over the appropriateness of jazz performance as an expression of the "primitive" folk, or working-class roots for black art and literature. All of these writers depicted or analyzed the participatory nature of jazz performance and its communicative strength, thereby testifying to the significant role of jazz performance in the Harlem Renaissance.

Harlem Renaissance writers analyzed the folk origins of black music in order to remind readers that it was indigenous to America and that it captured the particular experiences of Afro-Americans. James Weldon Johnson, Joel A. Rogers, and Alain Locke all commented on the folk origins of spirituals, work songs, ragtime, and blues. They were concerned with claiming a place for these musical idioms in American musical history.

James Weldon Johnson, a composer of ragtime and Broadway songs himself, used black music as a theme in much of his writing. His early novel, *The Autobiography of an Ex-Coloured Man* (1912), depicted a ragtime musician torn between composing great symphonies based on Afro-American music and passing into the white business world.

The unnamed protagonist chooses to pass, perhaps expressing Johnson's pessimism for the future of black composers. Johnson published *The Book of American Negro Spirituals* (1925) and *God's Trombones—Seven Negro Spirituals in Verse* (1927), both of which made valuable contributions to black music history and folklore. Johnson explained that the trombone had "just the tone and timbre to represent that old-time Negro preacher's voice," and at the same time, "there were the traditional jazz connotations provided by the trombone." Finally, in both *The Autobiography* and *Black Manhattan* (1930), Johnson provided cultural historians with a rich description of jazz cabarets and nightclubs.[6]

In his well-known introduction to *The Book of American Negro Poetry* (1922), Johnson asserted that the Uncle Remus stories, spirituals, the cakewalk, and ragtime "were the only things artistic that have yet sprung from American soil and been universally acknowledged as distinctive American products." Johnson's description of ragtime emphasized the ability of the music to provoke audience response and engage listeners:

> Any one who doubts that there is a peculiar hell-tickling, smile-provoking, joy-awakening, response-compelling charm in Ragtime needs only to hear a skillful performer play the genuine article, needs only to listen to its bizarre harmonies, its audacious resolutions often consisting of an abrupt jump from one key to another, its intricate rhythms in which the accents fall in the most unexpected places but in which the fundamental beat is never lost, in order to be convinced. I believe it has its place as well as the music which draws from us sighs and tears.[7]

Johnson's adjectives—"awakening," "provoking," "compelling," "audacious"—show his appreciation of the communicative power of black music to evoke emotions and audience participation. These kinds of descriptions were common in the Harlem Renaissance writing on jazz. Johnson's influential introduction provided an important early recognition of the relationship between music idioms and poetic voice in Afro-American literature.

Joel A. Rogers's "Jazz at Home," which Alain Locke included in his 1925 *New Negro* anthology, offered the comprehensive statement on jazz in the early literature of the Harlem Renaissance. Rogers's perspective was typical of Harlem Renaissance critics interested in jazz. He discusses the history of jazz performance, the influence of jazz on other music and entertainment forms, and jazz as a symbol of the modern age.[8]

Rogers attributes the distinctiveness of jazz performance to qualities derived from folk music. It is, he wrote, "of Negro origin, plus the experience of the American environment." Acknowledging the role of vernacular dance in the rhythmic development of jazz, Rogers further explains:

> It is in the Indian war dance, the Highland fling, the Irish jig, the cossack dance, the Spanish fandango, the Brazilian *maxixe*, the dance of the whirling dervish, the hula hula of the South Seas, the *dance du ventre* of the Orient, the *carmagnole* of the French Revolution, the strains of Gypsy music, and ragtime of the Negro.[9]

By locating the origins of jazz in worldwide folk music and dance, Rogers asserts a long and dignified heritage for jazz. Furthermore, identifying jazz with dance underscores its function as an expressive entertainment form.

Rogers's historical sketch of jazz also highlights the participatory qualities of jazz performance. Ragtime band performers, for Rogers, made their own instruments and used their bodies if necessary for "patting juba" rhythms. When itinerant stride and boogie-woogie pianists played the first jazz, according to Rogers, the audience became part of the show. Rogers recounts an apocryphal story that credits the audience with inventing the word jazz:

> Then came Jasbo Brown, a reckless musician of a Negro cabaret in Chicago, who played this and other blues, blowing his own extravagant moods and risqué interpretations into them, while hilarious with gin. To give further meanings to his veiled allusions, he would make the trombone "talk" by putting a derby hat and later a tin can at

its mouth. The delighted patrons would shout, "more Jasbo. More, Jas, more." And so the name originated.[10]

Rogers points out that when performers interacted with their communities in various call-and-response formats, they helped perpetuate a performance style typical of Afro-American sacred music, as well as blues and jazz.[11]

Rogers indicates further that the excitement and energy of jazz music and dance had inspired Broadway artists and that it continued to influence modernist European composers. "With the same nonchalance and impudence with which it left the levee and the dive to stride like an upstart conqueror, almost overnight into the grand salon," Rogers proclaims, "jazz now begins its conquest of musical Parnassus."[12] For Rogers, these new uses of jazz illustrate that black music was finally earning the respect it deserved.

Alain Locke's own essay on music in *The New Negro* calls for a serious study of the spirituals, which he believed were "the most characteristic product of the race genius as yet in America." But his appreciation of jazz grew during the 1920s and in his 1934 essay, "Toward a Critique of Negro Music," he expresses his admiration for a range of jazz artists including Duke Ellington, Noble Sissle, Cab Calloway, and Fletcher Henderson. In this latter essay, Locke tempers his earlier and fairly elitist disregard of jazz with a deepening critique of its origins and development through Afro-American musical traditions. His study culminated in *The Negro and His Music*, published in 1936. Locke's changing ideas on the subject of music underscore the value in seeing the Harlem Renaissance as an ongoing process of creation and evaluation rather than an event fixed in time.[13]

In all of his musical criticism, Locke argues for a painstaking analysis of how formal elements of black music are transformed in performance. His treatment of jazz was designed to show how ragtime and jazz embody "Negro rhythm and harmony" that had been lost through the dilutions of Stephen Foster, minstrelsy, and other popularizations of Afro-American music. For example, Locke used Abbe Niles's and W.H. Handy's *Blues: An Anthology* in his own history of jazz in order to emphasize the folk elements in the music. He notes that Handy attributed his inspiration for blues composition to the itinerant minstrels Handy witnessed at train crossings and to the lively responses from audiences who heard Handy play "hot."[14]

Locke also locates jazz rhythm and improvisation in folk music practice. The "tango rhythm," he wrote, was "characteristically Negro and its popularity among Negroes becomes very plausible when it is realized that it is originally an African Rhythm," and "basic in the purest and oldest strains of the Afro-Cuban music, in the folk music of Mexico and Brazil . . . and in Negro dances of even the Bahamas and Barbados." Improvisation, Locke writes:

> . . . came rocketing out of the blues. It grew out of the improvised musical "filling in" of the gap between the short measure of the blues and the longer eight bar line, the break interval in the original folk form of three line blues. Such filling in and compounding of the basic rhythm are characteristic of Negro music everywhere, from deepest Africa to the streets of Charleston, from the unaccompanied hand-clapping of the street corner "hoe-down" to the interpolation of shouts, amens, and exclamations in Negro church revivals.[15]

Locke aims to prove that jazz has a unique structure, history, and musical tone that originated in and continues to express the participatory traditions of black folk music—not only in America—but in Africa and much of the rest of the new world.

In addition to explaining the history and development of jazz, Johnson, Rogers, and Locke also refuted the charges of critics in the 1920s who complained that jazz was a "bunch of noise" lacking musical structure and requiring no skill or training to perform. All three of them were slightly more sympathetic to suggestions that jazz had a hypnotic effect on its listeners or that it symbolized the modern age.

For all of his alleged disdain for jazz, Locke disputes those who claimed the music was a "mere set of musical tricks by which any tune whatsoever can be 'ragged' or 'jazzed.'" Jazz had distinctive musical characteristics like other music genres, Locke insists, and could trace its lineage back to secular and sacred black folk music. He points out that it took talent and practice to play jazz and that black musicians in particular had mastered it. Accomplished jazz musicians needed to improvise, work with fellow bandsmen, and be skilled at head tunes and complex rhythms. According to Locke, jazz is characterized by a "freestyle" that "has generations of experience back of it; it is derived from the voice tricks and vocal habits characteristic of Negro choral singing."[16] The distinctiveness of jazz, then, derives from communal and participatory performance practice and continues to be expressed through improvisation.

Locke compares jazz to an "epidemic" that spread quickly and transformed tempo, technique, and themes in popular music. Johnson suggests a similar influence for ragtime when he describes it as music that "jes grew." Similarly, Rogers attributes a narcotic quality to jazz and believed that it offered psychological relief after World War I that was "safer than drugs or alcohol." Acknowledging potentially immoral influences of jazz, Rogers insists that its impact depends on the stability of its listeners: "Jazz, it is needless to say, will remain a creation for the industrious and a dissipator of energy for the frivolous, a tonic for the strong and a poison for the weak.[17]

Locke expressed fears that the growing commercial success of jazz undermines its folk heritage. The "common enemy" of all jazz musicianship is the "ever present danger of commercialization" as well as the "public taste," which he deemed a "notoriously poor judge of quality." Locke hoped jazz "experts" would exert more influence on public taste and encourage listeners to appreciate and thereby protect its folk roots.[18] Likewise, Locke measured the purported immorality of jazz against its origins in folk culture. He concurred with those who found an "erotic side of jazz." But, he explained:

> . . . there is a vast difference between its first healthy and earthy expression in the original peasant paganism out of which it arose and its hectic, artificial and sometimes morally vicious counterpart which was the outcome of the

vogue of artificial and commercialized jazz entertainment.
The one is primitively erotic; the other, decadently
neurotic.[19]

Locke carefully defines primitivism by its relation to folk
traditions, and in that context, he considers jazz a positive
influence on twentieth-century society. Noting that jazz had
been accused of being both "an emotional escape," and an
"emotional rejuvinator" for those trying to cope with post-
World War I America, Locke insists that jazz did not cause
immorality. Its popularity was a symptom of larger social
changes, he concludes. Much like Rogers, he sees jazz as a
"spiritual child of the twenties."[20]

James Weldon Johnson, Joel A. Rogers, and Alain Locke
see black music serving a dual role in the Harlem
Renaissance. Despite their proselytizing for jazz symphonies,
they nonetheless consider jazz and blues repositories of Afro-
American history and creativity and fascinating musical
idioms in and of themselves. The various perspectives offered
by Johnson, Rogers, and Locke acknowledge the power of
musical performance to express emotions through spontaneity
and audience participation, and each author documents the
unique strengths of ragtime, blues, and jazz that depended on
participatory musical traditions.

Both Rogers and Locke rebutted aesthetic and moral
accusations against jazz by condemning those with a prurient
or commercial interest in jazz. Because they located the
controversial qualities of jazz in the white-dominated
commercial music industry—not in black performance
traditions—these authors shifted the terms of the jazz
controversy. Furthermore, their criticism of the
commercialization of Afro-American folk culture encouraged
a serious analysis of the role of black music in American
popular entertainment. These concerns were not typical of
white jazz critics.

The poets and novelists of the Harlem Renaissance also
discovered a unique creative well in jazz performance.
Nathan Huggins suggests that the literary use of jazz as
background was casual—almost a convention required by the

cult of primitivism. But for some young artists, jazz and blues inspired new themes and language forms. Three young writers in particular—Claude McKay, Langston Hughes, Zora Neale Hurston—interpreted jazz and blues performance in provocative new ways. Black music also informed their attempts to formulate a new asthetic.

Claude McKay is perhaps the best-known Harlem Renaissance fiction writer to use primitivism self-consciously in his fiction. McKay's portrayal of exotic themes and atmospheres in *Home to Harlem* (1928), for example, drew on jazz performance. The music and the locations for its performance became a fundamental part of McKay's attempt to create a primitive urban world.[21]

In *Home to Harlem*, the protagonist, Jake, returns to Harlem following his desertion from World War I military service. He is entranced by "The noise of Harlem, the sugared laughter. The honey-talk on its streets, and all night long, ragtime and "blues" playing somewhere, . . . singing somewhere, dancing somewhere! Oh! the contagious fever of Harlem."[22] McKay uses this tone throughout the novel and evokes images of epidemic diseases much as Johnson, Locke, and Rogers had. The communicability of jazz pervades McKay's Harlem.

Much of the novel is set in the cabarets and nightclubs of Harlem. McKay's descriptions of performance locations stressed the exotic and the sensational. Nevertheless, they are fairly consistent with actual cabarets in the 1920s. McKay explains that some cabarets, like Barron's, relied "on its downtown white trade." Others, such as Leroy's, served as "the big common rendezvous shop for everybody." The "Congo" was typical of blacks-only clubs: "It was African in spirit and color. No white persons were admitted there." McKay bases his fictional Harlem nightlife on the actual clubs that existed in the 1920s, and he uses their differences to illustrate class and racial divisions.[23]

McKay also makes effective use of the decor of clubs to evoke images of hot-house or jungle-like worlds in which dancing, drinking, fighting, and flirtation were common. The environment relaxed the restraints of everyday life, and performers and patrons responded by expressing the emotions they normally held in check.

In a typical scene from *Home to Harlem,* for example, McKay offers his vision of how musical entertainment provided a welcome release for the "common workaday Negroes of the Belt":

> The orchestra was tuning up. . . . The first notes fell out like a general clapping for merrymaking and chased the dancers running, sliding, shuffling, trotting to the floor. Little girls energetically chewing Spearmint and showing all their teeth dashed out on the floor and started shivering amourously, itching for their partners to come. Some lads were quickly on their feet, grinning gayly and improvising new steps with snapping of fingers while their girls were sucking up the last of their creme de menthe. The floor was large and smooth enough for anything.[24]

The fictional nightclub scene, like others in McKay's novel, represents the nightclub as a place where patrons enjoy themselves and where the music and its setting are conducive to participation.

For McKay, working-class and peasant cultures contained a source of beauty that was relatively untouched by the civilized world. He believed that the Harlem he created in *Home to Harlem* was "similar to what I have done for Jamaica in verse." McKay used blues and jazz music in the American setting to establish an open, emotional, and participatory ambiance—what he considered "primitive." Despite a favorable reception by some reviewers, however, others claimed that *Home to Harlem* had strayed too far from a healthy grounding in folk cultures. He was accused of pandering to the exploitative tastes of white slummers by glorifying the Harlem underworld.[25]

McKay's portrayal of musical entertainment and its meaning for lower-class blacks challenges the assertion of Locke and others that "primitive" virtues belonged only to rural folk culture and that commercialization distorted "primitive" beauty. Likewise, McKay's suggestion that the power of music came from participatory performances located in dives and cabaret offended the more conservative Harlem Renaissance leaders. McKay later expressed his disappointment that "many of the talented Negroes regarded their renaissance more as an uplift organization and a vehicle to accelerate the pace and progress of smart Negro society."[26] McKay's controversial treatment of blues and jazz performance and the world of black entertainment drew criticism from W.E.B. DuBois, in particular, who could not accept the moral tone of *Home to Harlem*. McKay depicted an extreme potential of performance that challenged the norms of Renaissance leaders and set him apart from more genteel aesthetic values. As the reaction to McKay's work showed, however, black participants in the Harlem Renaissance debated the meaning and function of jazz. Theirs was not a simple argument between pro- and anti-jazz factions.

The richness of the discussion over jazz performance becomes clearer when we look at the writings of Langston Hughes and Zora Neale Hurston. Like Claude McKay, Langston Hughes found inspiration in the experiences of common people he saw in Harlem—many of them recent migrants from the South. Hughes did not try to develop a "primitive" vision. Beginning in the 1920s and continuing throughout his career, Hughes based his lyrical craft on the rich oral traditions of Afro-American folk tales and humor, blues and jazz, and sacred music. Musical performance and performers are prominent themes in Hughes's 1920s collection of poems, *The Weary Blues* (1926) and *Fine Clothes to the Jew* (1927).

Hughes used music, musicians, and dancers as the subjects of many early poems. *The Weary Blues*, for example, featured several poems that paid tribute to dancers, including: "Danse Africaine," "The Cat and the Saxophone," "Negro Dancers," and "Song for a Banjo Dance." The poems evoke various kinds of Afro-American dance, and one commentator has pointed out that "the poems are arranged in thematic pairs, each pair a contrast in mood, style, or point of view." All of them, nevertheless, capture the energy and grace of movement, and the relationship of dance to music. The poems reflect Hughes's appreciation of the richness of Afro-American dance as a performance medium.[27]

Performance environments are also important in Hughes's poems from the first volumes. "Jazzonia" and "Jazz Band in a Paris Cafe" capture the alluring world of the cabaret. In "Jazzonia," Hughes equates the effect of the performance atmosphere with that of the Garden of Eden and of ancient Africa:

> Oh! silver tree!
> Oh, shining rivers of the soul!
>
> In a Harlem cabaret
> Six long-headed jazzers play.
> A dancing girl whose eyes are bold
> Lifts high a dress of silken gold.
>
> Oh! shining tree!
> Oh, shining river of the soul!
>
> Were Eve's eyes
> In the first garden
> Just a bit too bold?
> Was Cleopatra gorgeous
> In a gown of gold?
>
> Oh, shining tree!
> Oh, shining rivers of the soul!
>
> In a whirling cabaret
> Six long-headed jazzers play.[28]

The performance in Hughes's cabarets are seductive, and the lyrical form echoes musical compositions with stanzas and refrains. Hughes uses the images and question marks in "Jazzonia" to suggest the power of music, rather than explaining it directly.

The most innovative aspect of Hughes's jazz and blues poetry is his combination of imagery from performance with music idioms. *The Weary Blues* and *Fine Clothes to the Jew* contain a wide range of blues, and many of them express the experience of migration and disappointment, as in "Bound no' Blues," "Homesick Blues," "Listen Here Blues," and "Po' Boy Blues." Hughes attributes his affection for the blues to his first exposure to them in the poor districts of Washington, D.C. In his autobiography *The Big Sea*, Hughes described the inspiration he found in the blues:

> I tried to write poems like the songs they sang on Seventh Street—gay songs, because you had to be gay or die; sad songs, because you couldn't help being sad, sometimes. But gay or sad you kept on living and you kept on going. Their songs—those of Seventh Street—had the pulse beat of the people who kept going.[29]

In *Fine Clothes to the Jew*, Hughes also explains the blues to his readers and notes: "The mood of the blues is almost despondency, but when they are sung people laugh."

Although Hughes would experiment a great deal in his later career with jazz forms, he offered an early example in "The Cat and the Saxophone":

EVERYBODY
Half-pint,—
Gin?
No, make it
LOVES MY BABY
corn. You like
liquor,
don't you honey?
BUT MY BABY
Sure. Kiss me,
DON'T LOVE NOBODY
daddy.
BUT ME.
Say!
EVERYBODY
Yes?
WANTS MY BABY
sweetie, ain't I?
DON'T WANT NOBODY
Sure.
BUT
Then let's
ME,
do it!

SWEET ME.
Charleston,
mamma!
!30

The alternation of capitals and lower case letters creates a
syncopated cadence, and Hughes incorporates jazz song lyrics,
as well as jazz dance and a sense of free improvisation. Much
of Hughes's 1920s poetry used music and performance themes.
The poems themselves are Hughes's own blues and jazz
performances.

The publication of Langston Hughes's jazz and blues
poetry did not generate the same kinds of criticism as
McKay's cabaret world of *Home to Harlem*. W.E.B. DuBois
praised Hughes in a 1924 *Crisis* article on "The Younger
Literary Movement," and Jessie Fauset and DuBose Heyward
both gave high praise to *The Weary Blues*. Locke commented
that Hughes's poetry did not have "the ragged provincialism
of a minstrel but the descriptive detachment of Vachel
Lindsay and Sandburg . . . the democratic sweep and
universality of a Whitman." Hughes's verse was often
compared with that of Vachel Lindsay and Walt Whitman.[31]

Countee Cullen also complimented his fellow poet, but
offered his reservations about the qualities of jazz poetry.
Cullen asked if poems like "The Cat and the Saxophone"
should be counted "among that selected and austere circle of
high literary expression which we called poetry." Cullen
voiced his concern that Hughes would become like those
writers who are "racial artists instead of artists pure and
simple." Cullen's questions were echoed by other critics like
George Schuyler who derided the "Negro Art Hokum" and
insisted that discussions of black cultural distinctiveness were
wrong-headed. According to Schuyler, folk art and folk
music, including blues and jazz, could have been "produced by
any group under similar circumstances."[32] These criticisms
challenged those writers who found in jazz a distinctive
Afro-American poetry and voice.

Hughes published a response to Schuyler's article in *The
Nation*. Hughes's essay asserted the position typical of young
and experimental Harlem Renaissance writers. Hughes

began by lamenting the lack of self-worth he felt was expressed by a young poet who remarked, "I want to be a poet—not a Negro poet." Hughes attributed the failure of this young man to appreciate his racial heritage to the dominance of black bourgeois cultural values. Hughes castigated the "Negro middle class" for "aping things white" and imitating "Nordic manners, Nordic faces, Nordic hair, Nordic art." Such aesthetic standards, according to Hughes, created "a very high mountain indeed for the would-be racial artist to climb in order to discover himself and his people."[33] Hughes's essay provided an impassioned defense of the distinctive qualities of black folk art. He also insisted that the common people continued to offer the best inspiration for great art because, unlike the middle class, they had not been entirely seduced by white artistic standards.

Hughes explained that he wanted to write about those blacks who "lived on Seventh Street in Washington D.C. or State Street in Chicago and they do not care whether they are like white folks or anybody else. Their joy runs, bang! into ecstasy! . . . They are not afraid of the spirituals and jazz is their child." Hughes was proud of the "racial" themes in his poetry, and he sought to grasp and hold some of the meanings and rhythm of jazz." His art was an expression of solidarity with the folks on Seventh Street. Langston Hughes concluded the essay with one of the most influential manifestos ever proclaimed by an Afro-American writer:

> Let the blare of Negro jazz bands and the bellowing voice of Bessie Smith singing Blues penetrate the closed ears of the colored near-intellectuals until they listen and perhaps understand. Let Paul Robeson singing "Water Boy," and Rudolph Fisher writing about the streets of Harlem, and Jean Toomer holding the heart of Georgia in his hands, and Aaron Douglas drawing strange black fantasies cause the smug Negro middle class to turn from their white, respectable, ordinary books and papers and catch a glimmer of their own beauty. We younger artists who create now intend to express our individual dark-skinned selves without fear or shame. If white people are pleased we are glad. If they are not, it doesn't matter. We know we

are beautiful. And ugly too. The tom-tom cries and the tom-tom laughs. If colored people are pleased we are glad. If they are not, their displeasure doesn't matter either. We build our temples for tomorrow, strong as we know how, and we stand on top of the mountain, free within ourselves.[34]

"The Negro Artist and the Racial Mountain" was punctuated with Hughes's "tom-tom" rhythms evoking music as a distinctive form of Afro-American culture. Hughes used music to celebrate the creativity of black people and to assert his own artistic independence. Jazz performance served as a fundamental measure of aesthetic development in his poetic vision.

Zora Neale Hurston's approach to folk culture provides a third distinctive vision of musical performance in Harlem Renaissance writing. Hurston became a legend of the Harlem Renaissance because her behavior shocked and amused contemporaries. Indeed, until recently many critics demeaned her talents and focused instead on her unconventional life. Hurston's biographer, Robert Hemenway, has pointed out that her flamboyant personal style and storytelling abilities derived in part from her childhood in the all-black town of Eatonville, Florida. More than any other Harlem Renaissance writer, Hurston had a firsthand knowledge and appreciation of folk tales and culture. This understanding set her apart from her literary contemporaries and formed the basis for her analysis of musical performance.

As Hemenway observes, Hurston did not try to preserve folk culture by advocating its transformation into "high culture." She did not see folk culture as a static object; instead, she recognized "no distinctions between the lore inherited by successive generations of folk and the imagination with which each generation adapted the tradition and made the lore its own."[35] Hurston refined her own understanding and knowledge of folk traditions by training in anthropology with Franz Boas. She drew on her own experiences in Eatonville for some of her earlier fiction, and as a practicing anthropologist, she contributed interesting observations on

black folk music to Nancy Cunard's 1934 *Negro Anthology*.
Hurston delineates "Characteristics of Negro Expression" that
were based on the ways blacks "modified language, mode of
food preparation, practice of medicine, and most certainly
religion." Hurston also describes the complicated
dissemination of jazz.

> Everyone is familiar with the Negro's modification of the
> white's musical instruments, so that his interpretation has
> been adopted by the white man himself and then re-
> interpreted. In so many words, Paul Whiteman is giving an
> imitation of a Negro orchestra making use of white-
> invented instruments in a Negro way. Thus has arisen a
> new art in the civilized world, and thus has our so-called
> civilization come.[36]

Hurston does not speculate on what *could* become of folk
traditions; rather, she records their transformation and
acknowledges the dynamic between popular and folk music
forms.

Zora Neale Hurston also provides her explanation for the
entertainment milieu in the South from whence jazz
developed: the jook. Her analysis of the jook is at once a
description of music, black women's social roles as
entertainers, and an analysis of black aesthetics. "Jook," she
wrote, "is the word for Negro pleasure house. It may mean a
bawdy house. It may mean the house set aside on public
works where the men and women dance, drink and
gamble." Hurston records that the piano had replaced the
guitar as the source for music in the jooks, and "player-pianos
and victrolas" were following. The significance of the jooks,
according to Hurston, was that "musically speaking, the Jook
is the most important place in America. For in its smelly,
shoddy confines has been born the secular music known as
blues, and on blues has been founded jazz. The singing and
playing in true Negro style is called jooking!" Hurston
emphasizes the communal creation of jook music that travels
"from mouth to mouth and from Jook to Jook for years before
they reach outside ears. Hence the great variety of subject
matter in each song."[37]

Hurston credits the jook with providing themes for black Broadway shows and noted that black audiences preferred a "girl who could hoist a Jook song from her belly and lam it against the front door of the theatre." Hurston lambasts "the bleached chorus" of some black theater reviews and concluded it was "the result of a white demand and not the Negro's." Hurston describes the effects of racism in black entertainment on black women, which was rarely noted by other Harlem Renaissance writers. Hurston also voices amusement at a famous white actress's use of blues on the stage:

> Speaking of the influence of Jook, I noted that Mae West in "Sex" had much more flavor of the turpentine quarters than she did of the white bawd. I know that the piece she played on the piano is a very old Jook composition. "Honey let yo' drawers hang low" had been played and sung in every Jook in the South for at least thirty-five years. It has always puzzled me why she thought it likely to be played in a Canadian bawdy house.[38]

Hurston records the creation of folk music as she saw it performed, and she notes its influence on both white and black music. Like Locke, she was concerned about the effects of commercialism on folk culture, but she did not call for it to be elevated to "high" culture.

In fact, Hurston upbraids the "Niggerati" who would have a renaissance at the expense of authentic black art:

> To those who want to institute the Negro Theatre, let me say it is already established. It is lacking in wealth, so it is not seen in the high places. A creature with a white head and Negro feet struts the metropolitan boards. The real Negro theatre is in the Jooks and cabarets. Self-conscious individuals may turn away the eye and say, "Let us search elsewhere for our dramatic art." They certainly won't find it. Butter Beans and Susie, Bo-Jangles and Snake Hips are the only performers of the real Negro school it has ever been my pleasure to behold in New York.[39]

Hurston's aesthetic differs both from the "folk" abstractions of other Harlem Renaissance leaders and white-influenced artistic standards. Her training in anthropology enabled her to document the relationship of folk music to jazz. She also shows a unique appreciation of black women's experiences as entertainers—a sensitivity that some critics find embodied in her literary performance.[40]

The well-documented criticism of jazz on moral values or bourgeois taste was only one response to jazz. Complex questions regarding the history and aesthetics of jazz performance also developed from the music and engaged prominent Harlem Renaissance writers. These discussions of jazz in the black community illustrated differing perspectives on music. James Weldon Johnson, Joel A. Rogers, and Alain Locke provided evidence for the existence of the New Negro by documenting the impact of folk music on ragtime, blues, and jazz. They acknowledged that participatory performance was the key to its creative power and lamented its trivialization through facile primitivism or commercial exploitation.

Claude McKay, Langston Hughes, and Zora Neale Hurston used jazz themes in their writing to communicate new and experimental ideas. Hughes, in particular, transformed the language and voice of musical performance into his poetry. These younger writers found jazz performance helpful to the creation of an Afro-American aesthetic based on folk and working-class culture. Their concerns put them at odds with more artistically conservative critics like W.E.B. DuBois and George Schuyler.

The Harlem Renaissance was pervaded by jazz performance. It was to be found on Broadway, in clubs, cabarets, rent parties, and even occasionally in early movies. Most Harlem Renaissance writers attended some or all of these performances, and it is curious that they did not say more about jazz. But even those who had reservations celebrated its popularity. A sincere appreciation of the unique participatory style of jazz performance sounds can be heard throughout Harlem Renaissance discussions of jazz. Those writers promoting the merits of jazz paid particular attention to the milieus of performance and the importance of traditions and practices in appreciating music. This understanding distinguished them from most whites debating the music in the 1920s and identified the centrality of performance in any future assessments of the cultural significance of jazz.

NOTES

1. Selections from this article will appear in a different form in a book entitled *The Jazz Revolution,* forthcoming from Oxford University Press in 1989. I would like to thank Ron Walters, Helen Horowitz, and Dan Shelton for their helpful readings of an earlier draft of this paper. Paul Burgett, Bruce Kellner, and other participants in the conference "Heritage: A Reappraisal of the Harlem Renaissance" also made several useful suggestions.

   None of the studies of the jazz controversy address issues raised in the Harlem Renaissance. These studies focus on the reception of jazz in the 1920s and attribute the controversy to social as well as musical causes. Morroe Berger and Neil Leonard describe the attempts of white and black critics and musicians to defend their aesthetic and behavioral values by denigrating or censoring jazz. Jazz historians and sociologists point out that the controversy subsided when white musicians, benefitting from racial prejudices against blacks, were able to play and record a cooler and more commercialized jazz that silenced critics. Morroe Berger, "Jazz: Resistance to the Diffusion of a Cultural Pattern," *Journal of Negro History,* 32 (1947), 461–494; Neil Leonard, *Jazz and the White Americans: The Acceptance of a New Art Form* (Chicago: The University of Chicago Press, 1962); Charles Nanry and Edward Berger, *The Jazz Text* (New York: Van Nostrand, 1979), p. 21; Frederick Ramsey, ed., *Jazzmen* (New York: Harcourt Brace Jovanovich, 1959), chapter 15.

2. The participation of black musicians in the Harlem Renaissance itself—as opposed to their acknowledgment of various discussions of music—is well documented in Eileen Southern's *The Music of Black Americans* (New York: W.W. Norton, 1971), chapter 14. Southern catalogs a wide variety of composers and performers influenced by "race consciousness."

3. Afro-American opposition to blues and jazz derived from the distinction drawn between sacred and secular music by black Americans throughout the nineteenth century. As John F. Szwed points out: "The significance of the Sacred-Secular distinction lies not just in their perceived difference as music, but also in their mutual exclusiveness: it was felt that performance of one or the other implied the social character of an individual." John F. Szwed, "Afro-American Musical Adaptation," in Norman E. Whiteen and John F. Szwed, ed., *Afro-American Anthropology: Contemporary Perspectives* (New York: Free Press, 1970). On primitivism and jazz, see Nathan Huggins, *Harlem Renaissance* (New York: Oxford University Press, 1971), pp. 89–90; and Michael B. Stoff, "Claude McKay and the Cult of Primitivism," in Arna Bontemps, ed., *The Harlem Renaissance Remembered* (New York: Dodd, Mead, 1972), pp. 126–146.

4. Huggins, *Harlem Renaissance*, pp. 9–10.

5. David Levering Lewis, *When Harlem Was in Vogue* (New York: Vintage, 1982), pp. 172–175, and "Parallels and Divergences: Assimilationist Strategies of Afro-American and Jewish Elites from 1910 to the Early 1930s," *Journal of American History*, 70, 3 (December 1984), 560–561.

6. The most influential essay on spirituals was, of course, W.E.B. DuBois's "The Sorrow Songs," in *The Souls of Black Folk* (1903; rpt. New York: New American Library, 1969), pp. 264–278. James Weldon Johnson, ed., *The Book of American Negro Spirituals* (New York: Viking Press, 1925); *God's Trombones: Seven Negro Spirituals in Verse* (New York: Viking Press, 1927); and *The Autobiography of an Ex-Coloured Man* (New York: Garden City Publishing Co., 1912).

7. James Weldon Johnson, ed., *The Book of American Negro Poetry* (New York: Harcourt, Brace, and World, 1922), p. 16.

8. J.A. Rogers, "Jazz at Home," in Alain Locke, ed., *The New Negro* (1925; rpt. New York: Atheneum, 1975), pp. 216–220.

9. Rogers, "Jazz at Home," p. 218.

10. Rogers, "Jazz at Home," p. 219. There is no certain single origin for the word jazz.

11. Jazz dance historians Marshall and Jean Stearns described a process of development for these vernacular dances very similar to Rogers's explanation in their book *Jazz Dance: The Story of*

American Vernacular Dance (New York: Schirmer Books, 1964), p. 78. One of the most comprehensive treatments of black dance generally is Lynn Fauley Emery's study, *Black Dance in the United States*, 1619–1970 (Salem, N.H.: Ayer Co., 1972).

12. Rogers did not complain about commercialization on Broadway; he considered the use of jazz in Broadway shows a high form of compliment.

13. Alain Locke's changing views on art, culture, and race relations are masterfully outlined in Jeffrey Stewart, ed., *The Critical Temper of Alain Locke: A Selection of His Essays on Art and Culture* (New York: Garland Publishing, 1983). On music specifically, Stewart explains, "Locke valued the spirituals as folk music and welcomed research into their African origins in his review 'The Technical Study of the Spirituals' (1925). But Locke also saw the spirituals as part of an evolutionary process of internal development in Afro-American culture. Thus 'the spirituals, ragtime, and jazz' constituted 'one continuous sequence of Negro music'" (p. 105).

14. W.H. Handy and Abbe Niles, eds., *Blues: An Anthology* (New York: A. & C. Boni, 1926).

15. Alain Locke, *The Negro and His Music* (New York: Associates in Negro Folk Education, 1936), p. 77.

16. Locke, *The Negro and His Music*, p. 78. Locke clearly challenged the claims made by jazz detractors that the music was formless and required little skill to perform. See Berger, "Jazz: Resistance to the Diffusion of a Culture Pattern," for an extended discussion of this aspect of the jazz controversy.

17. Locke, *The New Negro*, p. 223; James Weldon Johnson, ed., *Book of American Negro Poetry*, p. 12. Contemporary author Ishmael Reed used Johnson's "jes grew" analogy as a theme in his novel *Mumbo Jumbo* (New York: Avon Books, 1971).

18. Locke, *The Negro and His Music*, p. 87.

19. Locke, *The Negro and His Music*, pp. 82–85.

20. Locke, *The Negro and His Music*, p. 19 and pp. 89–90.

21. Michael B. Stoff offers a good description of McKay's primitivism: "For McKay this meant the conscious and studied illumination of a black folk-art tradition . . . whose central themes would be the indestructible vitality of the primitive black man

and the inextricable dilemma of the educated Negro," in "Claude McKay and the Cult of Primitivism," in Arna Bontemps, ed., *Harlem Renaissance,* (New York: Dodd, Mead, 1972), p. 132.

22. Claude McKay, *Home to Harlem* (New York: Harper and Row, 1928), p. 8.

23. For descriptions of Harlem cabarets, see Jervis Anderson, *This Was Harlem: A Cultural Portrait, 1900–1950* (New York: Ferrar, Straus & Giroux, 1981), pp. 161–180, and David Levering Lewis, *When Harlem Was in Vogue,* pp. 206–211.

    For a useful general description of how nightclubs and cabarets developed as intimate entertainment institutions, see Lewis A. Ernberg, *Steppin' Out: New York Nightlife and the Transformation of American Culture, 1890–1930* (Chicago, University of Chicago Press, 1981). Erenberg's analysis, however, tends to underestimate the contributions of black performers and performance locations.

24. McKay, *Home to Harlem,* p. 155.

25. W.E.B. DuBois gave the book a scathing review in *The Crisis:* "*Home to Harlem* for the most part nauseates me, and after the dirtier parts of its filth, I feel distinctly like taking a bath. . . . It looks as though McKay has set out to cater to that prurient demand on the part of white folks for a portrayal in Negroes of that utter licentiousness which convention holds white folks back from enjoying—if enjoyment it can be labelled" (June 1928).

26. Claude McKay, *A Long Way from Home: An Autobiography* (New York: Harcourt, Brace and World, 1970), p. 321.

27. Onwuchekwa Jemi, *Langston Hughes: An Introduction to the Poetry* (New York: Columbia University Press, 1976), p. 35.

28. "Jazzonia" in Langston Hughes, *The Weary Blues* (New York: Knopf, 1926), p. 25.

29. Langston Hughes, *The Big Sea* (New York: Knopf, 1940), p. 208.

30. Langston Hughes, *Fine Clothes to the Jew* (New York: Knopf, 1927). The title, "The Cat and the Saxophone," may be a reference to the nightclub with a similar name—Cat on a Saxophone—that Hughes patronized.

31. For reviews of Hughes, see Jessie Fauset, "Our Book Shelf," *Crisis* (March 1926), 30–31; Alain Locke, "Weary Blues," *Palms,* 1, No. 1

(1926), 25–27; and Countee Cullen, "Poet on Poet," *Opportunity*, 4 (March 4, 1926), 662–663 and 692–694.

32. George Schuyler, "The Negro Art Hokum," *The Nation* (June 16, 1926), 662–663.

33. Langston Hughes, "The Negro Artist and the Racial Mountain," *The Nation* (June 23, 1926), 692.

34. Ibid., p. 693.

35. See Robert Hemenway, *Zora Neale Hurston: A Literary Biography* (Urbana: University of Illinois Press, 1977); Alice Walker, "Zora Neale Hurston: A Cautionary Tale and a Partisan View," in *In Search of Our Mothers' Gardens: Womanist Prose by Alice Walker* (New York: Harcourt Brace Jovanovich, 1983); and Mary Helen Washington, "Zora Neale Hurston: A Woman in Half a Shadow," in *I Love Myself When I am Laughing and Then Again When I am Looking Mean and Impressive: A Zora Neale Hurston Reader* (Old Westbury, N.Y.: The Feminist Press, 1979), pp. 7–23.

36. Hemenway, *Zora Neale Hurston*, pp. 80–81. Hurston wrote a great deal more on music than I have suggested here. She, like Locke, was concerned that radio and phonograph recordings would commercialize folk music. She provided a controversial description of a cabaret in "How It Feels to Be Colored and Me," in 1928, which included some of the conventional primitivist literary devices. She also hoped to bring authentic folk music performance to the theater in the play *The Great Day*. See Hemenway, pp. 178–185, for a discussion of this subject.

37. Zora Neale Hurston, "Characteristics of Negro Expression," in Nancy Cunard, ed., *Negro Anthology* (New York: Ungar Press, 1934), p. 43.

38. Ibid., pp. 44–46.

39. Ibid.

40. For a comparison of Zora Neale Hurston and the 1920s classic blues artists, see Lorraine Bethel, "'This Infinity of Conscious Pain': Zora Neale Hurston and the Black Female Literary Tradition," *All the Women Are White, All the Blacks Are Men: But Some of Us Are Brave*, ed. Gloria T. Hull, Patricia Bell Scott, and Barbara Smith. (Old Westbury, N.Y.: The Feminist Press, 1982), pp. 176–188.

Europa Jazz in the 1920s and the Musical Discovery of Harlem

BARBARA L. TISCHLER

The history of American music for the concert hall has been punctuated by periodic calls for a compositional idiom that reflects the national experience and by an equally important debate regarding the best methods and materials with which to create such a national musical style. For all the nineteenth-century attempts to incorporate historical inspiration or ethnic musical motives into romantic symphonism, composers here found little in the way of an indigenous folk culture that could serve as the basis for a uniquely American music. We are unsure without program notes, for example, of what is "American" about Edward MacDowell's "Indian" Suite, and audiences outside the circles of American music enthusiasts have tended to ignore pieces with titles like "Yankee Doodliad" or "Tyler's Grand Veto Quick Step."

The turn of the twentieth century witnessed a brief period of enthusiasm for the folk music of Indians, white settlers, and Afro-Americans on the part of a small but vocal group of American composers. Henry F. Gilbert, Arthur Farwell, and their colleagues hoped to create an American concert music by quoting the spirituals, ballads, and tribal melodies of these groups in music that otherwise sounded as if it had been composed in Berlin or Vienna. While audiences often enjoyed this music, critics like Daniel Gregory Mason called its creators "polyglot parrots," and orchestras in the decades since its creation have offered few performances of works in this hybrid ethnic/romantic style. It took a new musical direction to bring composers to an awareness of the potential of Afro-American music and to put ragtime and jazz into the concert hall in a serious way in the 1920s.

The twentieth-century development of the modern musical aesthetic legitimized the use of folk and popular music, including the urban genres known as ragtime and jazz, which could be played in dissonant counterpoint, harmonized in new ways, even played upside down or backwards, and not simply quoted and clothed in the orchestral garb of the romantic symphony orchestra. Musical modernism also paved the way for the emergence of the American concert music composer as something other than the stepchild of his European teachers. The temporary but intense fascination with the popular music of Harlem prior to and during the 1920s, first exhibited by European modernist composers and later by Americans, was part of a broader search for the "new" and the exotic in the international language of musical modernism.[1]

Ragtime music and the cakewalk, which James Weldon Johnson had touted in 1912 as among those Afro-American cultural contributions "which demonstrate that they have originality and artistic conception, and, what is more, the power of creating that which can influence and appeal universally,"[2] attracted the attention of European composers. Claude Debussy used the rhythms of this music in the "Gollywog's Cakewalk" movement of his "Children's Corner" Suite (1908). Although the composer was offering a whimsical device for holding the attention of young piano students rather than exalting an Afro-American dance form, Johnson took pride in the international application of the cakewalk, arguing that in Europe the United States is popularly known better by rag-time than anything else it has produced in a generation. In Paris they call it American music. The newspapers have already told how the practice of intricate cake-walk steps has taken up the time of European royalty and nobility. These are lower forms of art, but they give evidence of a power that will someday be applied to the higher forms.[3]

For Debussy, Afro-American music was novel, but for the modernist composers of the 1920s, it provided material for serious compositional efforts. Even when the spirit of Dadaism pervaded a piece, as it often did in the music of Erik Satie and Darius Milhaud, the use of ragtime and jazz was serious in its attempt to create something new in the process of defying the compositional conventions of the past.

In the early 1920s, when many American modernist composers couldn't sail quickly enough for Paris or Berlin, composers in those same cities, fascinated by the versions of dance music and jazz that they heard, and intrigued by popular images of "roaring twenties" America (exemplified in particular by the image of night life in New York's Harlem), began to use elements of jazz in their own revolution against musical convention. Jazz was new, and its blue notes, quarter tones, muted trumpets, cymbals played with brushes, and instrumental and vocal *glissandi* were all grist for the modernist composer's creative mill. The best examples of 1920s Europa jazz do not attempt to re-create the exact sounds of jazz but to integrate its sounds and techniques into the fabric of modern music. Jazz, then, was useful as more than a simple device to evoke modern and exotic (and black) America. It was a source of technical material that could be refracted through the prism of the modernist perspective. For a brief period, the music of Harlem was, in Johnson's words, "applied to the higher forms" in works for the concert hall.

Jazz, the music that Jean Cocteau had called "une sorte de catastrophe apprivoisée," formed the basis of such pieces as Darius Milhaud's "Shimmy for Negro Dancer, Carmel Mou," and George Auric's fox trot, "Adieu, New York" (both 1921). Jazz was useful for its novelty and capacity to shock as well as

its synthesis of the Afro-American experience with that of
the cosmopolitan urban environment, a synthesis
accomplished through the transmission of the blues from the
country to the city. Jazz for many evoked faraway Africa and
conjured up images of the Harlem night club where Milhaud
heard the sonorities that would later appear in "La Création
du Monde."

The arrival of this new music in Paris from New York in
about 1918, in part through the influence of James Reese
Europe's army band, caused quite a stir. Milhaud wrote that

> a whole literature of syncopation grew up to convince a
> hesitant public. Stravinsky wrote his 'Rag Time' for eleven
> instruments, his "Piano Rag Music," his "Mavra." [Jean]
> Wiener wrote his "Sonatine Syncopée," his "Blues," and
> almost caused a great public scandal by bringing a famous
> jazz band into the concert hall.[4]

A comparison of the opening bars of Scott Joplin's "Maple Leaf
Rag" (recorded by the composer on a 1916 piano roll) with
the beginning of Igor Stravinsky's "Piano Rag Music" (1918)
reveals the utility of ragged time in modern composition.

In 1922, Darius Milhaud came to New York, as he said,
"looking for jazz." He looked, of course, to Harlem, which,
according to him, "had not yet been discovered by the snobs
and aesthetes." He goes on to add:

> we were the only white folks there. The music I heard was
> absolutely different from anything I had ever heard before,
> and was a revelation to me. Against the beat of the drums
> the melodic lines crisscrossed in a breathless pattern of
> broken and twisted rhythms. A negress, whose grating
> voice seemed to come from the depths of the centuries,
> sang in front of the various tables. . . . This authentic music
> had its roots in the darkest corners of the negro soul, the
> vestigial traces of Africa, no doubt. Its effect on me was so
> overwhelming that I could not tear myself away.[5]

The result was a ballet, "La Création du Monde," based on
a sketch by Blaise Cendrars drawn from African mythology.
"At last in 'La Création du Monde,'" Milhaud wrote, "I had

the opportunity to use elements of jazz to which I had devoted so much study. I adopted the same orchestra used in Harlem, seventeen solo instruments, and I made wholesale use of jazz style to convey a purely classical feeling."[6]

Actually, Milhaud enlarged the typical jazz orchestra to include solo strings, a bassoon, and an oboe, instruments not usually found in Harlem. He used a few jazz mottos, or riffs, which by 1923 had become almost clichés, employing them as subjects for counterpoint. The score also includes flutter tonguing for the flute, blues passages for the oboe, saxophone, and muted brass instruments, and sections that sound improvisational, even though they are precisely notated. These sections in particular sound like the product of an avant-garde creative mind rather than the spontaneous entertainment produced at a Harlem night club. Indeed, music historian Joseph Machlis noted that "La Création du Monde" has "a sensibility that is wholly French." To Machlis's assessment might be added the assertion that the sound of the piece is thoroughly modern for its time. It transcends the nationality of both its creator and of the jazz that inspired it. But the technical possibilities of jazz soon became too commonplace for Milhaud. He wrote that, even in Harlem, which he visited for a second time in 1926,

> the charm had been broken for me. White men, snobs in search of exotic color, and sightseers curious to hear negro music had penetrated even the most secluded corners. That is why I gave up going.[7]

Hints of American popular music can also be heard in concert music composed after World War I in Germany, but the effect is somewhat different from that achieved by Parisian "Le Jazz." Jazz elements synthesized with dissonant counterpoint or even serial technique sound ironic rather than playful and have more in common with a George Grosz painting than with Pablo Picasso's lighthearted scenes for Satie's ballet "Parade."

Ernst Krenek composed in a variety of music styles, but he became famous for his use of jazz in the 1920s in the opera *Jonny spielt auf!* (Johnny strikes up, 1926). This work was performed in one hundred cities and translated into at least twenty languages. The hero of the opera is Jonny, a black band leader and virtuoso violin player. The action is accompanied by an onstage band and is punctuated by much syncopation and a few "hot" numbers. *Jonny* was successful in Europe, but it failed at its American premiere at New York's Metropolitan Opera House. In the country where real jazz flourished, *Jonny* was perceived as merely a superficial evocation of a jazz mood. The opera's failure here only underlines the fact that what Krenek had written was not jazz at all; it was modern music. Audiences and critics looking for real jazz on the stage of the Metropolitan were disappointed,[8] as Krenek had utilized jazz sounds, techniques, and images to compose modern music.

Berthold Brecht and Kurt Weill used the sounds of jazz and popular music as a vehicle for political statement and agitprop theater in *Die Dreigroschenoper* (1928). The jazz elements in the instrumentation and the use of ballads, blues, torch songs, and tangos represent an integration of popular music into Weill's modern theater music style, one that was particularly appropriate to Brecht's declamatory idiom and sharp social commentary. As Weill would demonstrate further in his successful stage works composed in this country, he had mastered the art of creating modern music at least in part from the materials of jazz.

The music of urban America was not the only inspiration for modern European composers. The poetry of the Harlem Renaissance reached Europe in 1929 with the publication of *Afrika singt: Eine Auslese neuer Afro-Amerikanischer Lyrik*, a collection of works by eighteen Afro-American poets. These poems in German translation inspired six German and Austrian composers of various stylistic propensities to compose songs and choral works that expressed racial pride (as "Totes braunes Mädel" by Countee Cullen) and affirm a connection with Africa (as "Afrikanischer Tanz"). Wilhelm Grosz, Fritz Kramer, Edmund Nick, Kurt Pahlen, Erich Zeisl, and Alexander Zemlinsky shared a previous interest in jazz, which they had incorporated into their earlier post-romantic and modern music. For example, Grosz had composed a chamber piece, "Jazzband," around 1924, and a dance work, "Baby in der Bar," op. 23, in 1928, and Zemlinsky, Schönberg's friend and counterpoint teacher, had conducted early performances of Krenek's *Jonny spielt auf!* The synthesis of American jazz, blues, ragtime, and spiritual traditions with the European art song genre and the expanded harmonies of the twentieth-century modern movement in the music drawn from the *Afrika singt* collection represented an important American, *Afro-American*, contribution to the development of modern vocal music writing in Germany and Austria.[9]

By the end of the 1920s, European interest in jazz waned as American composers began to discover the potential of this important popular music for the creation of modern concert music. Works such as Adolph Weiss's "American Life: Scherzoso Jazzoso" and several works by Aaron Copland in the late 1920s revealed a cerebral interest in jazz, one that created modern compositions of limited appeal. Of course, jazz itself never lost its broad popular following, even as it traversed its swing, be-bop, and various modern phases. Certainly after World War II, jazz was claimed by all Americans, not just those who created it. The following excerpt from a letter written by Arna Bontemps to Langston Hughes on 23 October 1958 is not without its irony:

> I was interested last night in the TV readings by Carl Sandburg on the Milton Berle Show. Poetry with Jazz. Even he has gone for it. He gave 1919 as the date of his first poem: "Jazz Fantasia." He also talked on the first N.O. [New Orleans] and Memphis jazzmen to hit Chicago, at a time when he was a young newspaperman and very alert to such arrivals.[10]

Bontemps went on to suggest that Hughes should put *his* poetry on television, perhaps even on the Omnibus series. No longer exotic, jazz had become American family entertainment.

But for the first time in the 1920s, before Americans realized the potential of their musical resource in Harlem and other major urban environments, the path of serious cultural transmission was reversed, as European composers looked to the United States for musical inspiration and literary materials. The varieties of song, ragtime, and jazz that appeared in modern European concert music and stage pieces in this decade revealed a fascination with stereotypic American images of the time and, more important, a creative interest in the technical possibilities of jazz. Not all Americans thought of their era as a jazz age or a roaring decade, but the images that took hold in Europe (and in the American popular mind in later decades, in spite of the efforts of professional historians) were those of decadence and a Harlem subculture that brought vestiges of Africa to life after dark. If Europa jazz seldom sounded like the popular music of the real Chicago, Kansas City, or New York clubs, it mattered less than the fact that the modern composer was using jazz as a sound, a set of techniques, and as an idea as part of his departure from past conventions. Interest in jazz and a search for the new helped European composers to "discover" the New World in Harlem in the 1920s.

NOTES

1. The brevity of this fascination with jazz is illustrated in Darius Milhaud's comment in 1927, "Déja l'influence du jazz est passée comme un orage bienfaisant après lequel on retrouve un ciel plus pur, un temps plus sûr." See M. Robert Rogers, "Jazz Influence on French Music," *Musical Quarterly* 20, 1 (January 1935), 66.

2. James Weldon Johnson, *The Autobiography of an Ex-Coloured Man* (New York: Knopf, 1927), p. 87.

3. Ibid., p. 87.

4. Darius Milhaud, "The Day After Tomorrow," *Modern Music* 3, 1 (November–December 1925), 22–23.

5. Darius Milhaud, *Notes Without Music* (London: Dennis Dobson Ltd., 1952), pp. 117–118.

6. Ibid., pp. 147–148.

7. Ibid., p. 192.

8. See *Modern Music* 6, 4 (May–June 1929), 30 and 7, 4 (June–July 1930), 30, for reviews of "Jonny" in New York.

9. For a more detailed discussion of specific works, see Malcolm S. Cole, "Afrika singt: Austro-German Echoes of the Harlem Renaissance," *Journal of the American Musicological Society* 30 (Spring 1977), 72–95.

10. Cited in Charles H. Nichols, ed., *Arna Bontemps and Langston Hughes Letters, 1925–1967* (New York: Dodd, Mead, 1980), p. 367.

Early Recognitions:
Duke Ellington and Langston Hughes
in New York, 1920–1930*

JOSEPH McLAREN

In the 1920s, when Edward Kennedy (Duke) Ellington and Langston Hughes launched their careers in New York City, American artistic and popular culture had begun to accept and promote Afro-American literature and music in some measure. In assessing the contributions of Ellington and Hughes, it is essential to consider the outlines of American literary and musical culture in the post–World War I era. American writers such as Hemingway and Fitzgerald, as well as musicians such as Gershwin and Whiteman, had established, or were beginning to establish, reputations by the late 1920s that were international in scope and that assured for them economic and artistic success. However,

* This paper will appear as part of a forthcoming book entitled *Form and Feeling: The Critical Reception of Edward Kennedy "Duke" Ellington and Langston Hughes, 1920–1966*, to be published by Garland Publishing, Inc.

when one takes a broad view of the American artistic scene,
one becomes aware of certain levels of taste characteristically
divided into the categories of "serious" and "popular."
Literature and music can of course be divided into these
categories, and it is sometimes fruitful to do so because the
definitions of "serious" and "popular" (or "highbrow" and
"lowbrow") can often reveal the aesthetic preferences of
certain critics who are considered spokesmen for their
particular constituencies of American artistic culture.

Ellington and Hughes certainly fall into both these
realms of taste, the "serious" and the "popular," and in the
burgeoning years of their careers, their acceptance was
heralded by critics to varying degrees. For example, Duke
Ellington's engagement at the Hollywood Club in 1923 with
his first group of sidemen, then called the Washingtonians,
was not mentioned in the American journals of "serious"
orchestral music because this band was part of an
underground musical cult growing out of and representing
the post–World War I era of the "roaring twenties" when
jazz came of age and donned the cloak of respectability for
many white Americans—especially after Paul Whiteman's
introduction of symphonic jazz to New York in 1924.[1]

During the early 1920s, Ellington had not yet made a
significant impact on popular musical culture, although he
appeared to be destined to help maintain a style of raw jazz-
playing that had its source in New Orleans ragtime and the
blues. As a relatively unknown group, the Washingtonians
were mentioned in local newspapers that announced
upcoming engagements. Ellington's reputation as a New
York bandleader was especially solidified by his long
engagement at the Cotton Club (1927–1933), the underworld-
owned showplace of Afro-American entertainment in
Harlem. Duke Ellington's name then became firmly
associated with American popular musical entertainment,
just as jazz itself began to be accepted. Although the Harlem
Renaissance, the era during which both Hughes and
Ellington began their careers, received a serious setback from
the depression of the 1930s commencing with the stock

market crash of 1929, jazz continued to flourish with commercialization and symphonic elaboration.

One significant cultural reality in a comparative study of the acceptance of Hughes and Ellington is that Hughes, as a representative and practitioner of Afro-American literary expression, was reviewed by white critics of the "serious" literary world during his early career and especially with the publication of his first volume of poetry, *The Weary Blues* (1926). Reviews of Hughes's *Weary Blues* and his next volume of published poetry, *Fine Clothes to the Jew* (1927), appeared in the *New York Times Book Review* and the *New York Herald Tribune* as well as in Afro-American journals such as *Opportunity* and *The Crisis.*[2]

Criticism of the arts during the Harlem Renaissance, by such figures as W.E.B. DuBois, W.S. Braithwaite, Benjamin Brawley, and Alain Locke, did not discuss the development of jazz as an expression of "high" Afro-American art, and it is significant that Langston Hughes was one of the few Afro-American writers who lauded jazz and in fact structured much of his poetry on the blues form, a musical style that permeated the development of jazz during the 1920s and afterward.

As for Duke Ellington, the 1920s witnessed his rapid growth as one of the leading jazz bandleaders in America, a bandleader who in many ways surpassed such contemporaries as Don Redman, Fletcher Henderson, Jimmie Lunceford, and Chick Webb. It is significant that Ellington's growth can be measured in terms of his recorded works, his radio broadcasts from the Cotton Club, his night club performances and stage shows, and his popularity abroad, which proved especially consequential as the Ellington band made its first European tour in 1933.

If the success of Hughes and Ellington is any indication of the increasing acceptance of Afro-American literature and music, we must ask to what extent this acceptance contributed to the American artistic scene and American art forms. The Afro-American writer, from Wheatley to Dunbar, had been read and appreciated as an Afro-American. The nineteenth-century black American writer had been, for the most part, an imitator of European-American forms, a spokesman of protest as in Horton and Douglass, or a practitioner of plantation themes as in Dunbar and Chesnutt. Hughes's early work was published and promoted mainly because the American reading public, primarily whites, wanted to hear about the Afro-American experience, and publishers saw this experience as commercially profitable. Hughes is part of an Afro-American literary tradition of imitative art, of protest writing and of folk orientation. The Harlem Renaissance, however, brought to the fore a number of Afro-American writers whose race-consciousness found expression in works of radical artistic form. Originality in music at this time was exemplified by Duke Ellington.

Ellington's contribution to Afro-American music in the 1920s was in many ways a modification of essential elements of New Orleans jazz—African rhythmic and tonal qualities, blues structures, antiphony and polyphony—and a transference of these modified elements to a new mode of Northern jazz as played in New York. As a form of Afro-American music, jazz dates from Reconstruction and the post–Civil War period. Many jazz critics, such as Hobsen, Blesh, Jones, and Stearns, have demonstrated that blues, work-songs, and spirituals contributed to the development of jazz. Ellington's improvisational music, however, had its early and direct inspiration in the types of ensemble-playing that developed in New Orleans in the 1880s and afterward. It must be said that improvisation, altered tones, and blues elements had not been a primary concern of Afro-American musicians who, particularly in the North, had formed bands in the nineteenth century and were competent practitioners of traditional set-form band presentations. Departing from this, Ellington, it is clear, was working with the same kind of instrumentation as was found in the early jazz groups of New Orleans.[3]

As a product of American culture, jazz prospered through and along with many new mediums of entertainment— radio, motion pictures, and, especially for Ellington, recorded performances. That Ellington led one of the first bands to take part in a Hollywood film, *Check and Double*

Check, in 1930, is significant, for it indicates that jazz was becoming part of cinematic popular culture.

Regarding Afro-American literature, the spirit of the 1920s favored artistic expression by Afro-Americans; the Harlem Renaissance was proof of the craving for such expression. A number of scholars have attributed this growing interest in Afro-American literature to the hedonistic spirit of the 1920s and a resurgence of "primitivistic" ideas.[4] Although these conditions were certainly present—with the speakeasy, bootleg gin, and organized crime as a backdrop—the growth of urbanization and the fact that many Afro-Americans had access to higher education allowed room for artistic talent and the creation of forums for its expression. In short, Harlem was the mecca of black entertainment in the 1920s and there is a connection between its cultural milieu and the emergence of literary artists such as Langston Hughes.

If the 1920s can be viewed in American culture as an era of immigration and recession, of "do-nothing" presidents such as Harding, it can also be viewed as a period that marks the artistic and political reawakening of Afro-Americans. The relationship of American culture as a whole to the Afro-American literary renaissance is that its audience—the buyers of books and patrons of black writing—was formed mostly of white American intellectuals. In search of sensation and novelty, this literary elite found enjoyment in Afro-American literature that limned, for the most part, the conditions and cultural make-up of Afro-Americans. It is true, nonetheless, that many writers of the Harlem Renaissance were supported by Afro-American journals.

The acceptance and recognition of Afro-American literature and jazz in the 1920s and the elements that link these two manifestations of artistic expression raise important questions. Indeed, it appears that the poetry of Langston Hughes and the music of Duke Ellington satisfied a certain need: the need to experience the Afro-American reality that seemed grounded in an African "reality" or "primitive" folk qualities of expression. So the increasing taste for Afro-American literature and music showed a connection not only with the new political and social awareness gained by Afro-Americans but also with the realities of destruction brought on by World War I and its aftermath of widespread financial speculation. That taste appeared integral in the 1920s to this era of re-adjustment and rebellion. The white intellectuals who read Langston Hughes's poetry and listened to Duke Ellington's musical entertainment were moved to do so by dominant cultural forces of the times. Langston Hughes especially, among the Afro-American writers, wrote a kind of urban blues that had particular appeal for this urban audience concerned with the conditions of social change. It was an audience that supported Hughes's work because in this era when "the Negro was in vogue," it was "the thing to do." The taste of these patrons was anticipated by publishers who found new themes and new subjects of literary exploration in Afro-American life.

The Harlem Renaissance writers, including Hughes, were also encouraged by black periodicals such as *The Crisis* and *Opportunity*. The rising socialist press of the 1920s, notably *The Messenger* and *The Liberator*, could also be counted on to support the burgeoning efforts of Afro-American authors. It is clear, then, that Afro-American literature of the 1920s, with its themes of race pride, prejudice, folk ancestry, the African past, and the urban predicament, as well as traditional poetic lyricism, was supported by whites, encouraged by intellectual blacks, and published for the most part by the established publishing houses of the dominant literary culture.

The devotees of jazz, or Afro-American music, were also both black and white. Many of the Harlem nightclubs such as Smalls and the Kentucky Club, which could be called platforms for the presentation of "raw" types of ensemble playing that characterized Ellington's organization, allowed black patrons, but the Cotton Club, which was certainly the key booking in the development of Ellington's reputation, did not admit blacks; it was an entertainment arena for wealthy whites and gangland leaders. The Cotton Club is, thus, appropriately symbolic of the entertainment culture of

Harlem in the 1920s that catered primarily to white audiences.

One other aspect of American popular culture in the late 1920s helped contribute to the growth of jazz and to the development of Duke Ellington and his orchestra. This phenomenon was the rise of the recording industry and the mass production of phonograph records. During the late 1920s, Ellington and various sidemen recorded widely for many labels such as Okeh under the management of Irving Mills, the promotional agent and businessman who was responsible for securing the Cotton Club engagements and who rapidly accelerated the popularity of Ellington and provided key contacts for the band in the recording industry.[5] The first years of Ellington recordings were on various labels, some of them the so-called "race records" that had a specific audience and a particular method of release and sales. And yet the Duke's connection with a popular form of disseminating musical entertainment can be viewed as a major breakthrough in the history of jazz. It provided for him an audience that could share in and begin to be influenced by the kinds of musical expression that he and others were creating in the late 1920s.

The cultural importance of recordings that, unlike published sheet music, required no particular expertise in order to hear the reproduction, was similar to the aesthetic impact of the motion picture industry, for in both cases the audience needed only to let the product provide the entertainment. It was not essential to participate in the experience, although in the case of recorded music, the participation of the audience often took the form of dance. Recordings were also a way of bringing jazz to areas of the country that might not have been exposed to live performances of jazz, for many of the emerging black bands of the 1920s could not be booked in some areas of the country, especially the South, because of the then prevalent racial practices.

Afro-American literature as represented by Hughes and jazz as represented by Ellington wore different cloaks of respectability and acceptance among most white American

patrons of popular culture—in literature and in music—
during the 1920s. Like black intellectuals, socially conscious
white intellectuals enjoyed *The Weary Blues* and *Fine
Clothes to the Jew*. In certain respects, however, Ellington's
music and Langston Hughes's poetry corresponded to a
rebellious spirit on the part of certain segments of white
America and on the part of Afro-American artists. The
rebellious college-aged youth and upper-class whites listened
to "The Mooch" and "Black and Tan Fantasy" and "East St.
Louis Toodle-O."

A consideration of the level of the American population
that appreciated the creations of Hughes and Ellington leads
to a recognition of the cultural level exemplified by Hughes's
poetry and Ellington's music. As mentioned earlier, the
writers of the Harlem Renaissance were, for the most part,
non-supportive of jazz and considered it "low art." Writers
such as Countee Cullen and W.E.B. DuBois saw themselves as
promoters of a "higher culture" of the Afro-American
experience, and the development of big band jazz was often
viewed as an attempt to use coarser elements of Afro-
American culture for the purpose of art. Clearly, there had
been an ideological split in the attitudes of Afro-American
intellectuals toward jazz and its use of loud, so-called raucous
effects, especially in its development during the 1920s. In fact,
Hughes was perhaps the only writer of the Harlem
Renaissance who integrated an essential musical component
of jazz into his early poetry and into much of his later work;
this essential element is, of course, the blues.

If Ellington's brand of jazz in the 1920s was viewed by
some as a frivolous sort of background entertainment, as an
outgrowth of vaudeville entertainment, and as a purely
popular music designed to produce sensations of pleasure,
Hughes's work was regarded in some circles as a serious
attempt to promote the Afro-American contribution to
American literature. Hughes and Ellington were at different
stages of their artistic development in the 1920s, which is
evidenced by the types of critical responses their works
evoked. Again, jazz and Afro-American literature were not
exactly at the same point in their impact on various levels of

the culture. (Certainly, symphonic jazz had become by the late 1920s a kind of general popular music of America, but it must be remembered that it was Paul Whiteman who had been a major proponent of this adaptation of jazz characteristics to the symphonic form. At the same time, white American literary figures such as Eugene O'Neill, Sherwood Anderson, and Paul Green were exploring Afro-American themes and characters in their works of fiction and drama.)[6] It appears, however, that the dissemination of Afro-American cultural ideas that related to literature and music were unequally accepted and reproduced in the 1920s, so that by the time the stock market crashed in 1929, the American reading public had begun to move away from the creations of the Harlem Renaissance writers but had not, and would not, in fact, equally reject and move away from those elements of Afro-American musical expression that were popularly known as jazz.

Since the 1920s represent the development of Hughes and Ellington in their primary stages of artistic recognition, it is significant to examine some of the critical responses and references to their output in this period. For Duke Ellington, the 1920s (especially the first half of the decade) showed that the American musical world was not yet aware of or responsive to the talents and the innovative material presented by the Washingtonians (later known as "Duke Ellington and His Famous Orchestra"). In fact, if we survey two important American periodicals of the time, *Metronome* and *Etude*, we find hardly any mention of Duke Ellington in the beginning years of his career in New York City and the East. It is revealing to begin looking at these music periodicals from the year 1924, and, although it is practically impossible to find any mention of Ellington or other Afro-American jazz masters such as Louis Armstrong, one does become aware of the aesthetic issues of the times and the relevance of Afro-American music and jazz to American musical consciousness.[7] *Etude* and *Metronome* can serve as clear barometers of the opinions of the established voices of the American musical world of the time, of both the so-called "highbrow" and "lowbrow" levels.[8] Significantly, there appears to be only one mention of Ellington in the late 1920s and this is a reference to his name in the newly added section of *Metronome* called "Where They Are," a listing of club dates for bands and orchestras of the day: "Ellington, Duke—Cotton Club, N.Y." (October 1928). However, with the decline in the debate over jazz and an increased interest in Hollywood motion pictures, one begins to see the incorporation of musical advertisements in *Metronome* that used jazz personalities as "bait."

Certain *Metronome* issues of the 1920s had used important white dance bands and orchestral musicians as spokesmen for musical instruments and accessories— Whiteman and Wiedoeft, for example—but the "night club" hot musician had not yet been "taken up" as a popular selling, promotional and testimonial device. In addition to a general interest in the future of "bands," mostly high school and popular groups, by the close of the decade came the commercial advertising of "hot bands" and musicians. Bix Beiderbecke was part of a Holton trumpet advertisement and by April 1930, a number of Ellington tunes—"The Mooch" and "Birmingham Breakdown," "East St. Louis Toddle-O," and "Black Beauty"—appeared in an Irving Mills music advertisement.[9]

Unlike the development of Ellington's early career, Langston Hughes's recognition in the 1920s was both boldly apparent and significant. The differences in recognition are linked to previously discussed reasons, which suggest that Afro-American literature had progressed at a faster rate than Afro-American music, and that Langston Hughes first began to be published in periodicals that were controlled and edited by Afro-Americans, mainly W.E.B. DuBois's *The Crisis*, admittedly an organ of the "talented tenth" thinkers of the postwar generation. In comparing the development of Ellington and Hughes, it is critical to recognize that Hughes formed part of a tradition of Afro-American authors, beginning with Phillis Wheatley, who had been supported by certain "establishment" publishing houses and who were often considered spokesmen of the Afro-American experience.

Generally speaking, Hughes was lauded by both white and black literary critics. Because Hughes employed blues forms and themes in his first published work of poetry, *The Weary Blues* (1926), he was considered both innovative and radical, a poet of the people, a rhythmic syncopator. As early as 1924, DuBois had recognized the "exquisite abandon of a new day," and Alain Locke's landmark work, *The New Negro* (1925), had praised Hughes's "fervency of color and rhythm; and biblical simplicity of speech."[10]

In short, Hughes was a new poetic voice to be reckoned with by the critics, both black and white. The criticism of Hughes in the 1920s represents a dilemma expressed by both black and white critics over the value and importance of urban folk themes and "lowdown blues" elements in his work. This is particularly apparent in the responses to Hughes's second volume of poetry, *Fine Clothes to the Jew* (1927). Richard Barksdale has described the way in which *The Crisis* set out to defame and rebuke Hughes and other writers of the Harlem Renaissance who employed the facts of urban folk life as themes and structures of their works. Regarding an essay by Allison Davis in a 1928 *Crisis* issue, Barksdale comments:

> The objective of the essay was not only to censure with "learned rebuke" young writers like Hughes and Fisher and McKay but to end forthwith the diabolical influence of Carl Van Vechten on these writers.[11]

Clearly, both black and white critics were split over the significance of blues themes and style in Hughes's works that drew on the "real situation" of urban blacks in an undisguised form. The mention of Van Vechten reminds one that a cult of primitivism, although seemingly Afro-American, was in fact promoted by certain whites who saw the urban blues life as significant and exotic.

Like the issues surrounding the acceptance of jazz in the 1920s, the issues regarding the aesthetic correctness of Hughes's approach to verse point to the development of a black aesthetic as defined by Afro-American artists and critics. Ellington's brand of hot jazz was maligned by certain music critics because of its so-called "unrefined elements," just as Hughes's jazz and blues poetry was disliked because of its "raw folk" elements. Clearly, those Afro-American critics who deplored these elements in Hughes saw the development of unrefined jazz as equally denigrating to the image of the Afro-American in relation to white American society. And yet, as some others saw it, jazz represented a new form and a new approach to rhythm and tone, and Hughes's urban blues represented an emphasis on folk culture as the basis for poetry. And thus, despite lack of recognition by some contemporaries, both Hughes and Ellington were part of a whole wave of "newness" that influenced American cultural standards in the 1920s.

By examining the underpinnings of the critical approaches to Ellington's type of jazz and Hughes's type of poetry in this period, one is forced to return to what has now become a standard dualistic approach to judging the merits and cultural relevance of American art forms. The dualistic approach is based on a recognition of "high art" and "low art," of "serious" and "popular" culture. If "high art" became associated with the best artistic expression, the definition of "high" was closely linked to the class level of the audience that supported a particular form of "high art." If "low art" was associated with "popular" artistic expression, then "low" was closely connected with distinctly folk-oriented American models, which were offshoots of or improvisations on African and European designs and models. The poetry of Hughes and the music of Ellington were evidence of a re-emergence of contemporary folk expression that used rhythms and themes derived from the life of the folk as the basis of artistic material.

Although Ellington and Hughes developed their early careers in Harlem during the 1920s, they were not necessarily part of the same coterie of creative artists. However, as Faith Berry has pointed out, the two artists did collaborate during the 1930s in the writing of the musical play *Cock o' the World*.[12] Despite differences in critical recognition and reception, both Ellington and Hughes developed their individual artistic visions along similar aesthetic and cultural paths. This is demonstrated not only in their later collaborative efforts but also in the sources and designs of their early creative achievements.

NOTES

1. Much of the factual information on Ellington and the orchestra has been collected from Barry Ulanov, *Duke Ellington* (London: Musicians Press Ltd., 1946), and from the chronology of events in Derek Jewell, *A Portrait of Duke Ellington* (New York: Norton, 1977).

2. Hughes's two volumes of poetry published in the 1920s are *The Weary Blues* (New York: Knopf, 1926); and *Fine Clothes to the Jew* (New York: Knopf, 1927).

3. Four works on the development of jazz have been used for general factual information: Wilder Hobsen, *American Jazz Music* (New York: Norton, 1939); Rudi Blesh, *Shining Trumpets* (New York: Knopf, 1946); Marshall Stearns, *The Story of Jazz* (New York: Oxford University Press, 1956); LeRoi Jones, *Blues People* (New York: Morrow, 1963).

4. See Nathan Huggins, *Harlem Renaissance* (New York: Oxford University Press, 1971), ch. 3, for a discussion of primitivism. See also Amritjit Singh, *The Novels of the Harlem Renaissance* (University Park: Pennsylvania State University Press, 1976), pp. 21–25, 55–57.

5. Ulanov, pp. 73–74.

6. See Doris E. Abramson, *Negro Playwrights in the American Theatre, 1925–1959* (New York: Columbia University Press, 1967), ch. 2.

7. Editions of *Metronome, Etude,* and other jazz periodicals were found in the Library of Performing Arts at Lincoln Center, New York Public Library.

8. See Neil Leonard, *Jazz and the White Americans* (Chicago: University of Chicago Press, 1962), ch. 2. Leonard's is a cogent treatment of the controversy regarding the acceptance of jazz.

9. *Metronome*, 46 (April 1930), 10.

10. W.E.B. DuBois, "Younger Literary Movement," *Crisis*, 27 (February), 161–163; partially reprinted in R. Baxter Miller,

Langston   Hughes   and   Gwendolyn   Brooks: A   Reference   Guide (Boston: G.K. Hall, 1978), p. 7; Alain Locke, *The New Negro* (New York: Charles Boni, 1925), pp. 4–5.

11.   Richard K. Barksdale, *Langston Hughes: The Poet and His Critics* (Chicago: American Library Associaton, 1977), p. 26.

12.   Faith Berry, *Langston Hughes: Before and Beyond Harlem* (Westport: Lawrence Hill, 1983), pp. 263, 285, 313. Although this collaborative effort is mentioned a number of times, it is not clear how this effort was accomplished or exactly when it was initiated and completed. Evidently, Hughes had arranged for Ellington to write the musical score, and the project underwent revision during the latter half of the 1930s while Hughes attempted to find a producer. A later collaborative project, the writing of *Heart of Harlem* in 1945, also shows the compatibility of their artistic visions and styles.

Jean Toomer and the
Writers of the Harlem Renaissance:
Was He There with Them?

RUDOLPH P. BYRD

Like poets, critics are, for good or ill, image-makers. The medium for both is language and it is through language, sustained by some compelling purpose, that each seeks to impose an intelligible and meaningful order not only upon the page, but upon life itself. Of course, the task of the poet is different from that of the critic. The poet, seemingly with the blessing of the muse, uses language as a means to reveal some fundamental truth. The task of the critic, on the other hand, is to interpret, to evaluate, and finally to judge. The critic does not receive his inspiration from the muse, or at least he does not claim to, but from the scholarly tradition out of which he emerges and from the poet himself.

But the poet and the critic, in spite of the functional differences I have identified and others I have not, are essentially image-makers; that is to say, they are painters of verbal portraits that influence and carry meaning. The irony, however, is that the critic, in this important matter of image-making, is the more powerful, for his pronouncements to a very large extent determine the perception of a poet by both the contemporary reading public and posterity.

A critic's peculiar emphasis upon a particular feature of a poet's work—I am thinking, for example, of William Dean Howells's insistence that Paul Laurence Dunbar's greatest talent lay in writing dialect poetry—may have terrible consequences for the poet. In Dunbar's case, this public pronouncement rapidly became a public truth, which is why so many of his contemporaries were amazed to discover that he wrote sonnets. But if an undue emphasis can produce such regrettable effects, the damage that can be done to a poet's career as a consequence of a critic's distortion, purposeful or otherwise, is incalculable. I am thinking now of Jean Toomer and his fateful collision with Alain Locke.

When Toomer met Locke in the summer of 1923, *Cane* had not only been published, but Toomer had just returned from a two-month sojourn at the George I. Gurdjieff Institute for the Harmonious Development of Man in Fontainebleau, France. For some time, Toomer had been searching for what he called an "intelligible scheme" and he was certain that he had finally found it in Gurdjieff's psychological system. Gurdjieff was an enormously important figure in Toomer's life, and for a period it seemed that his involvement in the Gurdjieff work would eclipse his interest in literature and writing altogether. Recalling the force and effect of his duties as a Gurdjieff lecturer, Toomer wrote:

> These groups and the life that grew out of them became my life. I was worlds removed from the literary set. I knew little or nothing of what was happening in it. That I had once written a book called *Cain* [sic] seemed remote. What had happened to it I neither knew nor cared. . . .
>
> Gradually, however, I began making other contacts, I began awakening with interest to the wide activities of that time. Then I discovered, among other things, that a ferment was in the Negro world also, a literary ferment, and that it was producing a new literature. I was sufficiently moved to write an article. After this I viewed the movement as a splendid thing but something that had no special meaning for me.[1]

These are strange words from a writer whose first book is widely considered, as Robert Bone tells us, "the most impressive product of the Negro Renaissance."[2] Plainly, Toomer had no feeling left for the book that, in the words of Arna Bontemps, "heralded an awakening of artistic expression by Negroes that brought to light in less than a decade a surprising array of talents."[3] Nor apparently did Toomer have much feeling for the arts movement known as the Harlem Renaissance, an arts movement that Sterling Brown has labeled the New Negro Movement, since the former term confines what was really a national event not only to a portion of Manhattan, but to a particular region. In view of his unmistakable indifference to *Cane*, and his distance from the arts movement with which he is usually identified, how do we explain the perception, shared by students and teachers of American literature, that Toomer was an integral part of Harlem's literary scene? We return now to the notion of images and image-making, for the basis of this perception is in the pages of Locke's *The New Negro*, an anthology whose purpose was to initiate the uninitiated into the circle of concerns and interests of black American artists of the 1920s.

In his essay "Negro Youth Speaks," one of four essays by Locke in his anthology of verse, fiction, and cultural criticism, we are given a strong, promising, and oracular image of the new generation of Afro-American artists. The opening paragraph reads as follows:

> The younger generation comes, bringing its gifts. They are the first fruits of the Negro Renaissance. Youth speaks, and the voice of the New Negro is heard. What stirs inarticulately in the masses is already vocal upon the lips of the talented few, and the future listens, however the present may strain its ears. Here we have Negro youth, with arresting visions and vibrant prophecies; forecasting in the mirror of art what we must see and recognize in the streets of reality tomorrow, foretelling in new notes and accents the maturing speech of full racial utterance.[4]

In language that is lyrical and evocative, Locke conjures for us an image of a new generation of writers who are not only literate and articulate, but whose lives are joined together by one transcendent purpose: "full racial utterance." In phrases that are as subtle as Aaron Douglas's manipulation of lines and forms in *Building More Stately Mansions,* Locke suggests that the writers of the younger generation have all arrived together, and that they all stand together for the same ideals. There is also, and this is even more subtle, the implication that there is a sense of unity and coherence within this group that is not only a function of age and talent, but of an intimacy born of a shared vision and collaborative acts. The image, then, is both powerful and impressive. The words that support it are more than adequate to Locke's purpose, which is to place and explain the achievement of a group of writers of diverse interests and backgrounds. Locke cannot be faulted for his impulse to identify artistic patterns, but, as we shall see, there is a certain danger in such critical enterprises, for not every writer may conform to the pattern.

After identifying members of the older generation of writers—Charles Waddell Chesnutt, W.E.B. DuBois, Angela Grimké, and James Weldon Johnson, he proudly lists some members of the younger generation along with their preferred genre(s):

> Then rich in this legacy [the legacy of the previous generation of talent], but rather richer still, I think, in their own endowment of talent, comes the youngest generation of our Afro-American culture: in music Diton, Dett, Grant Still, and Roland Hayes; in fiction, Jessie Fauset, Walter White, Claude McKay . . . ; in drama, Willis Richardson; in the field of the short story, Jean Toomer, Eric Walrond, Rudolph Fisher; and finally a vivid galaxy of young Negro poets, McKay, Jean Toomer, Langston Hughes, and Countee Cullen.[5]

Toomer's name appears twice in this paragraph, as well as in other places in the essay, but it is one that does not fit so easily, for several reasons, into Locke's pattern.

First, when this new generation of writers began producing books—for example, Cullen's first volume of verse appeared two years after *Cane* and Hughes's followed it by three—Toomer had been immersed in the Gurdjieff work for at least three years, and would be leaving New York City in 1927 to lecture and establish study groups in Chicago. Thus, at the very moment when the Renaissance had found its voice, Toomer was not only in a different cultural orbit due to his duties in the Grudjieff work, but he was out of town. Even during the period when Toomer was a resident of Manhattan, he was not uptown in Harlem with Zora Neale Hurston, Langston Hughes, and Countee Cullen, but downtown in Greenwich Village with Waldo Frank and others. Recalling the excitement and pleasure of those early years, Toomer wrote:

> In New York, I stepped into the literary world. Frank, Gorham Munson, Kenneth Burke, Hart Crane, Matthew Josephson, Malcolm Cowley, Paul Rosenfield, Van Wyck Brooks, Robert Littell—*Broom*, the *Dial*, the *New Republic* and many more. I lived on Gay Street and entered into the swing of it. It was an extraordinary summer.[6]

Thus, Frank, Brooks, and others were Toomer's comrades in literature, and not Walrond or Fisher, as Locke suggests. Plainly, Toomer had very little contact with the writers of the Renaissance and when he did, as Hughes notes in *The Big Sea*, it was briefly and not as the author of *Cane*, but as a Gurdjieff lecturer.[7]

There is also a second reason why Toomer does not fit so neatly into Locke's generational scheme, and it is in many ways an extension of the first. Toomer did not identify with the writers of the Renaissance, or with their work. As we may recall, the list of writers who comprised New York City's literary scene for Toomer did not include any of the writers of the Renaissance, and it certainly did not include any of the writers to which Locke goes to great pains to link him.

Prior to Gurdjieff, the most potent figure in Toomer's imagination was Waldo Frank, who persuaded Horace

Liveright to publish *Cane*. After Toomer's break with Frank
(he made the unforgivable mistake of falling in love with
Frank's wife), he continued to share and discuss his own
work with Munson, who was also active in the Gurdjieff
work, with Paul Rosenfield, and also with Hart Crane.
Although Toomer's poem "Song of the Son" had appeared in
The Crisis, an important organ for the Renaissance writers,
prior to and after the publication of *Cane* his work appeared
in *Broom, The Little Review, Double Dealer*, and *S4N*. These
journals were a forum for an extremely self-conscious group
of writers now remembered for their experiments in the
new American idiom. Plainly, Toomer was a member of
this literary cadre not only by virtue of friendship and
professional ties, but because of obvious textual allegiances. In
Destinations, Munson, under his rubric of the "Younger
Writers," a later mutation of Locke's "younger generation,"
correctly links Toomer with such writers as Kenneth Burke
and Hart Crane, and describes Toomer as a "living symbol of
a really serious search for values."[8] Munson's placement of
Toomer with these writers is plainly more accurate, but
Locke, as we shall see, had his own reason for identifying
Toomer as a New Negro.

To me, the third and final reason why Toomer does not
conform to Locke's deceptively coherent pattern is Toomer's
reluctance or refusal to define himself as "Negro." Toomer
called himself an American, an American who was
"neither black nor white."[9] He insisted upon calling himself
an American not out of the need, as many have suspected, to
avoid the label of Afro-American author, but out of a
knowledge of his ancestry and a desire to define himself in
his own terms. Toomer writes that in his body were many
bloods: French, Dutch, Welsh, Negro, German, Jewish, and
Indian. He was keenly aware of the strangeness and even the
danger of his racial position in a nation preoccupied with
racial purity, but he strove "for a spiritual fusion analogous to
the fact of racial intermingling. Without denying a single
element," he sought to "let them function as complements."[10]
But Locke could not accept Toomer's self-definition and
labeled him Negro. Locke, however, was not the only

member of Toomer's generation whose traditional view of race made it impossible for him to accept any other. Waldo Frank was another, for in his foreword to *Cane* he identifies Toomer as Negro; this he did in spite of Toomer's several attempts to clarify his racial background and position.

On this important matter of race and self-definition, Toomer, who could have easily passed for white but did not, was generations ahead of his own generation. However, Nellie Y. McKay, in her recent book *Jean Toomer, Artist*, writes that Toomer was "hindered from developing relationships [with the writers of the Renaissance] because of his racial ambivalence."[11] I am not convinced that Toomer was ambivalent about race. Plainly, he saw race in all its baffling complexity. If he were ambivalent, he certainly would not have identified the darker strains in his ancestry as Negro. No, Toomer was not "hindered" from developing relationships with the writers of the Renaissance because of his alleged "racial ambivalence." On the contrary, he simply knew, in terms of his own artistic development, that his teachers and peers were not McKay and Hughes, but Frank and Crane.

In "The World and the Jug," in a stinging reply to public statements made by Irving Howe concerning his own literary influences, Ralph Ellison has perhaps given us the most useful framework to examine the issues surrounding a writer's place within a particular literary canon.[12] For Ellison there are "relatives," that is to say, writers who help another writer determine his growth, and "ancestors," or writers whose work becomes the standard by which a writer judges his own. If we apply Ellison's construct to Toomer's situation, we discover that Crane and Frank (and if we look backward to the previous century to Walt Whitman) were, just to name three, Toomer's "ancestors"; Hughes and Cullen, if they meant anything to him at all, were "relatives." But in tracing the development of Hughes and Cullen and their achievements as writers, we learn that Toomer was, to them, not a "relative" but an "ancestor."

Locke's placement of Toomer with the writers of the Renaissance—his artful image-making—becomes even more questionable and suspicious when we remember that the poems and stories from *Cane* ("Georgia Dusk," "Song of the Son," "Carma," and "Fern") that appeared in *The New Negro* were published there without Toomer's permission. In one of his several autobiographies, Toomer recalls his meeting with Locke and his response to the appearance of his materials in Locke's anthology:

> Locke said he was getting together a book of Negro materials and wanted something I had written, preferably a new story or a story from *Cain* [*sic*]. I replied that I had written no new stories of that kind and did not want *Cain* [*sic*] dismembered. He pressed. I thought of the article. I offered it to him. It turned out he did not want it. My expressed attitude was—the article or nothing. I concluded that the matter was finished. . . .
>
> But when Locke's book *The New Negro,* came out . . . there was a story from *Cane,* and there in the introduction, were words about me which have caused me as much or more misunderstanding than Waldo Frank's.
>
> However, there was and is, among other things, this great difference between Frank and Locke. Frank helped me at a time when I most needed help. . . . Locke tricked and misused me.
>
> For a short time after the appearance of Locke's book I was furious—. . . . Well, I shrugged and let it drop—but not without a pretty sharp sense of the irony of the situation.[13]

The article to which Toomer refers in these passages is one that contains his meditations on the rising prominence of black writers during the 1920s. This article was never published and is probably lost, as it seems not to be part of the Toomer Archives at Fisk University. The mention of Frank is an allusion to his foreword to *Cane* where he describes Toomer as Negro. As Toomer's remembrance of this event makes plain, he was quite angry with Locke, not only because he had reprinted excerpts from *Cane* without permission, but also because Locke had, in language that was suggestive, misleading, and, as Toomer himself points out, ironic, linked him to a group of writers with whom he did not feel the slightest connection.

Locke, however, had his own reason for appropriating Toomer's materials, and for promoting the image of Toomer as an important figure in his New Negro Movement. Since the critical acclaim of *Cane* had made Toomer an important literary success, Locke was extremely anxious to place him with his younger generation of black writers. In his search for shining and brilliant examples of the New Negro, Locke linked Toomer to Hughes and others because of the prestige that Toomer would bring to his efforts to increase national interest in what was then a burgeoning arts movement. If *Cane* had been published in 1913 or 1933, that is to say, ten years before or after its original publication date, Toomer's real relationship to the writers of the Renaissance would be astoundingly clear. In view of his involvement with the Gurdjieff work, his friendships and collaborations with Frank, Crane, Munson, and others, and his racial position, which prevented him from identifying with any group or movement that emphasized race, it is in many ways a historical accident that Toomer is grouped with the writers of the Renaissance at all.

Was Toomer then, as Locke's image of him in *The New Negro* suggests, a member of the Harlem Renaissance? Was he there with Hughes, Cullen, and the rest? Plainly, the answer is no. The facts of the relationship do not support the traditional view, and we are, therefore, moved to very different conclusions. All we can actually say about Toomer's relationship to the writers of the Renaissance is this: he was a member of this literary group to the extent that these writers read, admired, studied, and emulated his work—that is all. For these writers, Toomer was, to return to Ellison's construct, an "ancestor," not a "relative" or fellow participant, and it is in this manner that we must view him. Toomer was important to the Renaissance because he demonstrated to its writers that there was another way to see and treat Afro-American materials, and in the process he created a standard by which their work would be and has been judged. Of course, we should forgive Locke his manipulations and critical shortsightedness—his careless image-making—and hope that other critics will exercise more precision, judgment, and insight in their placement of writers.

NOTES

1. Jean Toomer, *The Wayward and the Seeking,* ed. Darwin Turner (Washington, D.C.: Howard University Press, 1980), pp. 131–132.

2. Robert Bone, *The Negro Novel in America* (New Haven: Yale University Press, 1958), p. 81.

3. Arna Bontemps, "The Negro Renaissance: Jean Toomer and the Harlem Writers of the 1920s," in *Anger and Beyond,* ed. Herbert Hill (New York: Harper & Row, 1966), p. 27.

4. Alain Locke, *The New Negro* (New York: Albert and Charles Boni, 1925), p. 47.

5. Ibid., p. 49.

6. Toomer, *Wayward,* p. 126.

7. Langston Hughes, *The Big Sea* (New York: Hill & Wang, 1940), pp. 241–243.

8. Gorham Munson, *Destinations* (New York: J.H. Sears & Co., 1928), pp. 9–10.

9. Toomer, *Wayward,* p. 126.

10. Letter from Toomer to McKay, 9 August 1922. Quoted in the 1969 introduction by Arna Bontemps in Jean Toomer, *Cane* (1923; New York: Harper & Row, 1969).

11. Nellie Y. McKay, *Jean Toomer, Artist* (Chapel Hill: The University of North Carolina Press, 1984), p. 58.

12. Ralph Ellison, *Shadow and Act* (New York: Vintage Books, 1953).

13. Toomer, *Wayward,* pp. 132–133.

Claude McKay's Marxism

GETA LeSEUR

Claude McKay remains today part of the acknowledged literary triumvirate of the Harlem Renaissance. He shares this prestigious position with Langston Hughes and Jean Toomer. Each in his own way made a lasting contribution to Afro-American literature and politics because of the uniqueness each possessed. McKay, however, was perhaps the most controversial of the three, because of his involvement with Marxism early in his career. The two primary dilemmas of McKay's life were as follows: the first was to resolve for himself whether socialism indeed was the answer to the "Negro question"; the second, the role of the black artist in a society that gives judgmental statements on both. The years 1922–1923, when he visited Russia to assess the workings and values of Marxism, were crucial for McKay. It took a lifetime to resolve these dilemmas and yet they were never satisfactorily resolved for him or his public. It was only during his final years that he found peace in the spiritual world of Catholicism.

In his study *Roots of Negro Racial Consciousness*, Stephen H. Bronz regards McKay's early understanding of socialism as having been "rooted in . . . racial equality and a return to the soil."[1] Bronz claims that McKay had not really seen Marxist doctrine in relation to the reform of industrialism.

This view is difficult to comprehend since McKay's knowledge and early experience of Jamaican communal life is evident in such works as *Banana Bottom* (1933) and "Boyhood in Jamaica." The emphasis on beauty and peace in an agrarian setting should explain his initial view of Marxism as applicable to racial prejudice and agrarianism, but it does not. McKay's 1921 description of himself as a "peasant" by birth and upbringing, i.e., one possessed by "the peasant's passion for the soil," is highly reminiscent of the mood and language of his autobiography. It is also peculiar, but true, that his peasant identity explains both McKay's appreciation of English Romantic poetry and his initial devotion to Marxism. Such a limited vision of a highly complex social and economic theory was "romantic," and foreshadowed an inevitable disillusionment.

McKay was strongly committed to international socialism, which in itself is far-reaching and utopian. His poetic outlook precluded objectivity, which most persons with political aspirations for uniting mankind should have. Men like McKay often fail because their romantic vision clouds the logical procedural tactics necessary to socialist goals. Even though McKay considered himself a poet first, the roles he had envisioned for himself posed a conflict in his soul or "rebel heart." The idea of being international, like most of McKay's other traits, was carried over into almost everything he did, including his letters to Max Eastman.[2] He mentions to Eastman that he would like to write a study about Russia, but adds, "I am paying for the penalty of being too naively internationally-minded . . . all that, in a subtle way, works against . . . me."[3]

In 1922 McKay left for Russia after having had a disagreement with his friend and editor, Max Eastman, over an edition of *The Liberator*, a socialist magazine devoted to art and literature. As an editor on the magazine and the only black there, McKay saw the feasibility of writing a chapter about the race question in America. Eastman and another editor, Mike Gold, thought the objective of the magazine would be lost if McKay emphasized this kind of issue; consequently, no gains would be made for the blacks.

McKay obviously disagreed, and in extended correspondence between him and Eastman, there were charges and counter-charges about where each specifically stood on the race question. Eastman wrote to McKay that

> . . . there was never any disagreement between you and the editors of the Liberator, so as far as I am aware, about the proper Communist policy toward the race question in the United States. . . . The disagreement which arose after I left was a disagreement about how to further those policies, along with the others for which the Liberator stood, in that particular magazine.[4]

Eastman insists that the effect of publishing McKay's article on the race question in *The Liberator* would be the "opposite" of the one desired. He goes on in this very lengthy letter to dissect McKay's capability as a writer of such a chapter. He continues,

> You cannot take two opposite positions with the same lofty and condescending tone of voice in the same chapter. . . . [It] will irritate and tend to alienate from you every one of them, and if they have, as you say they have, the "broadcast sympathetic social and artistic understanding of the Negro" of any white group in America, your chapter is a poor beginning of an effort to extend that understanding.[5]

The reader of this lengthy cryptic letter can assume that Eastman was not only angry but was indicating to McKay that there was also something wrong with his journalistic sense. Interestingly, a few years later while writing pieces for *Pravda* and *Izvestia*, McKay admitted that he had not quite mastered the knack of "journalese." His closeness to the subject matter in these cases resulted in the natural poetizing that got in the way of the objective perspective needed. To feel strongly about a subject is one thing, but to present it effectively is another. Paradoxically, however, one observes an acute sense of audience awareness throughout McKay's writing, even more so in the pieces he wrote during his Russian visit.

McKay's response to Eastman's attack was no less harsh
and analytical. Max Eastman has a memo in the manuscripts
that reads, "Claude's Brain Storm in Moscow." It is not clear
why he calls it that, but McKay goes through the origin of
the argument or disagreement with Eastman and *The
Liberator* staff, and writes, ". . . The Liberator group, revealed
to me that [it] did not have a class-conscious attitude on the
problem of the American Negro." McKay appears to
contradict himself because, in fact, he had not discussed the
labor movement seriously with *The Liberator* staff; rather, he
tells us that "I discussed [it] seriously only with the radical
Negro group in New York."[6] This last comment by McKay to
Eastman could have been one of the sensitive points that
made Eastman not wish to print the chapter. Perhaps he
sensed that groups sympathetic to McKay's view would reflect
an ideological perspective contrary to the socialist position
already established by *The Liberator*. It is obvious, too, that
McKay and Eastman were at odds regarding their views on
the right of a free press. McKay goes further to say that
Eastman did not even want to discuss Irish and Indian
questions, because they were "national issues." McKay felt,
however, that Eastman had said nothing at all on any
pertinent racial issues, including the Negro in the
Revolution. This is hardly a credit to a magazine's chief
editor. By way of supporting his argument for the publication
of the chapter in *The Liberator* on his experience, McKay
said that the article "He Who Gets Slapped," which appeared
in the May 1922 issue, got practical results. The most personal
attack on Eastman, though, is a response to the Tom
Paine/Lenin analogy in an earlier Eastman letter. He says:

> . . . Tom Paine was of his time and so is Lenin. To me there
> is no comparison. During the age of the French Revolution,
> Paine performed herculean tasks in England, France and
> America, and if you had in your whole body an ounce of
> the vitality that Paine had in his little finger, you, with your
> wonderful opportunities, would not have missed the
> chances for great leadership in the class struggle that were
> yours in America.[7]

Despite such "brainstorms," the two men remained lifelong friends, and their correspondence regarding all kinds of problems, literary, political, and personal, continued.

There had been many rumors and assumptions regarding Claude McKay's trip to Russia and they persisted for a long time. McKay had to live with not only rumors about how and why he went, but also whether he was Communist, Socialist, Marxist, or his own brand of any of these. It is no wonder, then, that critics have called his autobiography, *A Long Way from Home* (1937), unbalanced.[8]

Like Hurston's *Dust Tracks on a Road*, McKay's *Long Way* is a peculiar autobiography. The reader discovers very little about the innermost depths of McKay, the essential human being. The book is aimed mostly at clearing the air and setting the record straight about the annoying things in his life, from his first arrival in Harlem to his journeys to Europe and Africa. Three segments are devoted to his experiences, good and bad. Perhaps one of the most interesting is the section, "The Magic Pilgrimage," which consists of seven chapters dealing with the Russian Revolution, "Blackness" as an asset, the hostility of American Communists toward McKay, and the gossip that had been written about him.

Certain aspects of Communism excited McKay, and others repelled him. He had always felt the importance of belonging to a group because the group afforded strength, distinction, and assurance. Yet, one's individual identity can be lost in the group, and this was a dilemma he never quite resolved. The forsaking of Communism on these same grounds came about with time and experience in Russia. He had been to England in 1920–1921, had worked with the Pankhurst group there, and thought at that time that Marxism indeed was the answer to the race issue. It is interesting that McKay thought of England as the place of his first real active indoctrination. As a child of colonialism, with its class distinctions, McKay returned to the Mother Land to find that Englishmen were as much into socialism as colonialism. Perhaps that was a reinforcement for his subsequent leanings and European initiation. What was to haunt McKay and make him think of Communism as "dry rot" was that it, like the white patrons and the black bourgeoisie, attempted to exercise control over black writers and artists.

The Communist "killing off" of creativity was one of the experiences in Russia that he abhorred, and he saw it happening as he milled around with the "intelligentsia" transformed into "comrade workers." So, to set the record straight, McKay recorded in detail his entire Russian sojourn in "The Magic Pilgrimage." He became the darling of Russia, the first black to receive that honor even though he was not in 1923 an official candidate to the Fourth Congress of the Third Internationale. The mulatto officially appointed as a delegate to the Congress faded into the background as the dark McKay became the symbol of the Communist cause, an American prize who appeared like a miracle to the Russians. The timing for both him and the Russians was right.

In *A Long Way from Home,* he cites the fact that a cartoon had appeared in the American papers depicting him on a magic carpet sailing over the clouds from Africa (not the U.S.) into Moscow, and that his visit was much like that. In that "Moscow Brain Storm" letter can be found the clearest parallel to what McKay's real presence indicated for the Russians. He relates an earlier experience in New Hampshire about a black man in a white environment who is "down" on life, but eager to know the identity of both himself and his oppressor. He says:

> . . . I went into that hotel with the full knowledge that I was not merely an ordinary worker, but that I was also a Negro, that I would not be judged on my merits as a worker alone, but on my behavior as a Negro. Up there . . . the Negro (as in thousands of other places in America) was on trial not as a worker but as a strange species. And I went into that hotel to work for my bread and bed, and also for my race. This situation is forced upon every intelligent Negro in America. . . .[9]

The letter is important because it shows that despite the excitement, exposure and speeches, McKay didn't lose sight of who and what he represented. That portion of the letter to Max Eastman illustrated that he was clearly knowledgeable of his position. If the letters or words were transported from New Hampshire to Moscow, they would become equally meaningful in his understanding of his Russian experience and his role there. While enjoying the luxury of a "roaring good time," McKay was not naive, but took in all he saw, listened eagerly, and observed all facets of Russian life. To him, the Russian people and their politics were one. While McKay found many discrepancies in the socialism of Max Eastman, his co-workers at *The Liberator*, the black radicals, and American Communists in general, he admitted readily that his "senses were stormed by Moscow before the intellect was touched by the forces of Revolution."[10]

He had already observed that many Russians were "raggedy" and lived in poor housing, and in mingling with them he found that the majority did not understand the true nature of Communism. Some knew only that Lenin had replaced the Czar and that he was a "greater little father." Then, at the Fourth Congress McKay noticed that the American Communists were split on the direction the party should take. The more McKay became aware of what was going on with the American Communist delegation, the more he perceived their actions as affecting party unity negatively. The tension there was so great that they contemplated moving the party headquarters to another country. For the Russian Communists, however, McKay was an omen of good luck and while he was in Russia, only the actions and behavior of the American Communists who lied about the progress of the party takeover in America disturbed him.

There were obvious differences between the Russian and American labor organizations also. McKay admired the organization and platform of the Finnish delegation and saw a possible application of their tactics as a redemption for blacks. The Finns voted as a bloc, were never unprepared, and controlled their delegation because they had proper organization and money. As McKay says in *A Long Way from Home,* "every other racial group in America is organized except Negroes. What Negroes need is political union for strength like the Finns."[11] He also concluded that the only place where illegal and secret radical propaganda was necessary was among the Negroes of the South.[12] These thoughts and ideas were to find their way into some short stories he wrote in Russia for *Izvestia.* In Russia, Eastman, the pure American Marxist, was "shrugged off" at the Congress while McKay was asked to address the group, a fact McKay does not reveal in his autobiography although it is recorded elsewhere. The omission seems to be a deliberate one on McKay's part, in order to highlight the honors and attention accorded him in Russia.

McKay had many other concerns regarding the radical left, one of which was the explosive issue of the so-called "Jewish question." From his days on *The Liberator,* he had become aware of it much as he recognized the problems of the Irish, the blacks, and the American Indians. Jews, like Negroes, posed a problem for society, and he saw them as an oppressed, "lynched" people, among the masses of classless men. In a letter to Max Eastman, he asks:

> . . . Do you think the Communist leaders and the rank and file could by a single stroke change the minds of humanity that have been warped by hundreds of years of bourgeois traditions and education?[13]

He realized that the Communist regime had not swept away the deep-rooted prejudice against Russian Jewry. Max Eastman was also aware of similar problems in the U.S. and prior to McKay's observation had written:

> . . . The situation of the Jew in Russia before the revolution is the one thing in the world comparable to the situation of the Negro in the United States. A proletarian Revolution has occurred, or is occurring here. The persecution of Jews had ceased. The two most powerful men in the government at this moment are Jews. The race problem in its basic outlines has disappeared. For you, *the leading*

> *revolutionary figure in the Negro world* . . . to imagine that
> the race problem will be solved by the proletarian
> revolution (the triumph of labor) is really a tragedy.[14]
> [emphasis added]

Eastman calls McKay "the leading revolutionary figure in
the Negro World," an honor and recognition that McKay
did not assume for himself. McKay, however, responded to
Eastman's description in giving more serious thought to his
subsequent statements on race and revolution.

McKay goes on to tell Eastman that his revolutionary acts
started back in 1920 in London when he sold "Red" literature
on the street corners of London and also when he did
propaganda work among the colonial soldiers. When he
discussed political and race problems with fellow workers on
The Liberator in 1921, McKay was not play-acting, but was
very seriously committed despite the Justice Department's
persecution. Eastman, like most people, had been deceived by
him due to his "everlastingly infectious smile." This guise of
a relaxed attitude might have endeared McKay to the Russian
people, too. He did not have the intensity and brooding
attitude of a typical dedicated Communist. His was the image
they expected and wanted, naive and primitive, and they used
his "innocence" to further their aims. It is no wonder, then,
that they found his early poetry, that with which they were
familiar, proletarian—although his fascination was with the
past, not the future, and his point of view romantic.

When McKay finally left Russia in 1923 after seeing
much of the country and its political and social workings, he
was leaving at the height of his popularity. He had read his
poem, "If We Must Die," in the spirit in which he wrote it.
The poem evokes the ethos of radicalism and comradeship
the Russians admired:

> If we must die, let it not be like hogs
> Hunted and penned in an inglorious spot,
> While round us bark the mad and hungry dogs,
> Making their mock at our accursed lot.
> If we must die, O let us nobly die,
> So that our precious blood may not be shed

In vain; then even the monsters we defy
Shall be constrained to honor us though
Oh kinsmen! we must meet the common foe!
Though far outnumbered let us show us brave,
And for their thousand blows deal one deathblow!
What though before us lies the open grave?
Like men we'll face the murderous, cowardly pack,
Pressed to the wall, dying, but fighting back![15]

He had written a summary of these ideas for Trotsky, whom he had met there, and published them in *Pravda*. Russia had gotten a few poems out of him and some short stories. Though still puzzled by Trotsky's famous phrase, "Permanent Revolution," he moved on to view his Russian experience in retrospect. Although Russia had already "had her revolution," he found that Trotsky's statement, "one must be *Right* against the Party," contained practical wisdom of the highest order.

McKay did not meet Lenin or Stalin, but found Trotsky to be a magnetic personality. "Trotsky," he said, "wanted to know about Negroes, organization, political position, schooling, religion, grievances, and social aspirations." Trotsky told him that Negroes needed to be "lifted up" equal to whites and they must have education through all phases of their life. When Eastman wrote the book *When Lenin Died*, McKay thought highly of it and praised Eastman by saying that he [Eastman] was:

> . . . mountain high above any American leader. You occupy on your own ground as sure and important a place as did Lenin & Trotsky themselves. . . . It seems to me that you've given us one of the finest and most balanced political treatises of these times, a crystal-clear analytic study of the cooperative work of Lenin & Trotsky—their faults—their weakness—their greatness. And whatever happens to Trotsky this little book of yours will live and interest the world so long as it remembers Lenin & Trotsky. . . .[16]

While in Russia, McKay was supposed to write a book on the Russian Revolution for Negroes, but this never materialized. He had managed to write several articles, not all of which were "adulatory." The book commissioned to be written was *Negry v Amerike* (The Negroes in America) (1923) and had as its epigraph Walt Whitman's straightforward lines:

> My call is the call of Battle
> I nourish active Rebellion.[17]

The Russian experience stayed with McKay all his life. It left its great imprint on him. It is apparent not only from the content of the autobiography, but also from the letters written after 1930 upon returning to New York. In New York, he wrote to Max Eastman that he had eaten with a group of colored Communists whom he couldn't convince that he was not a Trotskyite, so, "some of them were sorry they had eaten with me. . . ." Also,

> . . . The Third Communist Internationale seems to me by far a greater tragedy than Trotsky. . . . [It] looks like a stuffed carcass and it seems to me it will be so as long as its siege remains in Russia. . . .[18]

From 1939 to 1944, when McKay joined the Catholic Church, his reflections became more somber and philosophical. He was asked to work with the CYO (Catholic Youth Organization) and advise them on the development of Communism, but he admitted that he had not followed the party's development or Russia "since Lenin died." Upon his conversion to Catholicism, he states that the Communists had no need to "gloat" over his conversion:

> Although I was once sympathetic to their cause I was never a Communist. I had a romantic hope that Communism would usher in a classless society and make human beings happier. All I saw in Russia was that Communism was using one class to destroy the other. . . . Besides, communism is quite a primitive ideal and I don't see how modern society could go back to it.[19]

McKay went to Russia to view a great social experiment which, in reality, was not an answer to his own problems.

He had argued with his friend, editor, and former boss Max Eastman about the positive effect of writing a chapter in *The Liberator* about the Negro question. Eastman saw it as negative and destructive to the magazine and the black masses. McKay, on the other hand, bound by duty, felt that this was positive and constructive. He felt that blacks needed to organize themselves into a power group and the closest thing he saw as a model was an international Communism separate from whites.

The real source of McKay's discontent was the beginning of his realization that the concept of a universal proletariat was not the solution to the black man's struggle. The Russian experience was enriching and confusing, as he did not see there the utopian solidarity he had envisioned. However, he used the experience, enjoyed the lionizing, managed to further a writing career (in prose), and came out of it still a "poet," not a politician.

For a few years McKay clung to the illusion that Marxism was the answer for the black man, and even when that illusion was shattered, he still wrote about the trip to Russia with a degree of nostalgia. The fact that he spent a large portion of his autobiography, *A Long Way from Home,* on this two-year phase of his life is evidence enough that Russia had made a lasting impact on him. Until his conversion to Catholicism, in the last few years of his life, the concept of a proletarian revolution was the strongest of all his temptations to desert his belief in a pure black identity.

NOTES

1. Stephen H. Bronz, *Roots of Negro Racial Consciousness* (New York: Libra Publishers, 1964), pp. 76–77.

2. McKay's unpublished letters are in the Lily Library, Indiana University, Bloomington. The references and excerpts are from the McKay Mss. there.

3. McKay letter to Eastman, 25 November 1934.

4. Eastman letter to McKay, March 1923.

5. Ibid., pp. 3–5.

6. McKay letter from Moscow, 3 April 1923.

7. Ibid.

8. Claude McKay, *A Long Way from Home* (New York: Harcourt, Brace and World, 1937).

9. McKay letter from Moscow, 3 April 1923.

10. McKay, *A Long Way from Home*, p. 138.

11. Ibid., p. 174.

12. Ibid., pp. 177–178.

13. McKay letter to Eastman, 18 May 1923.

14. Eastman letter to McKay, 12 April 1923.

15. Claude McKay, *Selected Poems* (New York: Bookman, 1953), p. 36.

16. McKay letter to Eastman, Avignon, May 1925.

17. Claude McKay, *The Negroes in America*, trans. from the Russian by Robert J. Winter (New York: Kennikat Press, 1979).

18. McKay letter to Eastman, 9 May 1934.

19. McKay letter to Eastman, 30 June 1944.

The Aesthetics of Community:
The Insular Black Community as Theme and Focus in Hurston's *Their Eyes Were Watching God*

MARY KATHERINE WAINWRIGHT

The publication of Zora Neale Hurston's *Their Eyes Were Watching God* in 1937 marked the beginning of a new tradition in black American literature. This novel deviates significantly from a mainstream black, predominantly male fiction, which finds its roots in the protests of male slave narratives, fiction that Sherley Anne Williams, among others, has characterized as generally "tragic," "violent," and "resentful."[1] In contrast, Hurston, whom Cheryl Wall has identified as the "first authentic black female voice in American literature,"[2] expresses in her novel what Roger Whitlow calls a "deep, warm, and honest affirmation of the worth of human life and love."[3] Her characters, according to Wall, attain identity not by "transcending" but by "embracing" their black culture.[4] And, as Alice Walker points out, Hurston's fiction depicts what "is lacking in so much black writing and literature: racial health; a sense of black people as complete, complex, *undiminished* human beings."[5]

Their Eyes Were Watching God presents the black cultural experience as an affirmative and validating experience instead of a "plight" to be either remedied or shed. It measures the worth of the black community in its own terms and not, as much traditional black literature does, against the touchstones of white society's values. It is this radical, alternative view of the black experience in America, a view of racial health instead of racial psychosis, that, in addition to being the basis for a continuing black women's literary tradition, accords Hurston a special position within the literary milieu of the Harlem Renaissance.

Hurston's novel stands apart from other novels of the Harlem Renaissance because within it Hurston projects what has been called her "folkloric ethos" into what I have identified as an aesthetics of community. Defined by Larry Neal as "the characteristic sensibility of a nation, or of a specific sociocultural group,"[6] this ethos, shaped by her anthropological involvement in black folklore and culture of the deep South and Haiti, embodies Hurston's belief, as Robert Hemenway phrases it, that "normality is a function of culture."[7] Refuting both prevailing social science "pathological" premises as well as theories of "cultural deprivation" on which a great deal of social protest literature and social legislation was based during her time, Hurston's folkloric vision, according to Hemenway, enables her to celebrate "the black folk who had made a way out of no way" and to liberate "rural black folks from the prison of racial stereotypes" by granting them "dignity as cultural creators."[8]

Hurston's folkloric ethos, infused with her belief in cultural relativity, provides the basis for an aesthetics of community because the community becomes the conditioning factor in Hurston's execution of fictional conventions as well as thematic concerns. First of all, the setting of the novel is the concretely conceived geographical communities of Eatonville and the Everglades migrant camp in "de muck." These communities are more than just fictional settings for Hurston's novel; in Hurston's hands, the community comes alive with a life of its own as in Chapter Six of *Their Eyes*, where the major plot of Janie and Joe's marriage plays a

secondary role to the community members and their storytelling rituals on the front porch of Joe Stark's store. But the
community serves the plot in more ways than just as setting.
It also becomes the vehicle through which other fictional
conventions are carried out. For instance, the community
plays an integral role in the character development of
Hurston's protagonist Janie Crawford inasmuch as her
maturation is fostered by her increasing ability to participate
fully in community life. Moreover, the conflict and
resolution of the plot center on the community and Janie's
ability to move from acceptance to questioning and, finally, to
challenging and overcoming community expectations about
the roles of women.

Besides serving as the central element in fictional
conventions such as setting, character development, plot
conflict and resolution, the aesthetics of community in *Their
Eyes Were Watching God* specifically allows Hurston to
develop certain thematic concerns shared by other artists and
intellectuals—Harlem Renaissance concerns such as the
definition, roles, and responsibility of the artist, the
definition of self, gender stereotypes, race and race building,
and social protest. Because her portrayal of these themes is
constantly informed by the values and qualities that she finds
in black folk life—in the community—Hurston's treatment of
these themes invites us to realize that art can function in the
service of consciousness-raising without losing its integrity as
art.

In *Their Eyes*, the protagonist, Janie Crawford, is an
artist-figure. If we pay close attention to the novel's framing
technique, we find the emphasis of the novel is placed on
Janie's return to her community to tell her story after her
adventures in "de muck." In the opening frame, Janie's
comment to her "kissin' friend," Pheoby, as they sit
conversing on the back porch steps initiates the importance of
Janie's quest to the community: "Ah been a delegate to de big
'ssociation of life. Yessuh! De Grand Lodge, de big convention
of living is just where Ah been dis year and a half y'all ain't
seen me."[9] But Janie's quest away from the relatively isolated
life in Orange County into the "big convention of living"

where she immerses herself in the life of the folk, a journey
that parallels the quest pattern of traditional romance
literature, is only half of Hurston's purpose. The concluding
frame in which Pheoby, after hearing about Janie's
adventures, says to Janie—"Lawd! . . . Ah done growed ten
feet higher from jus' listenin' tuh you, Janie. Ah ain't
satisfied wid mahself no mo'" (284)—illustrates my
contention that the function of art is reciprocal.

The artist, according to this dialogue between Pheoby and
Janie, is one who not only tells the story of going to the
"horizon and back" but who also has an effect on community
members, causes others to grow and not be satisfied with
themselves, and imparts visions to a particular audience, her
friends and neighbors. Through the reciprocal act of creation
that occurs between Janie and Pheoby, we find Hurston's
illustration of the idea that the artist is defined by her effect
on and responsibility to community members at the same
time that community growth is created through the artist's
vision of and model for attaining cultural dignity.

Hurston's strong belief in the dignity inherent within
the black folk community is attested to by her careful
documentation of the black oral tradition and folkways and
their effect on individual and group behavior in her two
collections of folklore *Mules and Men* (1935) and *Tell My
Horse* (1938). These anthropological observations carry over
into her fiction and become the underlying premises on
which her novel's portrayal of the role and responsibility of
an artist figure like Janie Crawford is based. In effect,
Hurston's novel expands the concept of the artist by suggesting
that the black woman artist is one who not only creates a
work of art but also contributes to the creation of the culture.
Also, reciprocally, the community is a significant factor in
the creation of the artist.

Next, the ethos of folklore (as it is channeled into an
aesthetics of community that informs Hurston's definition of
the artist) also provides the basis for her definition of the
self. That the community was the lens through which
Hurston ordered her world and her view of the self is
evident from both a comment in her autobiography and the

sequence of chapter arrangements. In *Dust Tracks on a Road* (1942), Hurston states, "Joe Clark's store [Eatonville's communal gathering place] was the heart and spring of the town."[10] Noteworthy, also, is the sequence of chapter arrangement in her autobiography. The first chapter, the place of prominence, is given to "My Birthplace," and it describes the founding and history of Eatonville. The second chapter, "My Folks," begins with a discussion of her immediate family and expands to incorporate community members. It is onto this backdrop of family and community emphasis that the "I Get Born" chapter is positioned. This sequence suggests, as I believe her novel does, that the self is a product of the environment, that it is through the vehicle of the community that the self is created, that the self is a composite, a relational entity instead of an autonomous one, compiled of group beliefs, values, and interactions, and that the self and the community are engaged in an interwoven process of creating and integrating each other. Janie Crawford, for instance, understands that being denied access to the community's gatherings on the store's porch has negative effects on the development of her self. In contrast, she is able to integrate her personality and arrive at mature self-awareness only after she engages in all aspects of community existence while she lives and works with Teacake in "de muck."

Hurston, however, does not always see the community as functioning in a positive way. Hurston's aesthetics of community also allows for her thematic criticism of the sexism inherent in black community and family life, a criticism that is unique to the literature of the Harlem Renaissance. While other writers continued to reify conventional and sexist gender roles and views, such as Claude McKay's perpetuation of woman as sex object in *Home to Harlem* or even Jean Toomer's portrayal of Fern in *Cane*, Hurston's *bildungsroman*, as S. Jay Walker concludes, offers a treatment of gender roles "virtually unique in the annals of black fiction" because it deals "far more extensively with sexism, the struggle of a woman to be regarded as a person in a male-dominated society, than racism, the struggle of blacks to be regarded as persons in a white-dominated society."[11]

Each of Janie's three relationships with men can be regarded as an exposé on the oppressive conditions and subservient roles of women within the black community. Her forced marriage to Logan Killicks represents the only role available to such women as her grandmother, who bitterly urges Janie to accept her fate as "de mule of de world." Janie's second marriage to Jody Starks represents the oppression of middle-class black women, who are expected to function only as symbols of their husbands' status and wealth without any regard for their own needs as human beings. Finally, her relationship with Teacake, despite its seeming perfection and equality, is marred by Teacake's belief in his right and duty to abuse Janie physically. He also thinks nothing of taking Janie's money after they run away together in order to bolster his ego by throwing a big party for his friends.

It is through the aesthetics of community that Hurston is able to fictionalize the destructive effects of sex-role stereotypes not only on individual characters but on the community as a whole. Just as Janie's self-growth is predicated on her participation in community life, so is a healthy community predicated on the participation and contributions of all its members. Each of her three life choices portrays Janie's increasing ability to function as a community member. She first moves away from her isolation on Logan Killick's farm to the pedestal on which she has been placed by Jody Starks, who insists that she is "too good" to attend community events such as the mule burial or to join other community members in the storytelling and "signifying" that take place on the porch of his store. But in her last marriage, she finally becomes the community member who works side by side with Teacake in "de muck." Thus, Janie's progress at transcending traditional sex-role stereotypes is paralleled by her ability to participate in community life. It is only when Janie merges with the community that her growth as an individual entity is achieved. The reverse is also true. The community, both at Eatonville and in the Everglades, becomes more complete and integrated as a result of Janie's equal participation in its activities. This merging of the self and the world, a merging which is clearly the central message of the novel, is evident in the final lines when Janie, alone in her room after returning to Eatonville, "pulled it [the horizon] from around the waist of the world and draped it over her shoulder. So much of life in its meshes! She called in her soul to come and see" (p. 286).

The idea of self and artistic integration resulting from mergence in black community life goes a long way in promoting race consciousness and elevating racial esteem, both of which appear as major concerns in the literature of the Harlem Renaissance. Aware that the previous artistic endeavors of black writers had often perpetuated the already prevalent doctrine of racial inferiority by reinforcing stereotypes that were demeaning and dehumanizing—the minstrel figure or the "passionate primitive," for instance—many black writers and theorists, as Nathan Huggins summarizes, "championed intellectual achievement" as the means to positive "race-building," to creating a consciousness of the "integrity of race and personality."[12] Hurston's novel is clearly in accord with this major aspiration of the Harlem Renaissance. To remove racially destructive stereotypes from the consciousness of blacks and whites alike by producing a black-centered literature and art would, according to the theorists, make visible and thus encourage a positive recognition of the enriching aspects of black culture and people.

Hurston's approach to race building, however, differs from that of her contemporaries of the Harlem Renaissance because her folkloric ethos provided her with a different framework by which to view the black community. She herself recognized that her approach differed when she once confided to Nick Aaron Ford that "many Negroes criticize my book [*Jonah's Gourd Vine*] . . . because I did not make it a lecture on the race problem." She continues by saying that while many black novelists "confuse art with Sociology," she wanted to write "a novel and not a treatise on Sociology."[13] In another context, Hurston continues to reject the kind of writing that was being done by other black writers:

> I saw that what was being written and declaimed was a
> pose. A Negro writer or speaker was supposed to say those
> things. It has such a definite pattern as to become
> approximately folklore. So I made up my mind to write
> about my people as they are, and not to use the traditional
> lay figures.[14]

Hurston establishes her own unique approach to the "race
problem" when she states, "I do not belong to the sobbing
school of Negrohood who hold that nature somehow has
given them a lowdown dirty deal and whose feelings are all
hurt about it. . . . No, I do not weep at the world—I am too
busy sharpening my oyster knife."[15]

Hurston, to use one of her favorite idioms and methods of
dealing with the white world, "hits a straight lick with a
crooked stick." By building a positive and affirmative racial
image through the depiction of her people with all their
virtues and foibles, a depiction of "undiminished" human
beings within the setting of an insular black community,
her novel neither elevates blacks who aspire to and succeed at
white middle-class standards (as in Jessie Fauset's four
novels), nor does she expose, with often tragic and violent
subject matter, the injustices and inequalities of blacks at the
hands of whites, as, for examples, Richard Wright does in
Native Son.

Hurston's ethos of folklore, her ability to fictionalize an
insular black community virtually free "from contact with or
economic dependence upon the white world," as S. Jay
Walker maintains,[16] is the philosophical foundation on
which her aesthetics and her humanist and revisionary
concepts of human life are based. It is also this ethos that is
responsible for Hurston's radical contribution to the social
protest literature of the Harlem Renaissance. As June Jordan,
for example, comments, "the affirmation of Black values and
lifestyles within the American context, is indeed, an act of
protest."[17] In *Their Eyes*, the community, while functioning
as a concretely conceived geographical setting, also
metaphorically and aesthetically structures racial, artistic,
self, and gender concerns. Because of the aesthetics of

community, Hurston is able to do what so many black fiction writers of the Harlem Renaissance failed to do. When she chose to dramatize the indigenous elements of an all-black world, Hurston refused to participate in an either/or logic (black versus white) that underlies much black fiction and that only confirms blacks' alienation from and battle against the prevailing white tradition.

In celebrating black folkways and culture, in presenting the black community as the necessary element in integrating the self and the artist, in depicting the imaginative creativity that characterizes black culture, even while criticizing the sexism that lies within it, Hurston's positive and affirmative racial images radically undermine and supplement the white tradition that determines power. By transforming an either/or logic into a both/and, Hurston reminds us that "normality" is indeed a "function of culture" and enables us to see, as Virginia Woolf has noted, that though we often "see the same landscape, we see it through different eyes."[18] Hurston's novel also illustrates her own belief that

> Nothing that God ever made is the same thing to more than one person. That is natural. There is no single face in nature, because every eye that looks upon it, sees it from its own angle. So every man's spice-box seasons his own food.[19]

The world that she asks us to envision, the culturally relative landscape of race, art, self, and gender, as seen through "the spice-box" of her aesthetics of community, is not judged as either inferior or superior, but rather is portrayed as itself in all its negative and positive aspects. As the "prototypical black novel of affirmation,"[20] *Their Eyes Were Watching God* needs to assume its rightful place in the canon of Harlem Renaissance literature and also to be seen as the genesis of a tradition of black women's writings that coexists with and provides a necessary corrective to black male literature of the twentieth-century America.

NOTES

1. Sherley Anne Williams, *Give Birth to Brightness: A Thematic Study in Neo-Black Literature* (New York: Dial Press, 1972), p. 72.

2. Cheryl Wall, "Zora Neale Hurston: Changing Her Own Words," in *American Novelists Revisited: Essays in Feminist Criticism*, ed. Fritz Fleischman (Boston: G.K. Hall, 1982), p. 371.

3. Roger Whitlow, *Black American Literature: A Critical History* (Chicago: Nelson Hall, 1973), p. 103.

4. Wall, p. 372.

5. Alice Walker, "Zora Neale Hurston: A Cautionary Tale and a Partisan View," in *In Search of Our Mothers' Gardens: Womanist Prose* (New York: Harcourt Brace Jovanovich, 1983), p. 85.

6. Larry Neal, "A Profile: Zora Neale Hurston," *Southern Exposure* 1 (1974), 162.

7. Robert Hemenway, *Zora Neale Hurston: A Literary Biography* (Urbana: University of Illinois Press, 1977), p. 332.

8. Hemenway, pp. 329–330.

9. Zora Neale Hurston, *Their Eyes Were Watching God* (1937; rpt. Urbana: University of Illinois Press, 1978), p. 18. All future references to this source are cited parenthetically in the text of this paper.

10. Zora Neale Hurston, *Dust Tracks on a Road* (1942; rpt. Urbana: University of Illinois Press, 1984), p. 61.

11. S. Jay Walker, "Zora Neale Hurston's *Their Eyes Were Watching God*: Black Novel of Sexism," *Modern Fiction Studies* 20 (Winter 1974–1975), 520.

12. Nathan Huggins, *Harlem Renaissance* (New York: Oxford University Press, 1971), pp. 56–58.

13. Nick Aaron Ford, *The Contemporary Negro Novel* (1936; rpt. College Park, Md.: McGrath Publishing Co., 1968), p. 96.

14. Cited by Evelyn Thomas Helmick, "Zora Neale Hurston," in *Feminist Criticism: Essays on Theory, Poetry and Prose*, ed. Cheryl L. Brown and Karen Olsen (Metuchen, N.J.: Scarecrow Press, 1978), p. 270.

15. Zora Neale Hurston, "What It Means to Be Colored Me," reprinted in *I Love Myself When I Am Laughing . . . : A Zora Neale Hurston Reader*, ed. Alice Walker and Mary Helen Washington (Old Westbury, N.Y.: The Feminist Press, 1979), p. 153.

16. S. Jay Walker, p. 215.

17. June Jordan, "On Richard Wright and Zora Neale Hurston: Notes Toward a Balancing of Love and Hatred," *Black World* 23 (August 1974), 5.

18. Virginia Woolf, *Three Guineas* (New York: Harcourt, Brace and World, 1938), p. 18.

19. Hurston, *Dust Tracks*, p. 61.

20. Jordan, p. 6.

Nella Larsen's Harlem Aesthetic

THADIOUS M. DAVIS

"I do so want to be famous," Nella Larsen wrote to Henry Allen Moe of the Guggenheim Foundation. She was in Spain for the completion of her year as the foundation's first black woman to receive a fellowship in creative writing: "The work goes fairly well. But I like it. Of course, that means nothing because I really can't tell if it's good or not. But the way I hope and pray that it is [is] like a physical pain. I do . . . want to be famous."[1] The statement in context is innocent enough, but it is an indication of the attitudes and values Larsen held throughout the 1920s and early 1930s when she was writing fiction.

At thirty-seven, Larsen had published her first novel, *Quicksand*, brought out by Knopf, but which she had considered submitting to Albert and Charles Boni, for as she said: "It would be nice to get a thousand dollars . . . and publicity."[2] *Quicksand*'s reception in 1928 fueled her determination to be a famous novelist. She promptly decided that she "was asking for the Harmon Award," because as she assessed her chances, "Looking back on the year's output of Negro literature I don't see why I shouldn't have a book in. There's only Claude McKay besides.—Rudolph [Fisher] is just too late—. . . ."[3] She immediately sought out recommendations from James Weldon Johnson, W.E.B. DuBois, and Lillian

Alexander when she discovered that one had to be *nominated* for the Harmon Award.

Larsen had already shaved two years off her age in order to comply with the image of youth promoted during the Renaissance. The daughter of an interracial union, Larsen had come a long way by the end of the 1920s when she no longer admitted to being from a working-class background on Chicago's South Side. However, it was not simply upward mobility that she sought during the Renaissance; by then, she had already been married to a physicist since May 1919. She was seeking instead to become someone important in her own right.

Nella Larsen, novelist, emerged from a particular cultural configuration—Harlem of the New Negro Renaissance; perhaps no other could have produced her. While her art was dependent upon a number of factors, it was obviously linked to her historical situation. With an influx of 87,417 blacks during the 1920s, the 25-block area above 125th Street was, as James Weldon Johnson declared, "the greatest Negro city in the world."[4] Harlem provided a place for black life, in Alain Locke's view, to seize "its first chances for group expression and self-determination. . . . There is a fresh spiritual and cultural focusing. We have, as the heralding sign, an unusual outburst of creative expression."[5] This "unusual outburst of creative expression" was possible in a particular environment not only conducive to black creativity, but also to inspire participation in that creativity.

In April 1927, when Nella Larsen and her husband Elmer Imes moved from Jersey City to an apartment in Harlem's 135th Street, they arrived seeking proximity to the "cultural Capital." Larsen especially welcomed the move as the convergence of her social and literary interests. Her initial aim was imitative; she wanted to join herself through writing to a particular phenomenon. The creative activity, whether a Zora Neal Hurston telling stories, an Aaron Douglas drawing illustrations, a Countee Cullen or Langston Hughes writing poetry, inspired confidence in artistic potential and promised rewards for involvement.

For Larsen, the activity was like a whirlwind. As she stated: "It has seemed always to be tea time, as the immortal Alice remarked, with never time to wash the dishes between while."[6] Her actions were controlled by her conscious desire to achieve recognition and were perhaps controlled too by her unconscious hope to belong. While for some the stirrings in Harlem may have been racial and aesthetic, for Larsen they were primarily practical. Her objective was to use art to protract her identity onto a larger social landscape as emphatically as possible.

Larsen had made her decision to become part of the growing number of "New Negro" writers in 1925 when, as Arna Bontemps recalled, "It did not take long to discover . . . the sighs of wonder, amazement and sometimes admiration . . . that here was one of the 'New Negroes.'"[7] The reception accorded young artists motivated Larsen to turn to writing, at first stories, which early in 1926 she sold to a ladies magazine. These stories, and especially her first novel, *Quicksand* (1928), were part of her attempt to "cash in" on the cultural awakening, to stake her own claim for the recognition and development of identity that other authors were accorded. Basically, it was not enough to write; it was *essential* to publish.

The writer during the Renaissance was just as often *made* as born. Walter White had written *The Fire in the Flint* (1924) in response to a wave of white interest in race material. And others had answered the call by publishers for "Negro" works by producing poetry, fiction, and drama. In that milieu it was possible to become a writer with an announcement to "friends" that a project was under way or through a notice that a publisher was searching for "Negro" materials. In 1927, for example, Larsen wrote to her friend Dorothy Peterson, "You'd better write some poetry, or something. I've met a man from Macmillan's who's asked me to look out for any Negro stuff and send them to him."[8] She would and did believe that any and all of her intelligent, lively friends could and would want to produce "poetry, or something" in order to take advantage of the opportunities for recognition and prestige that publishing,

particularly with a white firm, would bring. Talent or
inclination or aptitude or inspiration had little to do with it.

Larsen herself had become known as a budding writer
even before an audience had seen her fiction; rumor had it as
early as the start of 1926 that she was writing a novel. "How
do these things get about?" she asked Van Vechten, and
added, "It is the awful Truth. But, who knows if I'll get
through with the damned thing. Certainly not I."[9]

The two prongs of inspiration for Larsen were public
acclaim and social activity, both intricately tied to the climate
for publishing things "Negro." In this she may have been
similar to others; there were, however, writers who wrote
out of a different set of aesthetic values, such as Georgia
Douglas Johnson, who revealed in 1927:

> I wrote because I love to write. . . . If I might ask of some
> fairy godmother special favors, one would sure to be for a
> clearing space, elbow room in which to think and write and
> live beyond the reach of the wolf's fingers.[10]

Nella Larsen, however, functioned in what Gilbert
Osofsky called the "myth world of the twenties."[11] Described
in 1929 as having a "satin surface,"[12] she revealed her ritual
for reading a good book: "a Houbigant scented bath, the
donning of my best green crepe de chine pyjamas, fresh
flowers on the bedside table, piles of freshly covered pillows
and my nicest bed covers."[13] Her pretentious description
portrays not merely a sense of aesthetic pleasure, but also the
degree to which she was removed from ordinary black life.

Drawn to the class of blacks and of whites who could
ignore the poverty that Harlem bred along with the
possibilities for its residents, Larsen responded to a world of
glitter and potential that distanced itself from the teeming
masses. In the process, she created precarious boundaries for
her work and life: "I'm still looking for a place to move. . . .
Right now when I look out into the Harlem streets I feel just
like Helga Crane in my novel. Furious at being connected
with all these niggers."[14] Being ensconced in a five-room
apartment was not enough to make her forget that she was
trapped among lower-class blacks whom she once described

as "mostly black . . . quite shiftless, frightfully clean and decked out in appalling colours."[15] When she found a better apartment on Seventh Avenue, which she called "Uncle Tom's Cabin,"[16] she would more readily admit "that she would never pass" because, as she told a reporter, "with my economic status it's better to be a Negro [sic]."[17] She might have added—especially if she could be labeled one of the "talented tenth" of the race and associate with people accustomed to prestige, position, and comfort.

But, as Langston Hughes pointed out in *The Big Sea* (1940): "All of us knew that the gay sparkling life of the so-called Renaissance . . . was not so gay and sparkling beneath the surface. . . . I thought it wouldn't last long. . . . for how could a large and enthusiastic number of people be crazy about Negroes forever?"[18] Whereas Hughes's assessment is familiar, Alain Locke's is not. In 1936, eleven years after his confident pronouncements in *The New Negro*, and after the Harlem riots of March 1935, Locke wrote another Harlem essay for *Survey Graphic*, "Harlem: Dark Weather Vane," in which he broke what he called a "placid silence and Pollyanna complacency" about "the actual predicament of the mass of life in Harlem": "For no cultural advance is safe without some sound economic underpinning . . . and no emerging elite—artistic, professional or mercantile—can suspend itself in thin air over the abyss of a mass of unemployed [people] stranded in an over-expensive, disease- and crime-ridden slum . . . for there is no cure or saving magic in poetry and art, an emerging generation of talent, or international prestige and interracial recognition, for unemployment, . . . for high rents, high mortality rates, civic neglect, capitalistic exploitation."[19] Locke includes the two elements that were key components of Nella Larsen's Harlem aesthetic; the two are "international prestige" and "interracial recognition."

Partly because she was a black person in a predominantly white world in Chicago and a nobody in the primarily bourgeois world of elite blacks in New York, Larsen sought a career in writing as a way to become somebody. The single claim that she could and did make about being special was that she was a mulatto, daughter of "a Danish lady and a Negro from the Virgin Islands," as she wrote in her 1927 author's publicity sketch for Knopf; later, once *Quicksand* had been published, she could point out that she had not worked outside her home for three years, inflate her educational background and previous employment, and emphasize that her husband had a Ph.D. in physics and worked *downtown* for an engineering firm.

Larsen had married well, but the marriage did not guarantee her acceptance or prominence or make her comfortable within the black elite. She had neither college credentials to call upon, nor a prominent family to smooth her way. What she had was ambition and drive and intelligence. The ambivalences in her fiction and ultimately in her life result perhaps more from her attempts to enter into a class that never knew her for the person she had been in her early life—the child of a working-class immigrant family; it is the background that Larsen could never reveal once she had transformed herself from Nell*ie* to Nell*a*, member of a black society that was not only race conscious, but class conscious as well.

Larsen wanted her own life to become a kind of fairy tale, "like a princess out of a modern fairy tale," as she observed of Fania Marinoff, Van Vechten's wife.[20] But discontented with life in the limelight of her prince, she desired her *own* spotlight, as is indicated by her transition from calling herself Nella *Imes* to Nella Larsen, or Nella Larsen Imes when necessary, after she had finished her first novel. She confessed in 1929 that she "would like to be twenty-five years younger [and that] she want[ed] things— beautiful and rich things."[21]

Nella Larsen as a novelist was driven not by an inner need to write, but by a craving for what she called "fame" and what Locke described as prestige or recognition. Larsen, however, was not the only one whose values emphasized prestige and recognition: others such as Richard Bruce Nugent, Wallace Thurman, Albert Rice, Walter White, or Gwendolyn Bennett also wanted the fame that was almost assured by being part of the New Negro movement. I would not criticize the effort that such individuals put into their writing or dismiss the fact that the writing itself functioned as a means of insight.

I do not question Nella Larsen's effort or seriousness of purpose. Her hard work is a persistent refrain in her letters: "I have been working like a coloured person," she stressed repeatedly, and she would also, as she said, "sweat blood over her work, and console herself with Van Vechten's maxim: 'Easy writing makes bad reading.'"[22] Moreover, she saw herself as a serious novelist, despite being one who would underline the appositive "novelist" after her name in news items noting her attendance at social functions before sending the clippings to her friends. She never gave her occupation as anything other than "writer," and never referred to herself except as "novelist." My doubts about her work lie, therefore, in the somewhat inexplicable area of motivation and intention. I believe that Larsen's commitment to writing may have been inextricably linked to tangible social rewards. She seems to have valued social popularity on the same level as her writing, and it may well be that the publicity she received as one of the two black women *novelists* in the 1920s forced her to take the production of work seriously so that she could sustain her new identity.

Larsen "worked" privately on her writing and publicly on her social standing. She promoted herself on the stage that encouraged her transformation. Because she was bound by the larger expectations of the Renaissance and her own internal pressure to achieve, the measure she set for herself was public acknowledgment of her work and productivity. One result was the intensification of a split between her work as a creative process and her work as a source of public recognition—the standard by which she, like Locke and others, measured achievement. Because one of her objectives remained constant—reaping the benefits of social prominence—she was forced to set unreasonably short deadlines for her finished work and that self-imposed restriction ultimately frustrated her.

The tension between individual work and social interaction was exacerbated by her own underlying conception of writing, her Harlem aesthetic: writing was a "product," which could, upon reception, confirm self-identity as well as very self-worth. Larsen had in the Renaissance a formidable model for understanding writing in the contexts of upward mobility, status, and achievement, not in the private creative process but in the public end result. The result validates the power of the black writer to define the self in the larger world, yet validates as well the power of the larger world to determine and arbitrate the conditions of that validation.

Though Hughes had warned in 1926 that the "present vogue in things Negro . . . may do as much harm as good for the budding colored artist," and that the "Negro artist works against an undertow of sharp criticism and misunderstanding from his own group and unintentional bribes from the whites,"[23] his message was not heard distinctly. Tangible production was the most viable means of asserting the existence of the "New Negro" and measuring achievement. Locke's 1925 announcement of "outbursts of creative expression"—that is to say, published works—as a "heralding sign" established the stage in a way that he may not have fully intended. Achievement for Larsen and other racially defined writers was thus seemingly construed as public acknowledgment without which the creative act was incomplete. Achievement consisted of both publication and reception by an audience, preferably a white one.

Considered in this context, Walter White's letter to Claude McKay on 20 May 1925 is revealing:

> Things are certainly moving with rapidity . . . so far as the Negro artist is concerned. Countee Cullen has had a book of verse accepted by Harper . . . and . . . Knopf accepted a volume by Langston Hughes. Rudolph Fisher . . . has had two excellent short stories in *The Atlantic Monthly.* . . . James Weldon Johnson is at work on a book of Negro spirituals. . . .
>
> The Negro artist is really in the ascendancy. . . . There is unlimited opportunity . . . you will be amazed at the

eagerness of magazine editors and book publishers to get
hold of promising writers.

Let me as a friend urge you to get your novel ready for
publication as soon as possible.[24]

The trap here is evident. The black individual generally
has an internal barometer that measures, accurately or not,
his or her own selfhood in a society whose locus of meaning
has little to do with the meaning of blackness. However, the
black individual, who for whatever reasons wants and needs
a validation of the self in the external world, may well resort
to what that world has accepted as worthy of measurement.

This awareness is one that McKay had formulated when
he responded to White's letter: "I am so happy about the
increased interest in the creative life of the Negro. It is for
Negro aspirants to the creative life themselves to make the
best of it—to discipline themselves and do work that will
hold ground firmly [to] the very highest white standards.
Nothing less will help Negro art forward; a boom is a
splendid thing but if the masses are not up to standard people
turn aside from them after the novelty has worn off."[25]
McKay shifts his focus away from White's emphasis on
quantity and publication to "the creative life" and quality;
albeit he too leaves "white standards" as the aesthetic
measure.

For Larsen, too, in the sparkling social world of the
Renaissance with its interracial conclaves and its hope for
uplift, the printed product evidenced the New Negro's reality.
Each group of published works was carefully added to the list
of verifiable products, of achievement of oneself and the race;
each writer's productivity was dutifully proclaimed in the
records for the year. It is not surprising, then, that this tally-
sheet approach could not last, that most writers did not
endure, so that in a retrospective view of the Renaissance, one
can marvel not at the lists of works produced during a
relatively brief period, but instead take note of the casualties—
those black writers who, for whatever conjunction of personal
factors and external causes, simply did not make it into the
next decade, or if into it, then not out of it. By 1936 Locke
himself was to observe, "indeed, [we] find it hard to believe

that the rosy enthusiasms and hope of 1925 were more than
bright illusions or a cruelly deceptive mirage. Yet after all
there was a renaissance, with its poetic spurt of cultural and
spiritual advance, vital and significant but uneven
accomplishments. . . ."[26]

Few would quarrel with Locke here, and few would
challenge his interpretation of the accomplishments as
being "vital and significant but uneven." Too few have,
however, asked why the accomplishments were so uneven.
One answer to that question might pose as well an answer to
the questions of why the Renaissance ended so abruptly—a
question that is more frequently answered, but in such a way
as to link not aesthetics but economics to the decline of the
movement. Perhaps another answer to the question may lie
in the particular and personal motivations of individual
writers, in the impetus for their will to create. Their
aesthetics thus emphasized both the product and the status that
came with it, these two being more important to them than
either artistic creativity or economic gain.

For a brief time, one of these authors, Nella Larsen,
captured the spirit of a unique time for modern black writers.
She praised the activity as "writing as if [one] didn't
absolutely despise the age in which [one] lives. . . . Surely it
is more interesting to belong to one's own time, to share its
peculiar vision, catch that flying glimpse of the panorama
which no subsequent generation can ever recover."[27] In her
own words, in her own "flying glimpse of the panorama,"
Larsen saw a world of middle-class blacks that became the
basis for her fictional vision, but she saw, too, the
complexities of personal identification with that world.
While it cannot be claimed that she saw either steadily or
whole, it is evident that the angle and the scope of her vision
resulted from her particular involvement with her time.
Perhaps then, like others such as Thurman, Larsen was more
acutely a victim of the New Negro Renaissance than has been
assumed. Had she completed her three novels in progress,
she might have emerged from her age with a more
substantial canon, and with more of the fame that she so
wanted. Yet that canon, in all probability, would not have

altered the estimation of her relationship to her age, even though she had the individual talent to transcend "hack work," as she herself once labeled her early stories.[28] Larsen was a writer inspired to write by the confluence of activities in the Harlem of the Renaissance, and limited as well by that very inspiration.

NOTES

1. Letter to Henry Allen Moe, 11 January 1931, in the John Simon Guggenheim Foundation Files. Hereafter referred to as GFF.

2. Letter to Carl Van Vechten, 1 July 1926, in the James Weldon Johnson Collection, Beinecke Rare Book and Manuscript Library, Yale University, New Haven, Connecticut. Hereafter referred to as JWJC.

3. Letter to Carl Van Vechten, n.d., circa 3 September 1928, JWJC.

4. James Weldon Johnson, "The Making of Harlem," in *Survey Graphic*, 6 (March 1925), 635.

5. Alain Locke, "Foreword," in *The New Negro* (New York: Albert & Charles Boni, 1925), p. xvii.

6. Letter to Carl Van Vechten, Monday [1925], Carl Van Vechten Collection, New York Public Library, New York. Hereafter, CVVC.

7. Arna Bontemps, *Personals* (London: Paul Bremen, 1963), p. 4.

8. Letter to Dorothy Peterson, Thursday 21st [1927], JWJC.

9. Letter to Carl Van Vechten, 1 July 1926, JWJC.

10. Georgia Douglas Johnson, "The Contest Spotlight," *Opportunity* (July 1927), p. 204.

11. Gilbert Osofsky, *Harlem: The Making of a Ghetto, Negro New York, 1890–1930* (1965; rpt. New York: Harper & Row, 1968).

12. Mary Rennels, *The New York Telegram*, 13 April 1929.

13. Letter to Carl Van Vechten, Friday sixth. [1926], JWJC.

14. Letter to Dorothy Peterson, Tuesday 19th [1927], JWJC.

15. Letter to Fania Marinoff and Carl Van Vechten, 22 May 1930, JWJC.

16. Letter to Carl Van Vechten, 1 May 1928, JWJC.

17. Mary Rennels, *New York Telegram*, 13 April 1929.

18. Langston Hughes, *The Big Sea: An Autobiography* (New York:
     Knopf, 1940), pp. 227–228.

19. Alain Locke, "Harlem: Dark Weather-Vane," *Survey Graphic*, 25
     (August 1936), 457–462, 493–495.

20. Letter to Carl Van Vechten, Wednesday [1926], CVVC.

21. Rennels, *New York Telegram*, 13 April 1929.

22. Letter to Carl Van Vechten, 7 April 1931, JWJC.

23. Langston Hughes, "The Negro Artist and the Racial Mountain,"
     The Nation, 23 June 1926, pp. 692–694; reprinted in *Voices from
     the Harlem Renaissance*, ed. Nathan Irvin Huggins (New York:
     Oxford University Press, 1976), p. 307.

24. In NAACP Papers, Library of Congress, Washington, D.C.

25. Letter to Walter White, 25 June 1925, NAACP Papers, Library of
     Congress, Washington, D.C.

26. Locke, "Harlem: Dark Weather-Vane," *Survey Graphic*, 25
     (August 1936), 457.

27. Letter to Carl Van Vechten, Monday [1925], CVVC.

28. Guggenheim Application, 14 November 1929, GFF.

The Star of Ethiopia:
A Contribution Toward the Development of Black Drama and Theater in the Harlem Renaissance

FREDA L. SCOTT

At Fisk he sang. At Harvard he won second place in an oratorical contest and staged a reading of Aristophanes' *The Birds* with some black fellow students. When he went to teach at Wilberforce College, he imagined the possibility of a student production of *A Midsummer Night's Dream* in a beautiful campus glade. W.E.B. DuBois loved the theater, affectionately terming the unpublished dramas he wrote "my illegitimate children."[1] But drama was more than an interest and avocation for him. DuBois believed in drama as an instrument of instruction and enlightenment, and as a valuable weapon in the black cultural and political propaganda arsenal. He was an advocate for black drama in the Harlem Renaissance and helped usher in a resurgence of community interest in black drama and theater by writing and producing the pageant, *The Star of Ethiopia.*

When he chronicled a life of vast and varied achievement in his final autobiography, DuBois gave his theatrical contributions a spare paragraph:

. . . The pageant was an attempt to put into dramatic form
for the benefit of large masses of people, a history of the
Negro race. It was first attempted in the New York
celebration of Emancipation in 1913; it was repeated with
magnificent and breath-taking success in Washington with
1,200 participants; it was given again in Philadelphia in
1916; and in Los Angeles in 1924. Finally I attempted a little
theatre movement which went far enough to secure for our
little group second prize in an international competition in
New York.[2]

The Krigwa Players have often been discussed, as well as
DuBois's theater criticism and the *Crisis* literary contests he
instituted, of which playwriting was a part. Less has been
said about the pageants, and about their possible significance.

Pageantry was extremely popular in America during the
first quarter of the twentieth century; it was viewed by some
as a precursor to a national American theater, which became
an intensely sought after goal at a time when dramatists
were turning toward reflections of American life in an
American form, primarily through the study of American
folk ways. Thomas H. Dickenson, in his book *The Case of
American Drama*, published in 1915, saw the pageant as a
transitional form incorporating "primitive" art, which would
lead to a national drama:

Among the social developments of the past ten years
none has been more significant than the rapid growth of
pageantry. . . .
The significance of the pageant is thus a dual one. On
the one side it signifies an active society seeking an outlet
for its common energies. On the other side it represents an
appropriation on a large scale by the people themselves of
new agencies of artistic expression . . . and the use of these
agencies for their own purposes and according to their own
methods.[3]

DuBois was aware of this national enthusiasm and saw in it
an opportunity: "It seemed to me that it might be possible
with such a demonstration to get people interested in this
development of Negro drama to teach on the one hand the

colored people themselves the meaning of their history and their rich, emotional life through a new theatre, and on the other, to reveal the Negro to the white world as a human, feeling thing."[4]

DuBois started the first of several drafts of *The Star of Ethiopia* in 1911.[5] At first he called the work *The Jewel of Ethiopia: A Masque in—Episodes* (there were six in the first draft). Since the masque is more allegorical than commemorative, he began with a scene in which Shango, God of Thunder, gives the Jewel of Freedom to Ethiopia in return for her soul. The jewel finally reaches the United States after being lost and found several times. There the foundation stones of Labor, Wealth, Justice, Beauty, Education, and Truth are laid and the jewel is finally ensconced on a Pillar of Light and placed on this foundation. Finally, there is a celebratory tableau with the entire cast. The thirteen leading characters included the Queen of Sheba, Nat Turner, Toussaint L'Ouverture, and Mohammed Askia.

In subsequent drafts, the Jewel of Freedom became the Star of Faith, and some of the allegorical elements of the Masque were blended into a historical presentation. By 1913 the title had become *The People of People and Their Gifts to Men*, which was published in *The Crisis* after its presentation at the National Emancipation Exposition in New York on October 23, 25, 28, and 30, 1913.

A prelude was followed by six episodes. The setting was the Court of Freedom before the Egyptian-inspired Temple of Beauty, where heralds announced "the tale of the eldest and strongest of the races of mankind, whose faces be black." Each episode would illustrate the gifts of the black man to the world.

The first gift is the Gift of Iron. During a violent storm in ancient Africa, during which the men, women, and children of the tribe sing, dance, and pray to their gods, a Veiled Woman appears bearing the gifts of fire and iron. The storm is replaced by the sound of drums as a flourishing civilization grows amid feasting and dancing.

The second gift is the Gift of Civilization in the Valley of the Nile. There is a triumphant procession as Ra, the Black

Pharaoh, ascends his throne, to be joined later by the Queen of Sheba and Candace of Meroe. The third gift, the Gift of Faith, is announced.

There is a battle between the warriors of Songhay and the Muslims, who conquer them. Some of the Muslims retain captives as slaves. There is another procession, led by Mansa Musa on horseback, followed by Muslim priests and scholars.

The Gift of Humiliation is the fourth gift. Muslims and Black Africans trade slaves to Europeans. Christian missionaries enter, protesting to no avail. A silence falls, out of which the sound of moaning grows; the moaning gradually becomes the spiritual, "Nobody Knows the Trouble I've Seen." The slaves dance the Dance of Death and Pain, then clear the stage. The Dance of the Ocean follows, symbolizing the middle passage.

The fifth episode delineates a Gift of Struggle Toward Freedom. The history of blacks in the New World is illustrated, beginning with Alonzo, Columbus's pilot, and their introduction to native Americans. This is followed by Stephen Dorantes's discovery of New Mexico, and then we see slavery under the French and Spanish, culminating in the revolt of the Maroons and Toussaint L'Ouverture's leadership of Haiti's liberation. The British and Americans enter the action; suddenly King Cotton arrives followed by Greed, Vice, Luxury, and Cruelty. Nat Turner attempts rebellion and is killed; the slaves sink into despair.

The final, and longest, episode is the Gift of Freedom. The Veiled Woman reappears as slaves begin to escape. The abolitionists come, and then John Brown, Frederick Douglass, and Sojourner Truth. Union soldiers enter, then children, followed by the Laborer, the Artisan, the Servant of Men, the Merchant, the Inventor, the Musician, the Actor, the Teacher, Law, Medicine, Ministry, and the Veiled Woman, now called the All-Mother, who carries a bust of Lincoln. The heralds recapitulate the gifts, as banners, which were used to reinforce the announcement of each episode, proclaim that the play is done.[6]

The Star of Ethiopia is not directly mentioned in the first performed text, but the Court of Freedom before the Temple of

Beauty is shaped as a five-pointed star, according to an existing floor plan.[7] In subsequent productions, the Star is referred to directly and its symbolism enunciated:

> Hear ye, hear ye all them that come to know the Truth and forget not the humblest and wisest of the races of men whose faces be black! Remember forever and a day the Star of Ethiopia and its gifts to men: the Iron gift and gift of Faith, the Pain of Humility and Sorrow Song of Pain and Freedom, eternal Freedom underneath the Star. Children of [New York, Washington, Philadelphia, Los Angeles]: arise and go. The play is done! The play is done![8]

DuBois was a member of the Board of Governors of the National Emancipation Exposition of New York, held at the Twelfth Regiment Armory at 62nd Street and Columbus Avenue from October 22 through October 31, 1913, to commemorate the fiftieth anniversary of the Emancipation Proclamation. A few other states planned celebrations, but New York's was by far the most elaborate. The plan was that there would be exhibits to illustrate black progress and attainment and to indicate contemporary conditions; the pageant would provide a historical setting and lend an appropriate ceremonial feeling to the entire event. The entire budget for the Exposition was $25,000. From some portion of this, 350 participants in the pageant were costumed, musicians were hired, and the set was built. DuBois handled producing responsibilities, giving Charles Burroughs the position of Pageant Master. Burroughs, whom DuBois had taught at Wilberforce, directed all four productions of the pageant. It was Burroughs who provided the continuity and put the pageant in stageable form. DuBois reported that over 30,000 people[9] visited the Exposition; over 14,000 viewed the pageant.[10]

The effort was exhausting but rewarding. However, two years later, in 1915, funds became available for the repetition of the pageant in Washington, D.C., through DuBois's efforts. He formed an independent producing organization, the Horizon Guild; he contributed $500 of his own money and set out to raise $3,000 more. By the time the guild set up an office in Washington, it had only three weeks to prepare for the performance. A citizen's committee, The National Pageant and Dramatic Association, was formed in Washington to cooperate with the Horizon Guild.

There were over 700 additional costumes to be made, since 1200 people, including a chorus of 200 singers, would participate in the performances. These performances had 53 pieces of music by Afro-Americans and were held at the American League Baseball Park on October 11, 13, and 15, 1915. This time an admission fee of 25 cents was charged. The Manual Training Department of the Public Schools built the set and made the props; the cooperation of the Superintendent of Colored Education in providing space and manpower proved invaluable. The production aspect of the pageant was also enhanced by the addition of J. Rosamond Johnson, highly regarded composer and musicologist, and brother of James Weldon Johnson, as Director of Music. The form of the pageant itself was altered a bit; it was now and would remain *The Star of Ethiopia*.

There were five scenes: The Gift of Iron; The Relation of Mulatto Egypt with Black Africa; The Culmination of African Civilization (200 A.D.–1500 A.D.); The Valley of Humiliation (slavery); The Triumph of the Negro over the Ghosts of Slavery (ending in the building of the Tower of Light).[11] Symbolic representations of the rivers Nile, Niger, Congo, Zambesi, Mississippi, and Hudson were added. The Colored District Militia was enlisted for the battle episodes.

The Washington Bee, a black newspaper, ecstatically termed the pageant "The Greatest Event in the History of Colored America," and noted that "our most distinguished scholar" hoped to produce the pageant in ten more cities. Also noted was the fact what while some whites contributed substantial funds toward producing the pageant, only a negligible number of whites attended.[12]

The Washington production was a success in every way except financially. Since it cost a bit over $4400 to produce and took in $3176.35 at the gate, it ended up with a deficit of approximately $1226.[13] The committee of citizens guaranteed

The Crisis, 11, 2 (December 1915), Cover.

THE QUEEN OF SHEBA
(Miss Adella Parks)

ETHIOPIA
(Miss Eleanor Curtis)

CANDACE OF MEROE
(Miss Gregoria Fraser)

From the Pageant: "The Star of Ethiopia"

The Crisis, 11, 2, (December 1915), 90.

payment of all debts, but this deficit was a setback to DuBois's long-term plans.

DuBois thought the presentation of *The Star of Ethiopia* in Philadelphia would be the last. One thousand participants staged the pageant in the 15,000 seat Convention Hall on May 16, 18, and 20, 1916, "illustrating the history of religious faith in the Negro race and commemorating the 100th anniversary of the meeting of the General Conference of the African Methodist Episcopal Church."[14] With all funds exhausted and no further hope of production in sight, DuBois reflected on his pioneering efforts in *The Crisis*:

> For while it lacked the curious thrill and newness of the New York production and the mysterious glamour of shadow, star and sky which made the Washington pageant unforgettable, yet Philadelphia in its smoothness and finish was technically the best.
>
> . . . The Negro is essentially dramatic. His greatest gift to the world has been and will be a gift of art, of appreciation and realization of beauty. . . .
>
> All through Africa pageantry and dramatic recital is closely mingled with religious rites and in America the "shout" of the church revival is in its essential pure drama. . . .
>
> Recently . . . a new and inner demand for Negro drama has arisen. . . . The next step will undoubtedly be the slow growth of a new folk drama built around the actual experience of Negro American life. . . .
>
> The great fact has been demonstrated that pageantry among colored people is not only possible, but in many ways is of unsurpassed beauty and can be made a means of uplift and education and the beginning of folk drama.[15]

DuBois went on to comment wistfully that all that was left of the pageant was a thousand dollars worth of costumes and props; but he was pleased that the seed of Afro-American pageantry had been sown, noting that *The Star of Ethiopia* had inspired a Shakespeare pageant among Washington blacks and two masques in Cincinnati, with additional inquiries about the pageant pouring in from many other places. He also noted that the white community stood aloof from all this activity, and that "The American Pageant Association has been silent, if not actually contemptuous." DuBois also suffered the slings and arrows of petty jealousies and dissatisfactions within the black community.[16]

Problems notwithstanding, *The Star of Ethiopia* stands as a nearly phenomenal achievement. Tens of thousands witnessed it; several thousand were involved in its execution. This was truly a communal effort, a source of social cohesiveness and artistic pride. For a great number of those thousands, it must have been an introduction to both black history and drama. There is no way to measure what this effort must have meant in terms of audience development and interest in black drama and theater, but it had to be significant. Though the body of drama which was developed during the Harlem Renaissance years may not be remembered as great, *The Star of Ethiopia* helped prepare the way for much of the theatrical activity that DuBois had predicted. It helped sustain the hope that the presentation of blacks in a theatrical setting could be freed from the negative images that had dominated the American stage.

But Philadelphia was not the end for the pageant. Though DuBois remembered the Los Angeles production of *The Star of Ethiopia* as having taken place in 1924, the pageant was performed at the Hollywood Bowl, June 15 and 18, 1925. DuBois's records do not appear to be as extensive on this production, but his correspondence shows that he and Burroughs went to Los Angeles in May 1925. In a comment published in *The Crisis*, Dubois stated that over 300 performed in the pageant, which cost about $5,000 to produce. A few years earlier he had spent less to put 1200 onstage. He does not appear to have remembered the Los Angeles production as fondly as he did the others.[17] Since DuBois and Burroughs founded the Krigwa Players in August 1925[18] and the literary contests were under way in addition to DuBois's other activities, they may have felt it was time to move on to the next step toward a national Afro-American theater.

DuBois had originally thought that the pageants might raise funds for the National Association for the Advancement of Colored People. Later, he changed his goal and sought to form an independent, non-profit producing organization:

> The Horizon Guild, which will eventually be incorporated, proposes to present pageants of Negro history in the principal centers of Negro population during the next decade [1915–1925]. It is hoped in this way to form a sound basis for the dignified celebration of the adoption of the Fourteenth Amendment in 1916, the Ter-Centenary of the Landing of the Negro in 1919 and the Jubilee of the Fifteenth Amendment in 1920.[19]

DuBois felt strongly that the rendering of historical events in pageant form could have a greater, more lasting impact than any exhibit or lecture. Unfortunately, the funding base was never established; his plans were not to be. The only pageant produced was *The Star of Ethiopia*, and it was not performed in as many locations as DuBois had hoped.

DuBois did publish another pageant, *George Washington and Black Folk*, in *The Crisis* in 1932. This pageant commemorated the bicentenary of Washington's birth and told, through the actual words of those involved and through Washington's letters and documents, of George Washington's attitude toward and treatment of blacks at various stages of his life and career. Great black figures of the period and their contributions were featured. The construction of the text, held together through the sorcery of the Witch of Endor, who is a black seeress, is quite imaginative and interesting.

Other pageants among DuBois's papers include *The History of the Negro in America in Twelve Living Pictures*, which is undated, and *Nine Tales of Black Folk* (later *Ten Tales of Black Folk*) dated 1941, for which DuBois left a manuscript and notes for a film to be based on the material of the pageant. A pageant-play entitled *The All-Mother*, which is different from *The Star of Ethiopia* in its use of the All-Mother, is included in his unpublished volume of plays entitled *Playthings of the Night*. One manuscript of this book is dated 1931. DuBois's plays reflect his background in the classics and his love of fable, parable, and allegory.

DuBois created *The Star of Ethiopia,* and *The Star of Ethiopia* helped develop DuBois as dramatist and producer. He was responsible for a theatrical event for which there has probably been no single comparable event in black American theater before or since. This experience must have been helpful to him as producer of the Krigwa Players Little Negro Theatre, which he ran from 1925 through 1927.

The Star of Ethiopia is a component of black dramatic development during the Harlem Renaissance years which deserves further documentation and more than a passing reference in black theater history books. This pageant may also be viewed as the forgotten forebear to the pageant-like, ceremonially inspired, ritual dramas which were part of a search for a national black drama in the 1960s and 1970s. The objectives were the same: to instruct, to commemorate, to instill pride, and to foster a dramatic form truly reflective of African-American thought and culture.

NOTES

1. The Papers of W.E.B. DuBois at the University of Massachusetts at Amherst, microfilm reel 87 (Columbia University Library copy).

2. W.E.B. DuBois, *The Autobiography of W.E.B. DuBois* (New York: International Publishers, 1968), pp. 270–271.

3. Thomas H. Dickenson, *The Case of American Drama* (New York: Houghton Mifflin, 1915), p. 147.

4. W.E.B. DuBois, "The Drama Among Black Folk," *The Crisis,* 12, 4 (August 1916), 171.

5. DuBois, "The Star of Ethiopia," *The Crisis,* 11, 2 (December 1915), 90.

6. DuBois, "The People of Peoples and Their Gifts to Men (The National Emancipation Exposition)," *The Crisis,* 7, 1 (November 1913), 339–341.

7. The Papers of W.E.B. DuBois.

8. W.E.B. DuBois, "The Pageant of the Angels," *The Crisis,* 30, 5 (September 1925), 217.

9. DuBois, "The Exposition," *The Crisis,* 7, 2 (December 1913), 84.

10. DuBois, "The Star of Ethiopia," *The Crisis,* 11, 2 (December 1915), 90.

11. The Papers of W.E.B. DuBois.

12. Andrew Hilyer, "The Great Pageant," *The Washington Bee* (23 October 1915), n.p.

13. The Papers of W.E.B. DuBois.

14. *The Crisis,* 12, 1 (May 1916), rear cover.

15. DuBois, "The Drama Among Black Folk," p., 169.

16. Ibid., p. 171.

17. DuBois, "The Pageant of the Angels," p. 217.

18. DuBois, "In High Harlem—The Krigwa Players Little Theatre," *New York Amsterdam News,* 5 October 1927, 14.

19. DuBois, "A Pageant," *The Crisis,* September 1915, 231.

Negritude and Humanism:
Senghor's Vision of a Universal Civilization

ALFRED J. GUILLAUME, JR.

If the Harlem Renaissance of the 1920s served as the catalyst for the "New Negro" in the United States, the Negritude movement of the 1930s in Paris sparked a similar renewal for black students from Africa and the Caribbean, who rejected the assimilation of European values and redefined themselves as children of Africa. This journey to the ancestral sources ("pèlerinage aux sources ancestrales")[1] began in 1932 with the publication of *Légitime Défense*, a Communist and surrealist journal that opposed the bourgeoisie. Founded by Etienne Léro, Jules Minnerot, and René Ménil, all from the Antilles, the journal extolled black values and culture. But it was the 1934 literary journal *Etudiant Noir*, of Aimé Césaire, Léon Damas, and Léopold Sédar Senghor, that gave birth to Negritude, the second Negro Renaissance.

Although Césaire coined the word, Senghor, the poet/politician, became Negritude's principal apostle, promoting it in his poetry and essays as well as integrating it into his political posture. Senghor defined Negritude as the "sum total of black cultural values."[2] This ideology was as much a reaction against the imposition of European culture as a celebration of African civilization. Through Negritude, the

black rediscovers the self and reaffirms the riches of his own
heritage.

This reawakening of blackness by the students in Paris
did not develop in isolation. The Harlem writers were a
major source of inspiration. For Senghor, to proclaim one's
blackness, one's Negritude, was to reclaim one's humanity.
The Harlem Renaissance writers had done so, and Senghor
read them voraciously, even translating some of their work.
He admired particularly Langston Hughes, whom he met for
the first time in 1959 as a delegate to the U.N. General
Assembly. In a letter to Mercer Cook on 8 September 1967,
Senghor states that Hughes ". . . is the greatest Negro-
American poet. . . . He was, without doubt, the most
spontaneously Negro poet. In other words, he best fulfilled
the notions I have of black cultural values, of Negritude. I
believe, moreover, that Langston felt everything that linked
us—Césaire, Damas, and me—to him."[3]

This spontaneity that Senghor speaks about is emotion;
this, he says, is the special quality that makes one black. His
statement "emotion is black, reason is Greek" ("l'émotion est
nègre, comme la raison hellène")[4] is now legendary and
has caused much consternation among African literati who
feel that Senghor's theories reinforce ideas that the Negro is
inferior. Nevertheless, Senghor insists that emotion enables
blacks to grasp an object intuitively in its totality, its interior
as well as its exterior composition. This unique reaction,
according to Senghor, supersedes rational consciousness and
is a surreal participation of subject and object. He calls this
phenomenon an "attitude of abandon, assimilation, not
domination: attitude of love."[5]

In a 1976 interview with Senghor, I asked him to clarify
what he meant by object. His response was that "the European
seeks to dominate nature, as Descartes once said. He
transforms it to serve his own needs, whereas the Negro-
African considers nature as reality of the object, of that which
is in front of and which is beyond him; he blends into this
reality." To further illustrate his point, Senghor recalled a
dance of the bull that he witnessed at the home of President
Houphouet-Boigny of the Ivory Coast: "The bull's movements

bring forth fertility. Through his movements and gesticulations, [the dancer] allows himself to be seized by the bull's force. The dancer is totally identified with the object, bull. In contrast, the Albo-European sets himself apart from the object; he analyzes it; he uses it as an instrument. The black man abandons himself into the object to live its essence. This is called emotion."[6] Hence, for Senghor, the black man lives the object. There is a symbiosis of the real world and the imagination. In his response to nature as assimilator, he expands himself as subject and object.

That the Harlem Renaissance writers expressed a sensual celebration of life, is, according to Senghor, due to their African heritage. That they demonstrated a continuity of a past musical heritage (the link between the tom-tom and the swing of the trumpet), an outpouring of religious sentiment (the correlation between the African's respect for the cosmic forces and his ancestral dead and the Negro-Americans' image of God) is due to their shared Negritude.

Senghor's Negritude is a revalidation of the humanistic elements of African society. From Africa's innocence a new order of fraternal love and respect will emerge. Nowhere is this more apparent than in Senghor's poetic evocation of childhood. Through the exploration of this distant reality, Senghor rediscovers the lost world of unrestrained happiness. His intention is twofold: to become an individual mind united with nature and to retain the continuity that he associates with an African feeling for life. This emphasis on intensity and communion is the source of a profound feeling that progresses beyond personal fulfillment and in his poetry is often linked to a sociopolitical vision. Beginning with the emptiness of his Parisian environment experienced as a student, Senghor visualizes a fuller life for himself and all oppressed people through childhood innocence.

This retreat into memories of childhood is a rejection of Europe and a return to family, the ancestors, and the land, all of which represent a restoration of beauty and simplicity. This quest is not simply romantic idealization but a tangible reality that the poet can recall at will: "I only need to name things, the elements of my childhood universe, in order to

prophesy the City of Tomorrow, that will rise from the ashes
of the past. That's the poet's mission."[7] In order to purify
himself from the "contagions of being civilized" ("contagions
de civilisé") ("Que m'accompagnent kôras et balafong"),
Senghor uses the imagination to dissolve all conflicts
between himself and the external world; he recreates the
oneness with nature that he experienced as a child, thus
maintaining an indissoluble link with the splendor of
African life. He says of himself and of the other students
exiled in Paris: "We walked, equipped with the miraculous
arms of double vision, piercing the blind walls, discovering,
recreating the marvels of the Childhood Kingdom. We were
re-born through Negritude."[8] His poetry inevitably leads to
the complex questions of his attitudes toward Europe and of
the poetic and social function which he as a writer assigns
himself.

In Senghor's mind the innocence of Africa is somehow
the guardian of the innocence that Europe has lost:

> At the turn in the road, the river, blue in the cool
>   September fields
> A Paradise that protects from fevers a child with eyes
>   as bright as two swords
> Paradise my African childhood, which kept watch over the
>   innocence of Europe
>   ("Que m'accompagnent kôras et balafong")[9]

According to Senghor, the freshness of childhood assures the
triumph of what poetic reverie reveals, the possibility of a
future society of universal brotherhood. Although he does not
explain in detail how this will happen, childhood innocence
is thus broadened to include the promise of Africa's
sociopolitical future. What is certain is that his prophetic
vision involves a transcendence whereby the Europeanized
psyche of the poet dies in order to be purified in the child:

> Oh! to die to childhood, may the poem die[,] the syntax
>   disintegrate, may all the inessential words be
>   swallowed up.
> The weight of the rhythm suffices, no need of

words-cement to build on the rock the City of
Tomorrow.
("Elégie des circoncis," *Nocturnes*)[10]

These lines from an elegy recall a youth's initiation rites but
also the poet's re-initiation into the childlike universe that
he associates with a new society.

Senghor's messianic quest, as poet and politician, is to
seek the New Day, the Clear Dawn of the New Day ("Aube
transparente d'un jour nouveau") that will include the
emancipation of all colonized peoples and oppressed workers.
This metaphor of the "Clear Dawn" is of utmost importance
in his ideology and is the conclusion of "A l'appel de la race
de Saba" (*Hosties Noires*), a poem that shows the complexities
of Senghor's vision of Africa, nature, and politics. It
demonstrates how in the poet's mind the return to the
African experience of his childhood is identical to the
struggle for liberation. Part I of the poem introduces themes
of exile and nostalgia; Part II shows how the poet's memory
of family and community preserved him from the evils of
European society. Parts III and IV express Senghor's desire to
unite Africa and Europe, but also reveal the danger of
becoming an *assimilé*. But against that risk is the need to
engage in the communal combat for freedom. The poem thus
demonstrates how, in Senghor's mind, the return to the
African experience of his childhood is identical to the
struggle for liberation.

The child motif is a symbol of Senghor's political vision.
This is especially evident in "The Return of the Prodigal Son"
("Le Retour de l'Enfant prodigue"), a poem that contrasts the
childlike world with the destructiveness of war, the "mud of
civilization" ("la boue de la Civilisation"), that Senghor had
known during his sixteen years of separation from Africa.
Like a number of other poems, it is a stormy attack on the
oppressive aspects of European society, but the poet asserts that
he is preserved from hatred and favors fraternity. He is
willing to die for his people, but realizes that he can best
serve as "Master of Language—Nay, name me its ambassador"
("Maître de Langue—Mais non, nomme-moi son

ambassadeur"). He must stop European destruction of nature and resurrect his own past: "I resurrect my earthly virtues!" ("Je ressuscite mes vertus terriennes!"). Again, it is clear that Senghor's poetic-political undertaking springs from his adherence to the values of his African childhood:

> Oh! to sleep once more in the clean bed of my childhood
> Oh! once more the dear black hands of my mother tucking
>   me to sleep
> Once more the bright smile of my mother.
> Tomorrow, I will again take the road to Europe, the
>   road of my embassy
> Homesick for my black native land.[11]

Often in Senghor's poetry, his political mission presents certain ambiguities that appear to contradict this idealistic conception of justice inspired by childhood nostalgia, but a complete treatment of these issues is beyond the scope of this essay. It is instructive to note that in "Que m'accompagnent kôras et balafong," an early poem, Senghor's cleansing of the physical and psychic assimilation of European culture and his ultimate victory to restore Africa's dignity and nobility are not without violence and retribution. The poet as Archangel and trumpeter of justice purges his people of centuries of slave trade with a sword that spills the blood of colonizers into Europe's rivers. Similar ambiguities between Senghor the African and Senghor the European parallel the conflicts between Senghor the politician and Senghor the poet. These are especially apparent in the dramatic poem "Chaka."

Written about a Zulu chief who fought the whites early in the nineteenth century, the poem attempts at first to justify the use of violence to defend primitivistic values. Divided into two sections (*chants*), the poem is an apology for Chaka, who caused many Africans to suffer. Accused by the *Voix blanche* of killing Nolivé, an embodiment of woman-Afrika, Chaka responds, in the first *chant*, that her death is an act of love and ultimately the liberation of his people from European aggression. Her death is a new life that assures the continuity of African civilization. She is a sacrificial victim of the politician in his fight against the oppressor. A man of action and fortitude, Chaka destroys the poet within him. Both deaths are necessary for the liberation of the African people. Politics is Chaka's calvary, but it is an unselfish response to racism, exploitation, and colonialism. In spite of the suffering brought upon his people by the "Pink Ears" ("Roses-d'oreilles"), Chaka insists that his mission is not one of hate, but one of reconciliation and love.

In the second *chant*, however, Chaka loses his political persona and becomes Senghor, the poet. The violence-love of the first section is replaced by childhood-love that glorifies Africa's renaissance. As poet, Chaka envisions the serenity of childhood as a sociopolitical symbol of universal peace. Chaka is praised as a hero. His love for his people culminates in the sexual bond between him and Nolivé, a union that celebrates the living forces of African society. He is the prophet of a new order and the creator of life, a mission for which he was prepared by the serenity of childhood and the loneliness of exile.

From the union of lover and beloved, poet and Africa, arises the "new world" in an act of universal creativity. How this will come about remains unexplained. Perhaps it is mere mystification. Within the poem, however, it involves an ultimate triumph. Chaka's death is somehow an augury to the resurrection of the Africa to which Senghor aspires and to the creation of a future society void of oppression.

Senghor's vision of childhood, his idealization of an Africa of innocence and primeval goodness might appear diluted by his affection for France: "I have a strong weakness for France" (". . . j'ai une grande faibless pour la France") ("Prière de paix," *Hosties Noires*). And he wrote further: "Ah! don't say that I don't love France. . . ." ("Ah! ne dites pas que je n'aime pas la France. . . .") ("Poème liminaire," *Hosties Noires*). In fact, the series of poems, "Epitres à la Princesse" (*Ethiopiques*), written to a European princess and involving themes of love, separation, and death, seems to compromise his fidelity to Africa and to his mission. And yet he makes it clear in "Que m'accompagnent kôras et balafong" that if at any time he were forced to choose, he would choose Africa:

But if I must choose at the moment of ordeal
I would choose the verse of the rivers, of the
    winds and of the forests
The assonance of plains, and of streams.
I would choose the rhythm of the blood of my
    unclothed body
I would choose the trill of the balafongs and
    the euphony of the strings.
I would choose my weary black people, my peasant people.[12]

He reminds those who may consider him a servant of white European culture that before he was a teacher of French boys and an obedient civil servant, he was a child of Africa, nourished by the rich traditions of his people. The message of Senghor's Negritude, then, is that the humanity of Africa is preferable to the mechanization of Europe.

Some critics believe that Senghor's vision of Negritude fails because it appears to perpetuate the myth of the inferior Negro. Kofi Anyidiho, for example, referring to Senghor's romantic quest, states, "The only problem . . . is that he chooses the wrong myths for the cause of Negritude he claims to be championing. Not only are his myths compromised by his reliance on anthropological views of Africa; they conform too well to all the old stereotypes of colonialism, with their emphasis on the irrational, the sensuous, the luxuriant, the dark, the ingenuous, the compulsively self-giving."[13] Negritude, according to Stanislas Adotevi, is pure propaganda and "a panacea the president-poet uses for problems of government . . . an opium."[14] Frederick Ivor Case calls it a "philosophic aberration," and asserts that "the concept of Negritude cannot be the answer to any situation pertaining to the reality of the black masses."[15]

Yet fifty years after the founding of the Negritude movement, Senghor still tenaciously views it as the path to universal culture, conceiving his own childhood and youth as an ageless symbol of Africa's past, present, and future, a vibrant Africa, where rests the promise of mankind.

NOTES

1. Léopold Sédar Senghor, *Liberté I: Négritude et Humanisme* (Paris: Editions du Seuil, 1964), p. 103.

2. Ibid., p. 260.

3. Mercer Cook, "Afro-Americans in Senghor's Poetry," *Hommage à Léopold Sédar Senghor: Homme de Culture* (Paris: Présence Africaine, 1976), p. 154.

4. *Liberté I*, p. 24. (All translations are mine.)

5. ". . . attitude d'abandon, d'assimilation, non de domination: attitude d'amour," ibid., p. 71.

6. "L'Européen, aujourd'hui, cherche a être le maître de la nature, comme le disait Descartes. Il transforme la nature pour l'asservir aux desseins, aux désirs de l'homme, tandis que le Négro-Africain sent la nature comme une réalité de l'*objet*, de ce qui est posé en face de lui et qui le dépasse, et il se plie a cette réalité. . . . Le taureau est signe de fécondité. Ce jeune danseur dansiat la danse du taureau, en reproduisant les gestes caractéristiques de l'animal, pour mimer et faire venir la fécondité. Par les figures et le rythme de ses gestes, il se laissait saisir par la force du taureau. Il s'identifiait à l'objet taureau. Tout au contraire, l'Albo-Européen se distingue de l'objet. Il l'analyse et s'oppose à lui pour le maîtriser et s'en servir comme d'un instrument, quand nous, Négro-Africains, nous abandonnons à l'objet pour vivre son essence. C'est cela l'émotion.

7. "Il m'a donc suffi de nommer les choses, les éléments de mon univers enfantin, pour prophétiser la Cité de demain, qui renaîtra des cendres de l'ancienne, ce qui est la mission du poète," *Liberté I*, p. 221.

8. "Nous marchions, munis des armes miraculeuses de la double vue, perçant les murs aveugles, découvrant, recréant les merveilles du Royaume d'Enfance. Nous renaissions à la Négritude," ibid., p. 99. The "armes miraculeuses" of which the poet speaks is the power of the written word and an obvious allusion to the poem by Aimé Césaire, "Les Armes miraculeuses," that appeared in 1940 in the journal *Tropiques*. This title later appeared as a volume of poetry in 1970 published by Gallimard.

9.   "Au détour du chemin la revière, bleue par les prés frais de
     Septembre./Un paradis que garde des fièvres une enfant aux
     yeux clairs comme deux épées/Paradis mon enfance africaine,
     qui gardait l'innoncence de l'Europe," Léopold Sédar Senghor,
     Piènes (Paris: Editions du Seuil, 1964). All citations following are
     from this edition.

10. "Ah! mourir à l'enfance, que meure le poème se désintègre la
     syntaxe, que s'abîment tous les mots qui ne sont pas
     essentiels./Le poids du rythme suffit, pas besoin de mots-ciment
     pour bâtir sur le roc la cité de demain."

11. "Ah! de nouveau dormir dans le lit frais de mon enfance!/Ah!
     bordent de nouveau mon sommeil les si chères main noires/Et
     de nouveau le blanc sourire de ma mère./Demain, je repredrai le
     chemin de l'Europe, chemin de l'ambassade/Dans le regret du
     Pays noir."

12. "Mais s'il faut choisir à l'heure de l'épreuve/J'ai choisi le verset
     des fleuves, des vents et des fôrets/L'assonance des plaines et des
     rivières, choisi le rythme de sang de mon corps dépouillé/Choisi
     la trémulsion des balafongs et l'accord des cordes. . . ./J'ai choisi
     mon peuple noir peinant, mon peuple paysan."

13. Kofi Anyidiho, "Kingdom of Childhood: Senghor and the
     Romantic Quest," *French Review*, May 1982, p. 769.

14. Stanislas Adotevi, *Négritude et Négrologues* (Paris: Union
     générale 10:18, 1972), p. 114.

15. Frederick Ivor Case, "Negritude and Utopianism," *African
     Literature Today*, ed. Eldred Durosimi Jones, No. 7 (1975), p. 74.

Léopold Sédar Senghor's
Freedom I—Negritude and Humanism (1964)

WENDELL A. JEAN-PIERRE

In *Freedom I—Negritude and Humanism,*[1] Senghor focuses on the concept of Negritude as a cultural, racial, and humanist construct. He reiterates his definition of Negritude as the sum of the values of African civilization and, by extension, as a humanism transcending narrow racial particularisms in that it opens up a universal horizon embracing all mankind. According to this view, then, Negritude is racial but not racist. It does affirm, however, what Senghor asserts to be racial specificities peculiar to those of African descent. By cultivating one's "différence," to paraphrase André Gide, by affirming that which is seen as particular or unique to an individual or to a people, it becomes possible to achieve universality. The affirmation of blackness, historically determined by the thesis and practice of the doctrine of white supremacy and reinforced by oppression based on race and color, inevitably gave birth to the advent of Negritude and to the affirmation of one's humanity as a black member of the human community. Senghor's concept of Negritude of his more mature years, however, and his progressive elaboration of it during that period, are quite different from the Negritude he espoused in the 1930s during his student years in Paris when he defined the concept primarily to indicate a rejection of the French policy of cultural assimilation as practiced before World War II on the colonized peoples of Africa and the French West Indies.

> The French-speaking Negro-African elite were all fashioned during the interval between the two world wars in the same French rationalist school of thought. . . . We received the same education and docilely accepted its values. . . . Our ambition was to become negative copies of the colonizers, "black-skinned Frenchmen."
>
> Negritude, as we first conceived of it and began to define it, was a weapon of refuge and combat more than an instrument of liberation. We only retained those of its values which were opposed to the values of Europe. . . .[2]

Initially, therefore, Negritude as conceived by the founders of the movement was a violent rejection of French cultural assimilation. It signaled, simultaneously, the emergence of a black self-awareness ("prise de conscience") while celebrating the spiritual and traditional values of African civilization. These values were opposed to a way of life—Western civilization—that Senghor judged to "have died of machines and cannons."[3] Subsequently, Senghor's Negritude emphasized the preeminence of culture over politics and informed his efforts, as the President of Senegal, to formulate and implement political policies in Senegal and French-speaking West Africa in the light of this emphasis.

The affirmation of blackness was originally a negative postulate in that it was defined against a European humanism in which the intellectual black elite could not recognize all the dimensions of the black personality. This humanism, which was asserted as universal in scope, squared poorly with the practices of colonialism and racism. It led Senghor to maintain that "although universalist, the spirit of Europe, because it was European, was mutilated." Senghor felt that Africans were possessed of reserves of humanity that would enable them to "contribute, along with other peoples, to bringing about the unity of the World: to bind the flesh to the spirit, man to his fellow man, the pebble to God, in brief, reality to surreality."[4] African peoples, therefore, must root themselves in and profoundly live their Negritude.

Since Senghorian Negritude betrays itself as a heterogeneous mixture of ideas and influences drawn from disparate sources and fused together to accommodate a particular point of view, it has been criticized as an intellectual bazaar. This reproach merits appreciation, since Senghor, in his efforts to formulate what could be interpreted as the mystique of Negritude, has attempted to synthesize the influences he has assimilated. These influences include the views of the French Jesuit priest Pierre Teilhard de Chardin, Jacques Maritain and other French Catholic philosophers, the Negro Renaissance Movement, the group associated with the *Revue du Monde Noir*, Arthur de Gobineau, Sigmund Freud, Karl Marx, Henri Bergson, Paul Claudel, the French Surrealists, and more significantly the *Weltanschauung* particular to traditional African philosophy and religion. The development of his thought from the 1930s to the publication of *Freedom I—Negritude and Humanism* in 1964 must be assessed in terms of the historical itinerary of the above influences upon him. It was as a boy during World War I that Senghor, then at the missionary school of the Ecole des Pères du Saint Esprit in Joal (Senegal), first assimilated the seeds of self-alienation through the process of French acculturation:

> Those good missionary Fathers led Senghor and his classmates to disavow and scorn the culture of their ancestors. . . . the result was the complete destruction of the child's basic equilibrium. Many years went by before he acquired another.[5]

Years later in his collection of poems, *Chants d'Ombre— Hosties Noires* (Songs of shadow—black victims), the poet evoked this exile from the self occasioned by that experience:

> Bless you fathers, bless you!
> You who permitted mockery, contempt,
> polite offenses, sly innuendoes
> Deprivations and segregation.

And who snatched from this too loving heart
the ties that united it to the world's
pulse.[6]

And that other exile, more shattering to
the heart,
    the snatching of the self from the self
From the language of my mother, from the
skull of the Ancestor, from the tom-tom of
my soul.[7]

The policy of cultural assimilation, as Sartre pointed out in his preface to Fanon's *The Wretched of the Earth*, had made of the black elite in the French colonies "a new species of Greco-Latin Negroes."[8] Ultimately this policy proved to be counter-productive because it confined those it affected to the barren, psychological stretches of Limbo, to that no-man's-land that made for an unbearable psychic isolation. Refusing to be "thingified" ("choseité"), as Fanon labeled it, the leaders of the Negritude movement began to define themselves in opposition to the values associated with assimilation. This engendered a determination to search out and affirm the black deep inner self ("moi profound") and marked the beginnings of black self-affirmation among the French-speaking elite of African antecedents.

There were few blacks in the Paris of the late 1920s and early 1930s. Contact among those there was infrequent. Mutual antagonisms based on color and tribal prejudices kept alive the division that existed among them. With the introduction of French West Indian music into Paris, via the nightclub *Le Bal nègre* where they used to gather, the situation began to change. The prestige of Afro-American musicians and entertainers, carried to the skies ("portés aux nues")[9] by French critics, did much to improve the self-esteem of the black colony and gave impetus to a growing sense of solidarity among them. Writers and poets associated with the Negro Renaissance movement in Harlem began to flock to Paris after World War I and to exert an influence on their black French-speaking counterparts. The International Colonial Exhibition held in Vincennes in 1931 led to greater contact between black scholars and artists from different parts of the globe. Concurrent with the reassessment of the contribution of blacks to the arts and human advancement was the phenomenon of leading European intellectuals articulating their loss of faith in the basic values upon which their society reposed. Recurrent wars and increasing alienation, already the hallmark of a way of life dominated by machines, gave birth to a quest for spiritual fulfillment. An overwhelming desire among European artists and intellectuals to experience life on a deeper level led them to turn their attention to societies that they felt to be still in cosmic pulsation with the basic sources of life. As a result, the values of the "primitive" peoples of Africa, the Oceanic Islanders, and the Indians in the Americas were seen as being capable of furnishing the spiritual nourishment lacking in modern societies.

This development was certainly not unnoticed by Senghor. Moreover, the "flight toward singular and irrational values, desires, fervors, instincts, the pre-eminence of feelings," [10] as well as Henri Bergson's views regarding the primacy of intuition over intelligence, were not at all new to Africans and had indeed always been an integral part of their vision of the world.

It was within the framework of this deep discontent with a way of life whose values appeared to be no longer operative that the avant-garde of the Negritude movement decided to call a halt to the process of cultural assimilation, which Fanon in *Black Skin, White Masks*[11] characterized as a "whitening process that engenders neurotic behavior." The plunge into the *moi profond* became the *sine qua non* of self-recovery. In this attempt for self-recovery, Senghor affirmed the preeminence of culture over politics.

The Negro Renaissance movement served as an example to Senghor by emphasizing the contributions of African-Americans to the dominant culture. *The New Negro*, the anthology-manifesto of the movement, edited by Rhodes scholar Alain Locke, asserted the richness and dynamism of the race's cultural and humanist contributions. As a strategy, given the tenor of the times, it was felt that the race's image would best be redressed by cultural rather than political initiatives. Black Americans were urged to define themselves, affirm their distinctiveness as a people, and lay claim to their African heritage. Its orientation, was, however, frankly assimilationist and accommodationist. Alain Locke's article "The Legacy of the Ancestral Arts" in *The New Negro,*[12] established a connection between the dynamism of Afro-American culture and the African sources from which it originated. Senghor later expanded on this theme in postulating the future contributions of Africa to the world.

Paulette Nardal who, along with Senghor and a small group of Martinique students in Paris had founded the *Revue du Monde Noir* in 1931, urged her colleagues to move in the same direction as their counterparts in Harlem. Nardal and her group were proponents of the integrationist view, especially as far as French culture was concerned. Senghor was attracted to the *Revue's* anti-political stance and subscribed fully to the thesis of culture first of all ("culture d'abord"). Since that time Senghor has steadfastly maintained the primacy of culture over politics to achieve what he calls the "true revolution." Years later, at the First Congress of Black Writers and Artists held at the Sorbonne in 1956, he reaffirmed his position when he declared:

> Experience has proven that cultural liberation is the *sine qua non* of political liberation. . . . If Europe is now beginning to reckon with Africa, it is because African dance, literature, and its traditional philosophy are now imposing themselves upon a henceforth astonished world. . . . [13]

This claim is open to question since Europe was quite content for many years to escape boredom ("tromper l'ennui") by seeking release through the artistic offerings of blacks. If Europe is reckoning with Africa today, it is because European values are being re-examined now and because political developments have brought about changes that can no longer be ignored.

Senghor's view of freedom flows from his particular conception of what true freedom means. Political freedom for him is but an aspect of culture. Man is free when he becomes "integral man," as projected by the French Catholic philosophers whose views Senghor has to some degree assimilated. Senghorian freedom emerges, then, as an absolute freedom, an idea freedom—one that suggests a kind of Sysyphian effort to attain an unrealizable goal, but whose merit, hypothetically, is to be found in the constant effort to attain a height that will remain forever elusive. The attempt, however, may be seen as a purifying process that will enable man to become more man ("plus homme").

Humanism is the broad thematic background of *Freedom I—Negritude and Humanism*. But in this "humanism" to which all Senghorian paths lead are to be found the basic and familiar themes that he constantly reiterates. These themes are the "black soul," the African's unique degree of emotive sensibility ("Emotion is Negro, Reason is Greek"), the advocacy of cultural cross-breeding, integral humanism, the theme of a universal civilization, rhythm, and the black man's contribution to art and human advancement. Senghor has interwoven these themes into his concept of Negritude, which asserts the dominant role of intuitive knowledge and feeling among blacks, the African's community-based outlook on life, and the role dialogue plays in solving problems. These traits, supposedly possessed in some unique way by those of African descent, are opposed to Western man's technological mind, his discursive or analytical reasoning powers, and his individualism. They are seen as specific qualities that reflect themselves in the culture and art of African peoples.

Senghor believes that the "black soul," or the psychology of blacks, is basically explicable by the physical environment and agricultural existence the African lives. He admits that these factors condition the psychology of people living a similar experience, but not to the same degree as with Africans. The African climate, soil, and flora operate in such a way, he points out in "The Essential Elements of a Civilization of Negro-African Inspiration," that they provoke "psychic mutations which become hereditary" (p. 254). This explains the "permanence of psychic characteristics, particularly the gift of emotion . . . among the Negroes of America" (p. 254). This explains the "permanence of psychic characteristics, particularly the gift of emotion . . . among the Negroes of America" (p. 254). This also accounts for the unique degree of emotive sensibility of Africans and for their rhythmic or cosmic pulsation with telluric forces. As a result, the African may be compared to "one of those worms created on the Third Day, a pure field of sense impulses," discovering the other through his subjectivity "at the ends of his sense organs" (p. 259).

Senghor seems to resort here to the argument of geographical determinism to advance what he considers to be permanent racial traits identifiable among blacks, wherever they are to be found. In doing so, he also gives a biological or racial content to culture. This allows him to assign selective characteristics supposedly particular to blacks alone. But geographical determinism as a basis for racial constants seems to have been rejected by modern scientists who feel that man's enormous learning capacity is the most important factor in the development of culture. The influence of climate and ecology in the formation of human groups may be taken as a basic assumption. What is open to question, however, is whether this influence can induce permanent, exclusive racial traits. On balance, it appears that the "black soul" of which Senghor speaks is a product of lived sociogeographic experiences.

Senghor's views in this respect are not without a certain fascination and cannot be categorically refuted on a scientific basis. Nevertheless, the psychophysiology he postulates as being unique to blacks is largely a conceptual distinction that permits him to apply categories which he finds most useful to his personal views of Negritude. He has not successfully accounted for or systematically organized the independent variables of geography, culture, politics, physiology, psychology, and economics—something that must be done in order to establish beyond doubt the existence of what he calls the "black soul." Instead, he has stressed the intersection of ecology and climate to account for a permanent black psychology. The problem is to establish the exact role of ecology and climate vis-à-vis human groups rather than to formulate theories in which they are mobilized to explain all. In this respect, Senghor's approach parallels the Marxist tendency to explain everything in terms of economics.

The African's heightened sensitivity is also accounted for in terms of geographical determinism. This sensitivity is reflected in the relationship of the black man to the Other whom he discovers subjectively rather than analytically. He goes out to the Other. He abandons himself unto the Other in order to be reborn into the Other, declares Senghor, paraphrasing the French poet Paul Claudel (*Freedom I*, p. 259). This manner of discovering the Other is seen by Senghor as a form of knowledge. It is felt knowledge, intuitive knowledge. It transcends surface externals and immediately establishes vital contact with the Other. This emotive sensitivity, or heightened ability to feel, dictates the African's rhythmic rapport with the world. Rhythm is energy, an earth-force that repeats pulsating cosmic patterns. It makes for a characteristic attitude that attains to the essence of things. Senghor reduces the attitude to a syllogism: "I feel the Other, I dance the Other, therefore I am" (p. 259).

The basic intuitive rapport that defines the African's relationship to the world has led Senghor to claim that "Emotion is Negro, Reason is Greek" (p. 259). He has been widely criticized for this opinion by those who feel that it indirectly supports some racist theories that postulate that blacks have a limited intellect. Senghor responds to these attacks by reaffirming his position:

> I have often written that *emotion is Negro,* and have been wrongfully attacked for doing so. I fail to see how it is possible to otherwise account for our specificity, for this *Negritude,* which is "the sum of the cultural values of the black world," including the Americas.
>
> (p. 260)

Senghor also feels that intuitive knowledge represents a deeper dimension of knowledge. It is "integral knowledge," joining "subject and object in an indissoluble synthesis . . .

in a dance of love. Superior knowledge, therefore" (p. 264). By contrast, the analytical rapport of Western man with the world is one that dissects, transforms, and destroys. It defines an antagonistic relationship with nature (and by extension with other men as well). It seeks to impose its will upon nature and the Other. The African, by contrast, lives a symbiotic and empathetic rapport with nature and leaves it largely undisturbed.

In support of his stand that intuitive knowledge is a superior form of knowledge, Senghor refers to leading Western thinkers and scholars. Einstein is quoted as having declared that "mystical emotion" is the source of knowledge (p. 264). This same source informs "Negro art and knowledge," Senghor adds. Engels is cited as having pointed out in the *Anti-Dühring* that there are "laws of thinking and forms of thinking" (p. 259). Intuitive knowledge, therefore, cannot be dismissed as a lesser form of thinking. Finally, Senghor refers us to Marx's reported observation that reason has always existed but not in a rational form (p. 259).

René Ménil pointed out that if one follows Senghor's reasoning, neither the white man nor the black man can be a complete man without the other. They are, in the Senghorian universe, each of them, half a man. They must be joined together in order to produce a whole man:

> . . . On one side, emotion, magic, rhythm, imagination, dance, etc. This is allotted to the Negro. On the other side, reason, science, technicity, the faculty to reason logically. This is the white man's lot. We are in face of two mutilated and incomplete human worlds. The Negro is nothing more than the dark, reversed shadow of the white. Two halves of humanity in which certain faculties are lent to one on the condition that they be refused to the other. Neither L.S. Senghor's Blacks nor Whites are men, if being a man means to be in possession of all of the aptitudes of sensibility, reason, and will power, if being a man means that one must be capable of the infinity of operations peculiar to the human species. . . . In short, following Senghor's theory, it is necessary to add and combine a white man and a black man in order to have a man.[14]

> Senghor's Negro is the Absolute Negro, the Negro from
> nowhere, the Negro outside of social relationships, outside
> of the real world and national context.[15]

Neither Aimé Césaire nor Léon Damas, co-founders with
Senghor of the Negritude movement, share the belief that
"Emotion is Negro, Reason is Greek." For Damas, Negritude
is the rejection of cultural assimilation, which denied him
and his race an acceptable identity. For Césaire, it meant
largely the same thing, in addition to the right to exercise
options and initiatives inseparable from freedom and
sovereignty.

The striking contrast between the Negritude of Senghor
and that of Césaire inevitably invites comparison.
Senghorian Negritude seems to require constant elaboration
because of his attempts to formulate a political synthesis of his
religious, cultural, and humanist views. He advocates the
creation of an international community of nations. He is
willing to concede that Negritude is a myth, just as
democracy and communism are. But it is a dynamic, living
myth and thereby capable of adjusting itself to changes.
Césairian Negritude, on the other hand, stands in no need
of cosmic principles. It does not resort to complex elaborations
to deal with the reality of oppression and exploitation
confronting blacks in this cycle of human history. It simply
seeks to train blacks in an apprenticeship for freedom ("un
apprentissage de la liberté") in order to evolve political
responses leading to independence and to enable them to
create sociopolitical systems in which their personality as a
free people can develop in an unfettered fashion.

Senghor also believes that there is a characteristic "Negro
style" identifiable to blacks wherever they are. The tom-tom
beat discernible in the works of Césaire and Richard
Wright, according to Senghor, is discoverable in the final
analysis in their African racial roots. In the essay, "The
Poetry of the Negro," Senghor wrote:

> I should like to consider for a moment the *style* of our
> poets. I know that it varies according to respective
> temperaments and literary schools. But it is their common

characteristics, their Negro traits to which I wish to give
particular attention. I do not mean to say that similar traits
cannot be found among other peoples. But I do not believe
that they are brought together in so global and illuminating
a manner by which they reveal, more particularly, their
negritude.

(p. 110)

Césaire and Damas do not share this view. They do not deny
that a "Negro style" exists, but they believe that ultimately a
writer's style is a question of his individual temperament.
They do not discount the influences of sociohistorical
experiences that make for a certain similarity in the style of
black writers. This similarity has nothing to do with their
Negro traits ("leurs traits nègres"), but is explainable by the
contradictions of cultural cross-breeding ("métissage") and
the fact of racial oppression.

In *Freedom I—Negritude and Humanism,* Senghor
attempted to demonstrate a philosophy of Negritude based on
racial, humanist, and cultural qualities supposedly exclusive to
those of African descent. What emerges finally is not a
coherent, systematized philosophy, as much as a private point
of view that seeks to accommodate itself to various forces at
play while consistently subscribing to the basic premises the
author holds dear. As the foremost elaborator of a particular
concept of Negritude, Senghor's role seems more noteworthy
on the literary than on a political level. He has introduced
African themes into French literature. He must be counted in
the forefront of that small intellectual group of French-
speaking blacks who helped to raise the level of consciousness
of colonized people within the French orbit at that time. His
Negritude, however, is that of the transitional, French-
speaking African intellectual caught up in the contradictions
of cultural cross-breeding. It is as much Western as it is
African. In his elaboration of the concept of Negritude he has
provided valuable insights. But the "traits nègres" he assigns
as eternal to those of African lineage are not conclusively
demonstrated in *Freedom I—Negritude and Humanism.*
These traits do exist, but are seemingly more accountable in

terms of historical, political, and ecological particulars rather than in terms of race.

In its literary manifestations Negritude originated in the United States, and more particularly with the Harlem Renaissance that served as a model to the Negritude development in Paris among French-speaking blacks in the early 1930s. Whatever its limitation as a movement, the Harlem Renaissance occupies a decisive place in the literary itinerary beginning with W.E.B. DuBois's *Souls of Black Folk* (1903) to the new literary black consciousness unfolding currently in Brazil and elsewhere in the Americas. Included in that continuum are the indigenous movement in Haiti following the occupation of the island by American marines in 1915, and the flourishing output of poetry, novels, and plays that came out of the civil rights movement in the 1960s and the 1970s.

Both Senghor and Damas have expressed their indebtedness to the New Negro Renaissance and, in so doing, acknowledged its international dimensions. Although the Renaissance's emphasis on the cultural contributions of African-American poets, novelists, and musicians did not change the basic conditions which the masses of black people still endure,[16] the central role of both the Harlem Renaissance and the Negritude movement in laying claim to and affirming the distinctiveness of black specificity cannot be dismissed as insignificant. Contemporary black literatures, nourished out of the imperatives of the black-lived experience and a recreated consciousness that has emerged from it, may be viewed as a literary weapon with inevitable political consequences in the struggle to re-insert black humanity into the mainstream of history in the latter half of the twentieth century. The central importance of individual sensibilities and cultural specificities is reflected in the works of the poets and novelists of both the Harlem Renaissance and the Negritude movement.

NOTES

1. *Freedom I—Negritude and Humanism* is the English translation of the original French title *Liberté—Négritude et Humanisme* (Paris: Editions du Seuil, 1964). Unless otherwise indicated, page numbers in this paper refer to the original French text. The English translation of the original text is my own.

2. Léopold S. Senghor, "Négritude et Marxisme" ("Negritude and Marxism"), in *Cahiers Pierre Teilhard de Chardin*, No. 3 (1962), 17–20.

3. Senghor, *Chants d'ombre—Hosties noires* (Songs of shadow—black victims) (Paris: Editions du Seuil, 1948), p. 32.

4. Senghor, "Ce que l'homme noir apporte" (What the black man contributes), in *Liberté I—Négritude et Humanisme*, p. 38.

5. Jacques L. Hymans, *L'Elaboration de la pensée de Léopold Sédar Senghor: Esquisse d'un itinéaire intellectuel* (The elaboration of Senghor's thought: Outline of an intellectual itinerary) (Edinburgh: Edinburgh University Press, 1971), p. 9.

6. Senghor, "Le Retour de l'enfant prodigue" (The return of the prodigal son), in *Chants d'ombre—Hosties noires*, p. 754.

7. Senghor, *Selected Poems*, cited by Jacques L. Hymans in *An Intellectual Biography, Léopold Sédar Senghor* (Edinburgh: Edinburgh University Press, 1971), p. 9.

8. Jean-Paul Sartre, "Preface," in Frantz Fanon, *The Wretched of the Earth*, trans. Constance Farrington (New York: Grove Press, 1968), p. 8.

9. Interview with Léon Gontran Damas in Paris, November 1961.

10. René M. Albérès, *L'Aventure intellectuelle du XXe siècle—Panorama des littératures européenes 1900–1963* (Paris: Editions Albin Michel, 1959), p. 17.

11. Fanon, *Black Skin, White Masks: The Experiences of a Black Man in a White World* (New York: Grove Press, 1967).

12. Locke, *The New Negro* (1923; reprinted New York: Atheneum, 1969), pp. 254–267.

13. Senghor, "L'Esprit de la civilisation ou les lois de la culture négro-africaine" (The spirit of civilization or the laws of Negro African culture), *Présence Africaine*, June–November 1956, pp. 56–65.

14. René Ménil, "Une doctrine réactionnaire: la Négritude," (Negritude, a reactionary doctrine), in *Action, Revue Théorique*

et Politique du Parti Communiste Martinquais, I (August 1963), 7. Cited by J. Hymans in *L'Elaboration de la pensée de Senghor,* pp. 262–263.

15. René Ménil, cited by Hymans, p. 132.

16. Cf. Amritjit Singh, *The Novels of the Harlem Renaissance* (University Park: Pennsylvania State University Press, 1976), p. 131.

The Harlem Renaissance:
Sources of Information for Research

MARGARET PERRY

The scholar in search of information about the Harlem Renaissance now has no need to lament the scarcity of material. A wide variety of primary and secondary materials and sources throughout the United States and abroad can now be consulted. The descriptive approach of this paper is aimed at presenting the places and people that scholars might turn to in order to inform themselves about aspects of this fascinating period of Afro-American artistic and cultural expression. Materials of all kinds and formats can be found in several different categories of resources, including the following five:

I. The regular collection of monographs and periodicals in an academic or large public library.

II. Special collections in institutions, primarily academic. These collections form the richest sources for the researcher and include such items as manuscripts, correspondence, first editions, photographs, recordings, and interviews.

III. Foreign dissertations and other non-United States sources.

IV. Special collections in the hands of private
individuals.
V. Personal contacts.

I. The first knowledge that one must acquire, it seems
almost elementary to say, is accessible in any large or
medium research library. The monographs, periodicals, etc.,
that one might find in this category discuss the period and
help the researcher to build a preliminary bibliography for a
specific project. Specialists in the field already know these
basic materials: histories, commentaries, anthologies, and
the like, that explore the period, in depth as well as
superficially. The new researcher, including undergraduate
students, will need to look at a larger number of materials,
perhaps some that specialists might reject out-of-hand.* This
category includes general as well as specific bibliographies,
in addition to histories, written by such people as James
Weldon Johnson, Nathan Irvin Huggins, David Levering
Lewis, Amritjit Singh, Robert Bone, Bruce Kellner, Darwin
T. Turner, Jervis Anderson, J. Saunders Redding, Jean
Wagner, Hugh Gloster and Arna Bontemps—to name some
of the writers who have explored this great movement in
depth.

In some greater detail, depending on one's level of
expertise, it seems reasonable to examine specific histories
and surveys of the movement. One of the first books to
question the work of this period was Nick Aaron Ford's *The
Contemporary Negro Novel: A Study in Race Relations* (1936;
rpt. McGrath, 1968). Ford refused to bow to the hyperbolic
assessment of some critics concerning the Harlem
Renaissance and pointed out weak sociological writing by
many of the novelists and poets. Indeed, Ford suggested that

---

*This could range from Blanche Ferguson's inaccurate, soporific biography
of Countee Cullen to Nathan Huggins's *Harlem Renaissance*, which,
although the first major study of the period, continues to gather criticism as
time goes on.

the writers relinquish "the pretentions of pure artistry and boldly [take up] the cudgel of propaganda." One other early book, also by a black critic, is J. Saunders Redding's *To Make a Poet Black* (1939; rpt. McGrath, 1968). Chapter 4 covers the Harlem Renaissance, including some comments on fiction writers. Redding suggests that the movement started with Claude McKay and then was well under way by 1924, reflecting a move from the blacks' agrarian roots to an urban literature of escape. Hugh Gloster's *Negro Voices in American Fiction* (University of North Carolina Press, 1948) is another early history that presents a description of the period in chapters 3 and 4. Gloster felt the Renaissance period made a break with past stereotypes and produced more self-revelatory literature.

Sterling Brown, a reluctant member of the Harlem Renaissance (because he doubts the authenticity of such a movement), nevertheless reviewed this period in Rayford Logan's edited book, *The New Negro Thirty Years Afterward* (Howard University Press, 1955). Brown's essay (pp. 57–72) is entitled "The New Negro in Literature 1925–1955)," and he expresses some skepticism about the emphasis placed on the more exotic elements of Negro life rather than on the work of those writers, like Hughes, who tilled the soil of the common folk.

Although Langston Hughes presented a vivid, if not wholly intimate, portrait of the Harlem Renaissance in his autobiography, *The Big Sea* (1940; rpt. Hill and Wang, 1963), the period itself did not come into larger focus until the end of the 1960s and then, more forcefully, in 1971, with the publication of Nathan Huggins's *Harlem Renaissance* (Oxford). This book was preceded by Harold Cruse's controversial *The Crisis of the Negro Intellectual* (Morrow, 1967) where he characterized the Harlem Renaissance as crucial in the "black world's quest for identity and salvation," although he saw the period as one of "inspired aimlessness." Whereas Cruse devoted roughly two chapters to the Renaissance, Huggins devoted an entire book, the first full-length study, to this artistic, social, and cultural movement.

Since its publication, Huggins's book has received considerable critical comment, as well as plenty of competition as a source of information about this period. In addition to literature, Huggins explores art and theater. He emphasizes black-white relationships and sees the Renaissance as part of the great American quest for the self. One of his conclusions is as obvious as it is uncontroversial (many of his literary opinions are less so): "Whatever else, the era produced phenomenal race consciousness and race assertion, as well as unprecedented numbers of poems, stories, and works of art by black people" (p. 83).

The number of books devoted either fully or in significant part to the Harlem Renaissance is now phenomenal. Others no doubt will be written to revise or challenge earlier views or to explore individuals in greater depth, but this article is devoted to getting the scholar off to a start by describing what is already available. James Weldon Johnson's autobiography, *Along This Way* (Viking, 1933, 1961), and his history of Harlem, *Black Manhattan* (Knopf, 1930; rpt. Atheneum, 1968), both contain enough comments to be useful to researchers. After all, Johnson was important as a writer of the Renaissance and also as a strong supporter of the younger writers. Johnson, always upbeat in tone, gives a genteel yet authentic picture of the period and some of its writers—McKay, Larsen, Fauset, and Cullen.

Arna Bontemps wore the mantle of Johnson's successor as historian-participant of the movement and edited *The Harlem Renaissance Remembered* (Dodd, 1972) when he was curator of the James Weldon Johnson Collection at Yale. The essays are uneven in quality but provide a good coverage of people and literature, including a reprint of George Kent's sweeping, intelligent, inclusive overview of the whole period as well as pieces about some of the lesser-known figures of the Renaissance like Theophilus Lewis (theater critic) and Frank Horne. The book also highlights the role Charles S. Johnson played in fostering the movement and its writers and artists.

In Jean Wagner's monumental *Black Poets of the United States from Paul Laurence Dunbar to Langston Hughes* (University of Illinois Press, 1973) the author expresses a belief that the poets are the best writers of the Renaissance. Wagner sees the major themes of the writers as revolt, black pride, and a rediscovery of African-American cultural history. He demonstrated particular interest and insight into the poetry of Sterling Brown whom he describes as a "poet *par excellence* of the soil." Arthur P. Davis's first 135 pages of *From the Dark Tower . . .* (Howard University Press, 1974) has a discussion of the historical and social antecedents to the 1920s. As Davis points out, "Like all similar moments, the Renaissance had its roots in the past."

Robert Bone, who discussed Renaissance writers in his *The Negro Novel in America* (Yale, 1958; rev. ed., 1965), published a book on the major black writers of short stories in 1975, *Down Home: A History of Afro American Short Fiction from Its Beginnings to the End of the Harlem Renaissance* (Putnam). His examination of Hurston, Fisher, McKay, Walrond, Toomer, Hughes, and Bontemps explores his theory of the "pastoral and anti-pastoral" influences on these writers.

In 1976 two books entirely devoted to the literature appeared—this author's own survey, *Silence to the Drums . . .* (Greenwood), which provides a brief overview of poets and novelists and also devotes a chapter to short story writers, and Amritjit Singh's *The Novels of the Harlem Renaissance . . .* (Penn State). Singh discusses twelve novelists in relation to their themes, aesthetics, and values. He sees these writers as part of the Western literary tradition rather than as speakers for the masses. The novelists discussed are: Arna Bontemps, Countee Cullen, W.E.B. DuBois, Jessie Redmon Fauset, Rudolph Fisher, Langston Hughes, Nella Larsen, Claude McKay, George Schuyler, Wallace Thurman, Jean Toomer, and Walter White.

Three important books that have appeared in the 1980s are David Levering Lewis's *When Harlem Was in Vogue* (Knopf, 1981), Jervis Anderson's *This Was Harlem: A Cultural Portrait, 1900–1950* (Farrar, 1982), and Bruce Kellner's *The Harlem Renaissance: A Historical Dictionary* (Greenwood, 1984).

Lewis's book on Harlem was his fourth monographic publication; therefore, it is not surprising that he presented not only a highly readable but also a well-researched book about the Renaissance. It is a book of solid information written in a bold, stimulating style. He is sometimes chatty (which some scholars might abhor) and frequently irreverent; but he is never boring, and his assertions nearly always represent a challenge to the person looking for facts as well as opinions. The notes are full, and the photographs—familiar to any scholar who has done extensive Harlem Renaissance work—numerous, instructive, and enjoyable.

Jervis Anderson, a Jamaican-born staff writer at *The New Yorker*, serialized part of his book, *This Was Harlem: A Cultural Portrait, 1900–1950*, in that magazine. The writing is a pleasure to read, lucid and well-balanced. This is a broadly focused account of the period, episodic in nature (probably because of serialization) but possessing a sense of the spirit that pervaded the Renaissance scene.

Bruce Kellner, who has written about Carl Van Vechten and the Harlem Renaissance over the years and has been a correspondent with Richard Bruce Nugent (or just Richard Bruce—"Peck's Bad Boy," as someone has described him), published his latest book about this period in 1984: *The Harlem Renaissance: A Historical Dictionary for the Era* (Greenwood). After a brief but informative introduction and a few photographs, Kellner lets the reader plunge into a wealth of useful, sometimes fascinating, information about the Harlem Renaissance—from Robert S. Abbott and *Abbott's Monthly* to "Yeah Man!," a musical review of 1932. Do you know, for instance, George Alexander McGuire? What about "Oh Joy?" How about reflecting on the importance of Catherine Allen Latimer? The entries are generally short but supported by references. There are appendices, including "A Chronology of Significant Events, 1917–1935," and "A Glossary of Harlem Slang." The book ends with a useful 16-page bibliography.

The latest addition to the growing scholarly volumes on the period is *Harlem   Renaissance   Re-examined* (A.M.S.

Press, 1987), edited by Victor A. Kramer. It includes about twenty essays on theoretical issues and individual artists by scholars such as Amritjit Singh, Richard A. Long, Bruce Kellner, Leon Coleman, Darwin T. Turner, Charles T. Davis, Daniel Walden, Charles Scruggs, Lillie P. Howard, Margaret Perry, Deborah E. McDowell, John Lowe, Charles H. Rowell, and Robert A. Russ.

One of the most important points to remember always is to examine numerous articles in periodicals and chapters in books that contain observations and bibliographical information necessary for thorough research. In addition to the books dealing in part with the Harlem Renaissance, which have been mentioned above, several others are also worth noting.

Judith R. Berzon's study, *Neither White nor Black: The Mulatto Character in Fiction* (New York University Press, 1978), demonstrates that the mulatto as a favorite character did not fade from use during the Renaissance years. Works by DuBois, Hughes, Hurston, James Weldon Johnson, Larsen, Toomer, and George Schuyler serve as examples of this literary genre. Addison Gayle, Jr., in *The Way of the New World* (Doubleday, 1975), exalts social conscious writing and accuses Harlem Renaissance writers of conforming to white thought and standards "in a world where substance is more important than form." Many Harlem Renaissance writers would probably disagree with Gayle, even though he asserts—not too convincingly—that they started the shift from black middle-class concerns to those of the proletariat. Paul Carter Harrison's thesis in *The Drama of Mommo* (Grove, 1972) derives from African concepts; he thus examines work by Toomer, Hughes, and McKay from "a world-view peculiar to the African sensibility."

The author of *Native Sons . . .* (Lippincott, 1968), Edward Margolies, describes the Renaissance as romantic and self-congratulatory. But his approach to the literature of this period is sound as he explores the work of Hughes, Toomer, Schuyler, Thurman, and McKay. Roger Rosenblatt in his *Black Fiction* (Harvard, 1974) examines literature by a thematic concept approach and suggests the quest for the self to be the dominant theme in most Harlem Renaissance writings. Contrasts between the 1920s and 1930s are a feature of James O. Young's *Black Writers of the Thirties* (Louisiana State University Press, 1973). Young feels there was a shift in thought from black aesthetics to a concern for economic development in Renaissance writings.

Charles T. Davis's *Black Is the Color of the Cosmos* (Garland, 1982) contains several pieces on the Harlem Renaissance that deserve our attention. In *Black Women Novelists*, by Barbara Christian (Greenwood Press, 1980), and *All the Women Are White, All the Blacks Are Men, But Some of Us Are Brave*, edited by Gloria T. Hull, Patricia Bell Scott, and Barbara Smith (Feminist Press, 1982), there is some discussion of Fauset, Larsen, and Hurston that reinforces the thesis that there is a female tradition in Afro-American literature.

Other books containing examinations of Harlem Renaissance literature include the following: Catherine Juanita Starke's *Black Portraiture in American Fiction: Stock Characters, Archetypes, and Individuals* (Basic Books, 1971); Roger Whitlow's *Black American Literature: A Critical History* (Nelson-Hall, 1973); S.P. Fullinwider's *The Mind and Mood of Black America: 20th Century Thought* (Dorsey Press, 1969); Blyden Jackson's *The Waiting Years: Essays on American Negro Literature* (Louisiana University Press, 1976); Gilbert Osofsky's *Harlem: The Making of a Ghetto . . .* (Harper, 1963); Wilson Record's *The Negro and the Communist Party* (University of North Carolina Press, 1951).

The treatment of individual authors should be noted briefly. Langston Hughes has had an enormous amount of attention through critical monographs over the decades. His own literary autobiography, *The Big Sea* (1940), should not be overlooked because the tone Hughes uses for describing the times and people of the Harlem Renaissance has an immediacy even for today's reader. In 1967 Donald Dickinson's *A Bio-Bibliography of Langston Hughes 1902–1967* (Archon) appeared, detailing personal events and literary publications in "English and Foreign Languages up to 1965" (excepting newspaper items). Hughes had assisted in the compilation of this material. During this same year Twayne published a monograph on Hughes, written and compiled by James A. Emanuel, in its U.S. Authors Series (now with G.K. Hall). Milton Meltzer's biography, *Langston Hughes*, appeared in 1968 and two full-length studies, *Langston Hughes, an Introduction to His Poetry* (Columbia University) by Onwuchekwa Jemie and *Langston Hughes: The Poet and His Critics* (American Library Association) by Richard K. Barksdale, were published in 1976 and 1977 respectively. Therman B. O'Daniel's collection of edited essays, *Langston Hughes, Black Genius*, appeared in 1971, opening with a bio-bibliographical essay by O'Daniel. Edward J. Mullen, who wrote *Langston Hughes in the Hispanic World and Haiti* (Shoe String, 1977), edited a collection, *Critical Essays on Langston Hughes* (G.K. Hall) in 1986. This collection includes essays by many well-known Hughes critics: Onwuchekura Jemie, Emanuel, and Phyllis Klotman. After an introduction by Mullen, one finds reprints of many reviews of the poet's works, followed by essays on his poetry, prose, and drama. This is not a collection of new essays but the editor brings under one cover a variety of Hughes criticism. Faith Berry published a well-received biography, *Langston Hughes: Before and Beyond Harlem* (Lawrence Hill) in 1983. The first volume of Arnold Rampersad's *Life of Langston Hughes* (Oxford, 1986), the biography authorized by the Langston Hughes Society, is a thoughtful and well-researched literary work and is unquestionably a major work about Hughes. *Langston Hughes Review*, a semi-annual publication of the Langston Hughes Society and Brown University, reprints Hughes's writings and offers commentaries and other materials of interest to Hughes scholars.

The life and work of W.E.B. DuBois has been amply examined by the writer himself as well as by his biographers, critics, and editors. Although DuBois's autobiography did not appear in print in his own lifetime, he had expressed himself personally in such works as *Souls of Black Folk* (c. 1903) and *Dusk of Dawn* (c. 1940). Herbert Aptheker edited DuBois's autobiography in 1968: *The*

Autobiography of W.E.B. DuBois: A Soliloquy on Viewing My Life from the Last Decade of Its First Century (International Publishers). This book, according to Aptheker, "is more fully autobiographical than *Dusk of Dawn*." DuBois's personality is strong, of course, in his extensive correspondence (1877–1963) published by the University of Massachusetts Press (3 vols., 1973 to 1978). William L. Andrews edited the *Critical Essays on W.E.B. DuBois* (G.K. Hall, 1985), a collection that includes a bibliographical essay, discussion of DuBois's treatment of the Afro-American female, and a bibliography of his autobiographical writings. For more material on DuBois's writing style and subjects, one should also read Arnold Rampersad's *The Art and Imagination of W.E.B. DuBois* (Harvard, 1976). Julius Lester's long introduction to the two-volume anthology, *The Seventh Son* (Random House, 1971), is a valuable source. Addison Gayle is at work on an exhaustive bio-critical study.

Countee Cullen has yet to be the subject of a full-length critical biography; the author of this article published, in 1971 (Greenwood), a seminal work that has much bibliographical information—*A Bio-Bibliography of Countee P. Cullen, 1903–1946*. Although out of date, this work gives the researcher a good start on information about the writer. Darwin Turner's "Countee Cullen: The Lost Ariel," published in 1971 as part of his study, *In a Minor Chord* (Southern Illinois University Press), deserves attention. Houston Baker, Jr., in his 1974 book, *A Many Colored Coat of Dreams* (Broadside Press), explores Cullen's poetry from a black perspective, seeing his work as a "paradigm in the black creative experience." Alan R. Shucard published *Countee Cullen* in 1984 as part of Twayne's U.S. Author Series (G.K. Hall), where works are presented chronologically as well as historically. The author's life is explored briefly and bibliographical information is given in an up-to-date fashion.

There are numerous articles about McKay but just a few books that deal with him individually or in part. James Giles wrote a book, *Claude McKay*, for the Twayne U.S. Author Series (G.K. Hall) in 1976. After a brief biographical overview the author examines first McKay's poetry and then his fiction. Giles also discusses the nonfiction—*A Long Way from Home* and *Harlem*. In 1972 Broadside Press brought out a Critics Series selection entitled *Claude McKay: The Black Poet at War*, written by Addison Gayle. Stephen H. Bronz explored three Harlem Renaissance writers in his *Roots of Negro Racial Consciousness* . . . (Libra, 1964): Cullen, McKay, and James Weldon Johnson. The new biography by Wayne F. Cooper, *Claude McKay: Rebel Sojourner in the Harlem Renaissance, A Life* (Louisiana State University Press, 1987) is based on the author's doctoral dissertation at Rutgers.

   J.W. Johnson, who chronicled part of his own life in *Along this Way* (1933) and discussed the Harlem Renaissance in chapter 19 of *Black Manhattan* (1930), has now been receiving greater critical attention. A perceptive essay on *God's Trombones* appears in Jean Wagner's *Black Poets of the United States* (1973). An annotated bibliography by Robert E. Fleming appeared in 1978: *James Weldon Johnson and Arna Bontemps: A Reference Guide* (G.K. Hall). Articles, book chapters, and book reviews about Johnson are arranged chronologically by publication date up to 1976. As part of the University of Chicago's "Negro American Biographies and Autobiographies Series," Eugene Levy published *James Weldon Johnson: Black Leader, Black Voice*, in 1976.

   Zora Neale Hurston has come into her own in the world of literary criticism. She is the subject of an extensive biography by Robert Hemenway, who has specialized in her work for a long time. *Zora Neale Hurston: A Literary Biography* (University of Illinois, 1977) is well-researched and eminently reliable for its facts, analyses, and biographical portraits. Darwin T. Turner explores Hurston's work in his *In a Minor Chord* (1971) and emphasizes how her personal life adversely affected her writing. In the Twayne U.S. Authors Series (G.K. Hall), Lillie P. Howard has written *Zora Neale Hurston*, which one critic cites as "especially original when treating the fiction." Dr. Howard makes good use of unpublished correspondence in this work.

Jean Toomer is another author who is discussed in Turner's book. Articles about Toomer and his work abound; full-length works on Toomer are finally emerging to help the researcher explore every inch of Toomer's ideas, poems, and stories. Besides the long chapter in Turner's *In a Minor Chord*, some more recent works are: *Jean Toomer* by Brian J. Benson and Mable Dillard, in the Twayne series (G.K. Hall); *Jean Toomer, Artist: A Study of His Literary Life and Work, 1894–1936*, by Nellie Y. McKay (University of North Carolina Press, 1984), and Therman B. O'Daniel's *Jean Toomer: A Critical Evaluation* (Howard University Press, 1985). The most recent book about Toomer is *The Lives of Jean Toomer* (Louisiana State University Press, 1987) by Cynthia Earl Kerman and Richard Elderidge.

The Twayne Series of U.S. Authors (published by G.K. Hall) is a rich source for the study of individual authors (there is also, for instance, a book on George Schuyler) and will continue to be a source to consult for preliminary research information. Lastly, numerous dissertations have dealt with these and other Harlem Renaissance writers in great detail. *Dissertation Abstracts* may be checked for information, as well as this author's book, *The Harlem Renaissance* (Garland, 1982). Journals such as the *CLA Journal* and *Sage* also note the more recent dissertations concerning Afro-American writers.

Because the initial search is of prime importance, specific books are not the only ones emphasized by periodicals and bibliographies. The latter may be specific; but general bibliographies and those included in larger works also should be investigated. A few items in this category are:

> *Abstracts of English Studies* 1960–, Boulder, Colorado: National Council of Teachers of English; Walter Schatz, ed., *Directory of Afro-American Resources*, New York: Bowker, 1970; *Dissertation Abstracts*, 1938–1969, and *Dissertation Abstracts International*, 1969–; Carol Fairbanks and Eugene A. Engelidinger, comps., *Black American Fiction: A Bibliography*, Metuchen, N.J.: Scarecrow, 1978;

Edward Margolies and David Bakish, comps., *Afro-American Fiction, 1853–1976*, Detroit: Gale Research Co., 1978; William P. French, Amritjit Singh, Michel and Geneviève Fabre, comps., *Afro-American Poetry and Drama, 1760–1975*, Detroit: Gale Research, 1979; Haillie Q. Brown, Brown Memorial Library, comp., *Index to Periodical Articles By and About Blacks*, Boston: G.K. Hall, 1979; *MLA International Bibliography*, 1921–; Theresa Gunnels Rush, Carol Fairbanks Myers, and Esther Spring Arata, eds., *Black American Writers, Past and Present: A Biographical and Bibliographical Dictionary*, 2 volumes, Metuchen, N.J.: Scarecrow Press, 1975; Darwin T. Turner, comp., *Afro-American Writers*, New York: Appleton-Century-Crofts, 1970.

Some more specific titles would be:

Robert E. Fleming, *James Weldon Johnson and Arna Wendell Bontemps: A Reference Guide*, Boston: G.K. Hall, 1978; *Guide to the Microfilm Edition of the Countee Cullen Papers*, 1921–1969, prepared by Florence E. Borders, New Orleans: Amistad Research Center, 1975; Elizabeth W. Miller, comp., *The Negro in America: A Bibliography*, 2nd ed. rev., Cambridge, Mass.: Harvard University Press, 1970; Ruth Miller and Peter J. Katopes, "The Harlem Renaissance: Arna Bontemps, Countee Cullen, James Weldon Johnson, Claude McKay, and Jean Toomer," in *Black American Writers: Bibliographical Essays, Volume 1: The Beginnings Through the Harlem Renaissance and Langston Hughes*, edited by M. Thomas Inge et al., New York: St. Martin's Press, 1978, pp. 161–206; Martin Olsson, *A Selected Bibliography of Black Literature: The Harlem*

Renaissance, Exeter, England: University of Exeter,
American Arts Documentation Centre, 1973;
Margaret Perry, *A Bio-Bibliography of Countee P.
Cullen*, 1903–1946, Westport, Conn.: Greenwood,
1971; Margaret Perry, *The Harlem Renaissance:
An Annotated Bibliography and Commentary*,
New York: Garland, 1982; John M. Reilly, "Jean
Toomer: An Annotated Checklist of Criticism," in
Resources for American Literary Study, 4, 1 (Spring
1974), 27–56.

The magazines one should know as sources, both current
and past, seem legion today. It was not always so. Some
periodicals, such as *FIRE!!, Palms, The Stylus, Harlem, The
Carolina Magazine,* and *Black Opals* have moved into a
pantheon of special reference material. Other journals—
some still being printed, some not—at the risk of stating the
obvious are: *CLA Journal, Black American Literature Forum,
The Crisis, Black World* (especially the November 1970
number); *Freedomways, Negro History Bulletin, Studies in
Black Literature, The Messenger, Opportunity, Black Scholar,
Phylon, Journal of Black Studies,* and *Umoja.* We are
indebted to Jean Fagan Yellin now for the literary index to
The Crisis, a tremendous aid in one's search for specific
information in this notable magazine that served so many
writers of the Harlem Renaissance.

Those are periodicals primarily devoted to the black
experience, but other more general magazines cannot be
overlooked: *Survey Graphic* of 1 March 1925, which led to the
now-famous *The New Negro* (see the end of this article).
Hughes's explosive essay, "The Negro Artist and the Racial
Mountains" first appeared in *The Nation*, another magazine
frequently open to exploring issues connected with the
Harlem Renaissance. Other magazines that can be cited are:
American Mercury; *The Atlantic* (where Rudolph Fisher
published some stories); *The Saturday Review*, *Harper's*; and
Century Magazine.

II. Moving to the wider world, another step is to select
the institution whose research collection meets one's needs.

The James Weldon Johnson Collection at Yale University is replete with materials and is broad in its coverage of numerous authors. The collection has been enriched recently by the Jean Toomer papers that Fisk has had to turn over to it, in accordance with Mrs. Toomer's wishes. The Johnson collection is in the Beinecke Rare Book and Manuscript Library and contains a vast array of materials for the Harlem Renaissance scholar. The collection is strong in original manuscripts as well as in correspondence among the authors. All of the major Renaissance writers are represented in this enormous collection.

Fisk University, however, still has a significant oral history collection, the Charles S. Johnson papers, some W.E.B. DuBois papers (notably, a typed manuscript of *Dark Princess*, with handwritten revisions), and the Aaron Douglas papers. Among the oral history individual accounts are comments of Arna Bontemps, Ethel Ray Nance, and Aaron Douglas. There is also a picture file and an unpublished anthology, edited by L.M. Collins, that contains material not published in any other anthology as far as can be ascertained.

The papers of Countee Cullen at Amistad Research Center, Tulane University, are available on microfilm (7 reels). This is a treasure trove of materials—correspondence, manuscripts, a diary, scrapbooks, clippings—and one can order a shelf list of the contents for only $7.00.

The Locke papers at Howard University are essential for work on McKay and Fauset, as well as for work on Locke himself.

At Atlanta University, the Trevor Arnett Library collection contains many valuable manuscripts and papers for serious work on the Harlem Renaissance. Included are photographs, sheet music, tapes, and broadsides. The Claude McKay papers at Atlanta are valuable for understanding this often difficult personality. The photographs, too, are valuable as well as interesting.

A list of places a research scholar might visit is long and varied: Brown University (Rudolph Fisher); Columbia University, because of its oral history project; the University of Florida at Gainesville; the Indiana Historical Society; Indiana University's Lilly Library; the University of Massachusetts at Amherst; the Library of Congress; and, of course, the Schomburg Center of the New York Public Library. The archival material at the Schomburg is now on microfilm. Some of the correspondence in Schomburg's file is especially interesting; for instance, McKay has many letters to Schomburg between the years 1920 and 1937.

The content of these different collections is described in my book, *The Harlem Renaissance,* where there are brief descriptions of the holdings; see pp. 211–232.

Of course, a general description cannot give a researcher the opportunity to discover information that might be specifically relevant to his or her area of research. It may be a word, a line, a marginal note in someone's book; it may be a line that is scratched out in a manuscript. While McKay's *Constab Ballads* may be available, this does not mean that one gains full insight into McKay's mind; a copy at Yale, for instance, is inscribed by the author later in life with the following sentiment—"My one book I should like to see destroyed." This is the same author who berates blacks in his *Banjo* for being ashamed of their own culture, their past, their "racial roots." The researcher has to take all of this into consideration. Once again, an example of what a visit alone can do for the researcher: at Fisk, there are notes and comments concerning submissions to the *Opportunity* contest; to my knowledge, these materials have never been published.

The preceding description of special collections represents only a broad range of possibilities for the researcher. In the acknowledgments to David Levering Lewis's *When Harlem Was in Vogue,* there are indications of many other places where one might seek information about the Harlem Renaissance. The institutions listed on p. xiii, along with people thanked, should help scholars seek more specialized materials.

There are also printed catalogues for some of these collections; and these are helpful in assessing the strength of specific holdings:

Chicago Public Library. Vivian G. Harsh Collection. *The Chicago Afro-American Union Analytic Catalog: An Index to Materials on the Afro-American in the Principal Libraries of Chicago.* 5 vols., Boston: G.K. Hall, 1972.

Howard University Library. Washington, D.C. *Dictionary Catalog of the Jesse E. Moorland Collection of Negro Life and History.* Boston: G.K. Hall, 1970. First Supplement, 3 vols., 1976.

New York Public Library, Schomburg Collection. *Dictionary Catalog of the Schomburg Collection of Negro Literature and History.* 9 vols., Boston: G.K. Hall, 1962. First Supplement, 2 vols., 1967. Second Supplement, 4 vols., 1972.

III. Foreign dissertations concerning the Harlem Renaissance are numerous, although a comprehensive guide to them has not yet appeared. In Perry's *The Harlem Renaissance*, there was a concentration on French theses because of her own special knowledge in that area. The work of Spanish, or Latin American, scholars on Langston Hughes should be explored, just as the theses in German and, indeed, English materials from Great Britain, need illumination. Those scholars from institutions that hold membership in the Center for Research Libraries in Chicago can expect to have a reasonable chance of securing foreign dissertations. Information on dissertations done in India is available from the American Studies Research Center, Hyderabad. Contact with scholars in foreign lands might also help in the search for what is admittedly a more specialized branch of source material for studying the Harlem Renaissance.

IV. The materials in private hands form a small, select category, and they need to be pursued, edited, and published. One could classify the Anne Spencer materials in this category because her memorial foundation is primarily a family affair (Address: 1313 Pierce St., Lynchburg, VA 25401). Robert Hemenway, from the University of Oklahoma at Norman, is well known as a specialist in the work and

life of Zora Neale Hurston, and he has letters to and from
her agent, a film she made, and letters from her to her ex-
husband. It is often items such as these, no matter how brief,
that give the scholar a new or different view of a segment of
study concerning the Harlem Renaissance. It is possible that
Dorothy West may still have some items; and that most
elusive of families, the Rudolph Fisher family, still has the
yellowing, frail papers containing Fisher's last works (e.g.,
his last story, "The Soldier.")

There is, in other words, the challenge of discovery as
well as the challenge of getting specific information in this
area of source material.

V. The last category, personal contacts, is closely related
to the foregoing because one may assume that many of the
persons one might contact may still be holding onto useful
material. The author of this paper can be used as an example:
working on Cullen, she had to secure permission from Edna
St. Vincent Millay's family to quote some lines of poetry. She
received the permission plus a brief personal note from
Norma Millay Ellis in which she states the following—"He
had a charming English accent. I danced with him after a
party given by 'The ten of us' at Madame Walker's in
Harlem. At Small's *old* place after our dance he offered me
his arm to take me to my table and said charmingly 'You
Bump divinely, Miss Millay.' And that from a black man was
praise indeed. He had an elegance."

There are others, including historians of the period: Dr.
Arthur P. Davis, of Washington, D.C., for instance, is
willing to talk via the telephone to information seekers. He
is known for his work on many of the Harlem Renaissance
authors. One must make one's own list, of course. Dorothy
West has been a willing conversationist about the Harlem
Renaissance—this period during which she first started her
writing career.

The list of these individuals may not be long—but it is a
distinguished one. Each one can bring history alive in an
intimate and rewarding fashion.

The reader, at this point, may detect (or at least sense) a
serious omission from the materials cited: *The New Negro*,

edited in 1925 by Alain Locke and published by Boni. Indeed, more than the publication of "If We Must Die" (1919) or even *Cane* (1923), the appearance of this collection of stories, poems, essays, and artwork helped to herald the period and to give it presence in an organized fashion. If the editors of *FIRE!!*, which appeared the following year, felt *The New Negro* was too tame for their tastes, it mattered not; the "establishment" reader bought and sometimes even discussed *The New Negro*. As a publication, it helped to call attention to some of the new writers; it also helped to expose blacks and whites alike to some significant information about the cultural heritage of African-Americans. The book grew out of a special issue of *Survey Graphic* (1 March 1925) and this also helped get the book attention when it appeared. If the movement of the "New Negro" did not reflect the optimism expressed by Locke, the period at least received the formal announcement of its existence with the publication of *The New Negro*.

These are the resources: they are written, they are recorded, they are human. Ultimately, the story will be told and retold. The histories will tumble, one after the other, and the fascination with this golden period in our cultural history will be sustained not only by those of us who have done work in the past but by scholars to come—scholars who will have these and even more sources of information for research, as we deal in an organized and systematic fashion with our past.

NOTES ON THE CONTRIBUTORS

Richard Kenneth Barksdale graduated from Bowdoin College (B.A., 1937), Syracuse University (M.A., 1938), and Harvard University (Ph.D., 1951). He is Professor Emeritus of English, University of Illinois, Champaign-Urbana. Currently, he is Visiting Professor of Afro-American Literature at the University of Missouri-Columbia. He has written *Langston Hughes: The Poet and his Critics* (1977) and several journal articles on Afro-American Literature and is co-editor (with Keneth Kinnamon) of *Black Writers of America* (1972).

Paul Joseph Burgett took undergraduate and graduate degrees from the Eastman School of Music of the University of Rochester. His Ph.D. dissertation treated the aesthetics of the music of black Americans. This subject continues to occupy him as a teacher in the classroom, in papers which he has authored, and in presentations on various aspects of the subject. Recently, he was named Vice-President and Chief Student Affairs Officer of the University of Rochester, a position to which he acceded after eight years as Dean of Students at the Eastman School.

Rudolph P. Byrd is Assistant Professor of English at Carleton College, North Field, Minnesota, and Director of the African, African-American Studies Program.

Robert A. Coles is Assistant Professor of English at Berea College, where he teaches American literature. His articles have appeared in *Modern Language Studies* (NEMLA), *Dictionary of Literary Biography, CLA Journal,* and the *Journal of Popular Literature.*

John Cooley is Professor of English and Director of Environmental Studies at Western Michigan University. He is the author of numerous scholarly articles and the critical study, *Savages and Naturals: Black Portraits by White American Writers* (Delaware, 1982). He is listed in *Who's Who in the America: Writers, Editors and Poets.*

Thadious M. Davis, Professor of English at the University of North Carolina, Chapel Hill, is the author of *Faulkner's "Negro": Art and the Southern Context* (1983) and co-editor of several volumes of the *Dictionary of Literary Biography* on Afro-American writers. She has also completed a critical biography of Nella Larsen.

Alfred J. Guillaume, Jr., is Dean of the College of Arts and Sciences and Associate Professor of French at Xavier University of Louisiana. He received his Ph.D. in French Studies from Brown University and has published articles on nineteenth-century French literature, African and Caribbean literature of French expression, and nineteenth-century Louisiana literature in French in journals such as the *French Review, College Language Association Journal,* the *Langston Hughes Review, Louisiana Literature,* and the *New Laurel Review.*

Diane S. Isaacs completed her Ph.D. dissertation on Ann Petry as a graduate student in Afro-American Studies at the University of Minnesota. She has served on the staff at Fordham University and published articles on Afro-American women writers. Currently, She is chair of the English Department, grades 7-12, Nyack High School, in Nyack, New York.

Wendell A. Jean-Pierre is Chairman of the Afro-American and African Studies Department, Rutgers University at

Newark. He received his Ph.D. in French Letters from Brown University. He holds diplomas from the Universities of Paris and Aix-Marseilles and is the author of numerous articles on the concept of Negritude, and on Third World countries and the West. Currently in progress is a study focusing on the Afro-Russian poet, Alexander Sergeyevitch Pushkin.

Vincent Jubilee is Associate Professor of English at the University of Puerto Rico in Rio Piedras. He attended New York University as a Woodrow Wilson Fellow and received his M.A. in English there in 1967 and was awarded a Ph.D. in American Civilization from the University of Pennsylvania in 1980. The essay included here is part of a book in preparation on Philadelphia's black literary activities during the Harlem Renaissance.

Bruce Kellner is Professor of English at Millersville University in Pennsylvania. He has written six books, including *Carl Van Vechten and the Irreverent Decades* (1968), *The Harlem Renaissance: A Historical Dictionary for the Era* (1984), and *Content With the Example: A Gertrude Stein Companion* (1988).

Geta LeSeur is Assistant Professor of Women Studies and English at the University of Missouri-Columbia, where she teaches courses on women, race and class, and Commonwealth literatures. She received her Ph.D. from Indiana University and recently received a two-year Chancellor's Postdoctoral Fellowship at the University of California-Berkeley, where she worked on her forthcoming book, *The Afro-Caribbean Bildungsroman*. She has published articles on black women's rites-of-passage and narratives, including those in the American West. Her current research focuses on Black Anglophone female writers and Barbadian-Canadian writer Austin Clarke.

Joseph McLaren is currently Associate Professor of English and Humanities at Mercy College, Dobbs Ferry, New York.

He received his Ph.D. in American Civilization from Brown University. His publications include a book entitled *Form and Feeling: The Critical Reception of Edward Kennedy "Duke" Ellington and Langston Hughes*, to be published by Garland Publishing.

Charles H. Nichols, Professor of English at Brown University, is a graduate of Brooklyn College. He received his Ph.D. in English from Brown University in 1948. He was formerly Professor of North American Language and Literature at the John F. Kennedy Institute for American Studies, Free University, Berlin, Germany, 1959–1969. He is the author of *Many Thousand Gone: The Ex-Slaves' Account of their Bondage and Freedom* and editor of *African Nights: Black Erotic Folk Tales, Black Men in Chains: An Anthology of Slave Narratives*, and *Arna Bontemps and Langston Hughes: Letters, 1925–1967*.

Assistant Professor Kathy Ogren teaches American History at the University of Redlands. She is the author of *The Jazz Revolution*, forthcoming, 1989. She also serves as an associate editor for "Jazz: History, Culture, Analysis," a publication series of Wayne State University Press.

Margaret Perry, Director of Libraries, Valparaiso University (Indiana), is the author of four books about the Harlem Renaissance. The latest is an edited work, *The Short Fiction of Rudolph Fisher* (Greenwood, 1987). She also writes poetry and short stories and soon will have a story in *Forum* (Ball State University).

Arnold Rampersad is the Zora Neale Hurston Professor of English at Columbia University. He has published widely on American and Afro-American literature. His books include *The Art and Imagination of W.E.B. DuBois* (1976) and the two-volume *Life of Langston Hughes* (1986, 1988).

An instructor at City College, Freda L. Scott is at the dissertation level in the Ph.D. Program in Theatre at the City University of New York Graduate School. Her topic concerns black drama during the Harlem Renaissance period. She has contributed papers to several conferences and has had articles published in *Theatre Journal* and *Overture.*

Robert B. Stepto teaches American literature at Yale University, where he is Professor of English, Afro-American Studies, and American Studies. His publications include *From Behind the Veil: A Study of Afro-American Narrative, Chant of Saints* (with Michael S. Harper), and *Afro-American Literature* (with Dexter Fisher).

Barbara L. Tischler is Director of American Studies and Assistant Professor of History at Barnard College, Columbia University. She earned a Ph.D. in History from Columbia University and has a Master of Music degree from the Manhattan School of Music. She has published articles and reviews on cultural, labor, and women's history. *An American Music: The Search for an American Musical Identity* was published in 1986 by Oxford University Press, which will also publish her forthcoming book on wartime cultural propaganda and protest.

James W. Tuttleton is Professor of English and Associate Dean of the Graduate School of Arts and Science at New York University. He is the author of *The Novel of Manners in America* (1972) and *Thomas Wentworth Higginson* (1978). He has also edited Henry James's *The American* (1978) and *The Works of Washington Irving* (1984).

Mary Katherine Wainwright is Associate Professor of English at Manatee Community College, Bradenton, Florida. For the 1988–89 school year, she has been awarded a McKnight Junior Faculty Fellowship in order to complete her dissertation-in-progress—"Black American Women Writers: The Neglected Tradition"—for the American

Studies Program at Purdue University, West Lafayette,
Indiana.

ABOUT THE EDITORS

AMRITJIT SINGH, Associate Professor of English at Rhode Island College, has taught at universities and colleges in Delhi, New York, Hyderabad, and Jaipur. Books written and edited by him include *The Novels of the Harlem Renaissance* (1976), *Afro-American Poetry and Drama, 1760–1975* (1979), *Indian Literature in English, 1827–1979* (1981), *India: An Anthology of Contemporary Writing* (1983), and *The Magic Circle of Henry James* (1988). Dr. Singh is currently at work on a study of Richard Wright's later non-fiction, for which he has received ACLS and NEH awards.

WILLIAM S. SHIVER has been Associate Professor of French at Clark University and at Hofstra University. At Hofstra, he also taught courses in Comparative/African/Afro-American literatures. His current scholarly interests center on Afro-French literature, especially on the Senegalese writer Cheikh Hamidou Kane, author of the prize-winning novel *Ambiguous Adventure* (1961). Dr. Shiver's long-time interest in the Negritude movement was perhaps responsible for the Hofstra-NEH conference on the Harlem Renaissance in May 1985; it received sympathetic attention early on from the late Dr. Joseph G. Astman, Professor of Comparative Literature and founding director of the Hofstra University Cultural Center.

STANLEY BRODWIN is Professor of English at Hofstra University. He has published extensively on nineteenth-century American writers, notably on Mark Twain, in journals such as *American Literature, PMLA, Criticism, Journal of Black Studies, Journal of the History of Ideas*, and *Mississippi Quarterly*. In 1981, he received from the late Mrs. Ida Cullen the Countee Cullen Literary Award for his contributions to the teaching of Afro-American literature. Dr. Brodwin is currently preparing a book-length study on the theological dimensions of Mark Twain's writings.

INDEX